The Literary Imagination

By the same author:

Criticism

The Truest Poetry: an Essay on the Question, What is Literature?
The Truthtellers: Jane Austen, George Eliot, Lawrence
The Uses of Nostalgia: Studies in Pastoral
An Introduction to English Poetry
Love and Marriage: Literature in its Social Context

Poetry

Domestic Interior
The Directions of Memory
Selves
The Man I Killed
A.R.T.H.U.R.: the Life and Opinions of a Digital Computer
A.R.T.H.U.R. and M.A.R.T.H.A.: the Loves of the Computers

Fiction

The Englishman
A Free Man

The Literary Imagination.

Essays on Literature and Society

LAURENCE LERNER
Professor of English, University of Sussex

THE HARVESTER PRESS · SUSSEX

BARNES & NOBLE BOOKS · NEW JERSEY

First published in Great Britain in 1982 by
THE HARVESTER PRESS LIMITED
Publisher: John Spiers
16 Ship Street, Brighton, Sussex
and in the USA by
BARNES & NOBLE BOOKS
81 Adams Drive, Totowa, New Jersey 07516

© Laurence Lerner, 1982

British Library Cataloguing in Publication Data
Lerner, Laurence
   The literary imagination.
   1. Literature and society — History and criticism
   2. English Literature — History and criticism
   I. Title
   820'.8'0355   PR149.S/

   ISBN 0-7108-0097-5

Library of Congress Cataloging in Publication Data
Lerner, Laurence.
   The literary imagination.

   1. Literature and society — Addresses, essays, lectures.
I. Title.
PN51.L39   1982   801'.3   82-1612
ISBN 0-389-20270-3   AACR2

Typeset in 11 point Garamond by Alacrity Phototypesetters,
Banwell Castle, Weston-super-Mare.
Printed in Great Britain by
Mansell Limited, Witham, Essex

PN
51
L39
1982

To Patrick Grant

Contents

Preface

It is of the nature of art, I believe, that it is relatively independent of its context, including its social context; but these essays are mainly concerned with how the literary imagination sees society. This paradox can be defended on two grounds. First, that the autonomy of the poem or novel is best understood in relation to the context from which it breaks free; and second, that the experience of responding to literature is not the same as that of discussing and interpreting it — that autonomy belongs to the experience, and the social context grows more important in its interpretation. This in turn raises the issue whether interpretation imposes social and ideological concerns on a relatively timeless reading, or simply brings to the surface those limiting social factors that were unperceived in the apparent universality of the reading experience. Whichever is truer (and neither seems to me tenable in extreme form), I believe that it need not be reductive to relate literature to the society which produced it; and I believe there is that in literature which ought not to be reduced.

All the essays address themselves to a general critical problem, illustrating it from a range of examples. They thus lack the free-floating speculation of a wholly theoretical article (nothing but argument), and the richness and subtlety of a commentary on a single work (where there may be so much flesh on the bones that the argument it hard to make out). I believe literary discussion is usually the better for avoiding these two extremes. To study a single work without raising general questions about its genre, its social, political or even merely human function, its aesthetic value or its linguistic form, is narrow; but to discuss literary theory without making significant contact with the experience of reading actual works is barren. The essays are therefore concerned with the points where theory and particularity meet.

If I were to state the general position informing the book, the best single word I could offer would be agnostic. It is my experience that when I have disengaged the underlying philosophical issues in a critical dispute, I cannot choose between them. When I find a battle raging over whether a literary work shows *profondeur* or *complexité*, whether literary space must be located in the world or in its symbols, I constantly react by thinking that either word, or either position, would do. The great Victorian agnostics struggled to show that their inability to take up a firm religious position need not mean that they were people who didn't care, for they cared passionately about morality, about their society, about the future of mankind, and worked together with those who knew all the answers, without needing either to accept or denounce the religious beliefs of others. In the same way, I care passionately about literature, and strongly about interpreting it, but I do not greatly care about taking up a rigid theoretical position from which to do so. Hence the pluralism that is implicit all through the book, and explicit in the first essay.

One other generalisation about its position is possible. Insofar as form and content can usefully be separated (and however much it may fail us in the last resort, I believe such a separation is useful, indeed essential), I am more concerned with the meaning and function of literature than with its form. If we divide critics into those who see literature as a way of *saying* something, and those who see it as a *way* of saying something, I have to place myself clearly in the first group. Only one of these essays begins with formal questions, and even it does not stick rigorously to them. In what follows, formal rigour takes second place to human content. Which is not to say that literature is to be seen as biographical documents.

Some of the essays have already been published, as follows: 'The Determinants of a Literary Work' (in much shorter form) in the *Times Literary Supplement*; 'Literature and Money' in *Essays and Studies 1975*; 'Psycho-analysis and Art' in *Literature and Psychology: Yearbook of Comparative Criticism, Vol. 7*; 'Literature and Social Change' in the *Journal of European Studies 1977*; 'Lukacs' Theory of Realism' in *Encounter 1977*; 'The Bourgeois Imagination' in *The Literature of the Western World, Vol. V: The Modern World – Realities*, edited by David Daiches and A.K. Thorlby. To all the editors and publishers of these, thanks are due; and much warmer and more personal thanks are due to those friends who have read or listened to some of the essays, and helped by their comments to remove some of the most glaring faults: Patrick Grant, Tony Nuttall, Barry Supple, Alan Sinfield and Tony Thorlby.

The essay on 'Literature and Social Change' and that on Lukacs represent different developments of the same concerns, and there is thus a slight overlap between them, for which I must apologise to the reader. Rather than tidy this up, I have thought it best to leave each in its complete form, so that they can be read independently of each other.

1

The Determinants of a Literary Work

The concern of this essay is not the analysis or appraisal of literary works as finished product, but the aetiological question of how they come to be as they are. What are the possible factors that determine the nature of any play or novel? I want to suggest as a simple model, perhaps in the first instance no more than a rule of thumb, that there are three: tradition, individual and society. From already existing literature certain ways of telling a story, certain character types, plot structures, metrical forms, image patterns and rhetorical devices offer themselves as elements in each new work: that is the literary tradition, either explicitly formulated as conventions, or half-consciously followed as habits. From the personal life of the writer certain concerns, preferences, emotional needs, aspirations, disappointments and personality traits push themselves forward and lead to the choice of particular subjects or particular ways of treating them: that is the individual element, and it too can function at varying levels of consciousness. And every work is produced at a particular time and place; in a particular society, whose beliefs, assumptions, problems, conflicts and habits set limits to what can and can't be expressed, and how it will be treated: that is the pressure of society, and it can be seen in two ways. If our conception of society stresses consensus, we shall look at the shared assumptions of the whole society, and say, this work is the product of eighteenth-century England or the Greek city state; if it stresses conflict we shall look more at the particular

1

group, sub-culture or social class, and say this work is bourgeois, clerical or by a woman. I believe that all three factors always operate, but that their relative importance can vary: and I am not sure that there are any others.

What is the origin of Mr Micawber? He can be seen as a version of Don Quixote — feckless, given to fine speeches, well-intentioned, never quite master of any situation, the accidental instrument of goodness; though his gusto, his delight in fleshly pleasures, and the fact that his one skill seems to be making punch suggest a different pedigree. He is Don Quixote with a touch of Falstaff. But he also has a personal origin, for it is well-known that Dickens used his father as a model. Since he also used his father as a model for the more selfish and less comic Mr Dorritt, we can identify the attitude towards each character by contrast with the other: indulgent forgiving and affectionate in *David Copperfield* (the incompetent substitute-father offers more true fatherly warmth than the stern and competent stepfather), perceptive, fascinated and in the last resort deeply hostile in *Little Dorritt*. Whether this difference is due to Dickens' changing feelings towards his father between 1849 and 1855, or to a deliberate selection of what would fit each book, is arguable: insofar as we say the second, we are departing from the personal factor as explanation. And Micawber too can be related to the society in which Dickens wrote, if we think about the difference between property and income. One of the most important social changes of the past two centuries is that which has produced the assumption that every young man will enter paid employment and earn his own living: this has reduced — almost eliminated — the financial anxiety of fathers needing to 'provide' for their children, and removed the expectation that one's family, or one's wife's family, will 'do something' for one. This change is clearly connected with the growth of capitalism that makes trade respectable, and even more with the rise of the professions. On this matter, Mr Micawber belongs to the old world, not the new: his constant confidence that something will turn up is based on no systematic efforts to find employment and constantly linked with his feeling that his wife's family should have done something for him. The comic treatment of Micawber — the ridiculousness of his hopes —

reveals Dickens' consciousness that this older world is no longer viable. In contrast, the final glimpse of Micawber making good in the never-never land of Australia reveals a nostalgia for a world in which something *does* turn up. The almost universal critical agreement on the artistic success of Micawber and the unconvincing perfunctoriness of the happy ending would then show the difference between purveying a truth about society, and replacing it with easy wish-fulfilment.

A very similar discussion is possible about Thackeray's Colonel Newcome. He too can be seen as a version of Quixote (and we know Thackeray reread Cervantes' novel when he was writing *The Newcomes*), or as Major Carmichael-Smith, the author's stepfather (and we know Thackeray declared him to be the original), or as deriving from the Victorian respect for manliness, sentimentality, family affection and the stiff upper lip, and so as a figure who could never have been depicted before the nineteenth century. Or let us take Caleb Garth, in George Eliot's *Middlemarch*. Here the literary origin is not a particular figure but a type, the sober prentice or industrious workman; and the personal origin is, once more, the author's father, and once more there is another version of her father available for comparison. There is much less difference this time between the two versions: both Adam Bede and Caleb are almost completely admiring portraits. Caleb is free from the self-righteousness of Adam (he is meant to be cured of this, but it cuts deeper than the author intended); and Caleb is certainly the more successful portrait artistically, because the fact that he has a family to support and cannot easily afford the complete integrity that comes so naturally to him yields a more interesting situation. This difference is not due to the author's personal involvement but to her craftsmanship; and the fact that the tensions which we know to have existed between her and her father find no place in either portrait indicates the very limited sense in which she 'used' him as an original. In this case it also limits the subtlety of the portraits and it is tempting to see this as cause and effect: if Marian Evans had had the brutality to put into the characterisation some of the resentment her father must have aroused in her at times, she might have written more powerfully.

The social explanation of Caleb will begin by observing that the society of *Middlemarch* is pre-industrial, but a society on which industrialism is beginning to make an impact, most notably in the form of the railway: Caleb is in favour of this, as he no doubt would be in favour of any form of 'businesslike' economic progress. His attitudes were formed in the economy of craftsmanship, agriculture and estate management, but they represent that element in the older world that is needed by industrialism. The gap in time between the writing and the setting of the book (1871-1832) is important here: the author is aware of subsequent economic progress, though she does not mention it, and this implicit awareness produces a sense which may even spill over into the plot, that Caleb is on the winning side.

Let us turn from individual characters to a whole book. Conrad's *Heart of Darkness* belongs to a very old literary kind, the journey to the underworld, as found in the *Odyssey*, the *Aeneid*, the *Divine Comedy*, the *Faerie Queene* (II v) and the story of the Harrowing of Hell: it is so impregnated with ideas of exploring the forbidden, of the dangerous journey that brings self-discovery, that the resonances of this type of tale are certainly meant to sound through it. The personal origin of *Heart of Darkness* lies in Conrad's trip to the Congo in 1890, which has many resemblances to the story, and which he regarded as perhaps the crucial experience of his life. And that *Heart of Darkness* is about colonialism, and the scramble for Africa is obvious: it explores both the idea of Africa as an extreme situation in which normal habits are dropped, and the darkness of men's hearts made plain; and as a set of alternative cultures as strongly entrenched and as effective for social control as the 'civilisation' which the Europeans bring. That makes it a contribution — shrewd radical and terrifying — to contemporary debates on the White Man's Burden.

We need a poem to set beside these examples from prose fiction, and I will take Auden's love lyric 'Lay your sleeping head, my love'. The simple fact that this is a love poem enables us to place it in a tradition, that by which love creates a shelter or retreat, a self-contained world, magically protected from the difficult reality that surrounds it:

> Lay your sleeping head, my love,
> Human on my faithless arm;

Time and fevers burn away
Individual beauty from
Thoughtful children, and the grave
Proves the child ephemeral:
But in my arms till break of day
Let the living creature lie,
Mortal, guilty, but to me
The entirely beautiful.

Soul and Body have no bounds:
To lovers as they lie upon
Her tolerant enchanted slope
In their ordinary swoon,
Grave the vision Venus sends
Of supernatural sympathy,
Universal love and hope;
While an abstract insight wakes
Among the glaciers and the rocks
The hermit's sensual ecstasy.

Certainty, fidelity
On the stroke of midnight pass
Like vibrations of a bell,
And fashionable madmen raise
Their pedantic boring cry:
Every farthing of the cost,
All the dreaded cards foretell,
Shall be paid, but from this night
Not a whisper, not a thought,
Not a kiss nor look be lost.

Beauty, midnight, vision dies:
Let the winds of dawn that blow
Softly round your dreaming head
Such a day of sweetness show
Eye and knocking heart may bless,
Find the mortal world enough;
Noons of dryness see you fed
By the involuntary powers,
Nights of insult let you pass
Watched by every human love.

'But in my arms till break of day': the rhythm asserts blissful surrender, the meaning insists on the brevity. The speaker is faithless, the beloved is guilty, but love for that one night makes her the entirely beautiful: this maintains the paradox that love both admits and denies its element of self-deception, its knowledge that the surrounding world is not changed by love's assertions.

The third stanza asserts this more explicitly. If they tempt fate with fortune-telling, and the cards tell them what is impending, they will cling all the more fiercely to the experience of the night. This is the paradox that Donne so memorably inserted into love poetry, the vindication of 'let us possess one world' against the 'cities, towns, courts' of the ordinary world.

Between these comes the second stanza that asserts the paradox of soul and body, how a full experience of either somehow turns into the other. The spiritual vision of Venus can also be traced back to Donne

—Love's mysteries in souls do grow
And yet the body is his book—

and the sensual ecstasy of religious vision to, say, Crashaw:

Ah how oft shall she complain
Of a sweet but subtle pain…

By asserting his paradox Auden is joining two poetic traditions, the metaphysical line in love poetry and the baroque line in religious poetry.

All this seems to suggest that placing this poem in a literary trdition enables us to say all we need to say about it. What have the two other factors to offer? Let us take the social first: has the poem any social context at all? That is not easy to answer. The outside reality that presses may be timeless and universal ('time and fevers', 'nights of insult'); even 'fashionable madmen' could exist at any time. It is only if we regard it as part of the larger whole that is Auden's poetry, or at any rate the Auden of the thirties, that we will be led to set the lovers in a world where war impends, where 'all the dogs of Europe bark', where

Above them, expensive and lovely as a rich child's toy,
The aeroplanes fly in the new European air,
On the edge of that air that makes England of minor importance.

The sense of political threat is important in Auden's poetry, the sense of a particular kind of surrounding anxiety, an awareness of the troubles of the age that are perceived in their specificity before being universalised. And Auden is so brilliantly and wittily aware of class guilt, of the public school communist ethos, of the fear of impending war, that his poems may be enriched as well as limited if we set them firmly in their time.

As for the third factor, the personal, now that Auden is dead we can observe that since he was a homosexual the 'love', if it is a particular person, must be a man; and even if the love is no more individual than the Delias and Julias of traditional love poetry, it was imagined as a man by the poet and by his circle of friends. There is nothing in the text of the poem — or of any of the *Collected Poems* — to suggest that it is addressed to a man: just as the social context has to be brought to this poem from a reading of the author's other poetry, so the homosexuality has to be brought to all his love poems from his biography. Whether we now regard it as part of their meaning will be a question of definition.

§

What objections can be made to this threefold scheme? I cannot of course deal with those objections so fundamental that they consider the inquiry itself illegitimate. A structuralist claim that critical inquiry should concern itself with how the reader constitutes literary discourse, rather than with the determinants of individual works, or a Marxist claim that we should study the social function of the institution of literature and how it maintains a privileged class in power, can be met in two ways: either with a polite pluralism which replies that those are worthwhile aims but they do not invalidate the different aim of this essay, or with the counter-claim that such general aims will remain at the level of shadow-boxing with abstract nouns until they seek to apply their general concerns to individual works, for the way in which we constitute literary discourse means the way we discover the meaning of particular works. Both these replies seem to me valid, but the second only arises when making objections to a structuralist or Marxist undertaking; for the purpose of this essay I am content to say to the Marxist that no study of the social function(s) to which literature is now put can remove the need to study its meaning and origin, and to the structuralist that no study of the reader's activity in general can abolish the existence of particular works and the consequent need for literary criticism.

But there can still be objections, and the obvious way to classify them is into those which say that three is too few, and that it is too many. The first objection requires us to name others which cannot be fitted under these headings, and there are two others in particular which are clearly of enormous importance, language and ideas. The question whether they should be regarded as a fourth and a fifth determinant is really a matter of logic and convenient classification.

Of course the English language makes Auden's poem possible: the jagged clash of sound that evokes the tenseness of the hermit's nerves

> — And an abstract insight wakes
> Among the glaciers and the rocks —

would vanish in any translation. Nothing I say is intended to diminish the importance of language itself, or to be incompatible with Richards' belief that our words are sometimes wiser than we are. But language, being the medium of the creative act, cannot also be its cause: it has the same status logically as the artists' pigment or the acoustic qualities of the violin chamber. Both Mozart and Brahms use the same violin, both portraits and still lives use the same pigment, and one could not therefore use the medium as the defining factor in explaining why a sixteenth-century Venetian portrait differs from a still life by Cezanne. What we are trying to explain is the different use made of the same violin, the same syntax: the medium functions within the finished work, not as an external cause. If we do not accept this, we are led into tautology. Just as the personality of Keats cannot explain the difference between two poems by Keats, so qualities of English phonology or syntax that were available to two poems cannot explain the difference between them.

The exception will be when language imposes restraints on (or offers possibilities to) one work and not another. Language, in other words, becomes a determinant when different languages operate: this will include different phases, dialects and even registers of the same language, as long as these are differences in what was available to the poet, not choices made by him from a common stock. A very simple example will be the brilliant *tour de force* in the eighth chapter of Gautier's *Mlle de Maupin*, in which the hero confesses that, to his horror, he has fallen in love (as he thinks) with a man, saving this point for the very last sentence of his letter. This is only possible in a language in which the words for 'his' and 'her' are the same. It is untranslatable, and there is a clear sense in which this effect, not available to the English or German novelist, is caused by the French language. Or take a linguistic effect like

> Through half the night
> Scudding away from snare to snare, I plied
> That anxious visitation: — moon and stars
> Were shining o'er my head. I was alone
> And seemed to be a trouble to the peace
> That dwelt among them.

There are only four words of Latin origin in this passage. The simplicity of the episode and its closeness to nature is rendered almost wholly in Anglo-Saxon vocabulary, except for the poly-syllables that suggest how the closeness is marred by uneasy elements in consciousness: first the fact that his presence in the hills is an 'anxious visitation', second the fact that he is a 'trouble' to peace. As the Romance language troubled the innocence of English, so Wordworth uses the consequences to express the alienation that troubles his boyhood innocence. This is only possible because our Latinate vocabulary is so important, yet has never captured the heart of the spoken language. The insertion of Fremdwörter in a similar context in German would be far less natural, and quite impossible in Old English. So if we are contrasting *The Prelude* with *Beowulf* or *Faust* we can attribute this effect to the English language itself, but not if we are contrasting it with *Paradise Lost* — though there may be other changes in the language to explain some of those differences too. The medium is never static: oil paint is invented, the piano replaces the harpsichord, the *passé simple* declines. When that happens, it becomes a determinant.

For precisely analogous reasons, we cannot usefully include the natural world among our determinants. The way night-ingales sing is not an explanation why the *Ode to a Nightingale* is as it is (the same song lies behind Crashaw's *Music's Duel*); the fact that we all die is not an explanation for Gray's *Elegy* (it would equally be an explanation for *The Rubaiyat of Omar Khayyam*). Once again, the exceptions will be when there has been an actual change in the circumstances: the decline in infant mortality is one reason why Marvell's *Picture of Little T.C.* could not be written today.

The remaining candidate will be the most difficult to dispose of: that is ideas. A good deal of literature takes its origin from ideas which have already been independently formulated (as politics, as theology, as morality) and which are then given imaginative life by the poet. Is not Christian theology a major determinant of *Paradise Lost*, Aristotelian ethics of the *Faerie Queene*, Neoplatonism of *The Witch of Atlas*? The aim of the *Faerie Queene* is 'to fashion a gentleman or noble person in virtuous and gentle discipline': for this purpose, Spenser tells us, he chose the history of King Arthur, and 'I labour to portray in Arthur, before he was king, the image of a brave knight, perfected in the twelve private moral virtues, as Aristotle hath devised, the which is the purpose of these first twelve books.' Or — to take a very different theology — the aim of some of Hardy's poems is to expose the absurdity of Christianity. In *God's Education* he invents a dialogue between God and a human being about the destruction of beauty by age.

> I saw him steal the light away
> That haunted in her eye:
> It went so gently none could say
> More than that it was there one day
> And missing by-and-by.
>
> I watched her longer, and he stole
> Her lily tincts and rose;
> All her young sprightliness of soul
> Next fell beneath his cold control,
> And disappeared like those.
>
> I asked: "Why do you serve her so?
> Do you, for some glad day,
> Hoard these her sweets —?" He said, "O no,
> They charm not me; I bid Time throw
> Them carelessly away."
>
> Said I: "We call that cruelty —
> We, your poor mortal kind."

10

> He mused. "The thought is new to me.
> Forsooth, though I men's master be.
> Theirs is the teaching mind!"

This is meaningless except in relation to the Christian ideal of an omnipotent and benevolent God. The difficulties of such a belief have often been stated, but never so wittingly revealed: Hardy's God is benevolent but not omnipotent, not even all-comprehending, and the pathetic, well-meaning figure we are shown is meant to clash in our minds with the traditional conception. It is not a literary but a theological tradition that is being used.

For an example from fiction I turn to Arthur Koestler. The purpose of his novel *Arrival and Departure* is to set against each other the analysis of a situation in political and psycho-analytic terms. A young man having escaped from totalitarian tyranny during the war has to decide whether to shelter from the conflict or return to it. A long encounter with a psycho-analyst teaches a good deal about his own personal motivation in taking this decision; but in the end he puts this insight aside and replaces it by the political. The decision involves a response to the outside world, and it must be taken on the basis of a judgement on the nature and needs of that world. The more famous *Darkness at Noon* is an illustration of the problem of political ends and means. Rubashov, the old Bolshevik has based his career on the communist doctrine that ends justify means; now that he is no longer necessary to the revolution, this principle can be used against him. Since someone has to decide when it is necessary to the movement that a member be 'administratively liquidated', the principle gives unlimited power to the Party. The whole story of Rubashov is an explanation of these central questions of political morality. Koestler's novels spring from political philosophy.

Perhaps the threefold scheme ought to be turned into a fourfold one: yet my hesitation at adding ideas as a fourth determinant may not spring entirely from the feeling that all good things go in threes. (Would it be entirely discreditable if it did? May the critic not show his respect for tradition too?) It springs in part from the fact that authors are so untrust-worthy about their ideas. If they feel a strong ideological conviction — or rejection — they are likely to attribute to an ideological position a work which was written out of other and deeper insights. This may not matter much if it is question of which side the author is on. If we believe that *Paradise Lost* does not justify the ways of God, because it makes so good a case for Satan, or for Adam, or for a world needing to break free from so tyrannical a Deity, it remains true that the poem is dealing with that set of ideas, and its language and structure are determined by theodicy. But what of the *Faerie Queene* and the twelve Aristotelian virtues? C. S. Lewis does not believe they have anything to do with the poem:

> The account of the poem given in the Letter to Raleigh is demonstrably untrue... *I labour to pourtraict in Arthure... the image of a brave knight, perfected in the twelve private morall vertues, as Aristotle hath devised* — yet already in the First Part of your poem you have introduced Holiness and Chastity, which Aristotle would never have dreamed of including among his virtues.

Lewis makes two points (though he does not separate them) in his reply to Spenser (or whoever wrote the prefatory Letter), first that though the poem does depict moral virtues, they are not the Aristotelian ones, and second that Spenser 'has no full understanding of what he is really doing.... His poetry... depends for its success on his obedience to the images that rise out of [his] brooding'. These points can be paraphrased to make them fit my argument: first, that if we use a philosophical scheme to understand the poem we cannot assume that the author's own account of that scheme is reliable; and second, that the poem is not based on a philosophical scheme at all — we can impose one if we wish, and it may fit (philosophy is not totally useless after all), but it will be like imposing such a scheme on life itself. The second point is certainly saying that ideas are not determinants of the poem, and so really is the first, for a determinant must pre-exist what it determines, and if we derive the scheme from the poem itself it may be an admirable explanatory device but it is certainly not a cause.

A rather different objection is suggested by the Koestler example. Koestler is seen by many as a 'novelist of ideas': his fiction seems to be written in order to illustrate some political or ethical dilemma, rather than to spring more directly out of a human situation. This opinion may be offered as derogatory or

— conceivably — with cautious respect, but it will never be intended as the highest praise. It is certainly true that to explain Koestler's fiction in terms of the ideas it exemplifies is easier than with the fiction of (say) James or Conrad or Proust; and that in the case of (say) Mann and Lawrence, the parts most easily explained in this way are often the least admired. But this is not necessarily an objection: this factor could apply in varying degrees to different works. In principle, there will be ideas behind *The Mayor of Casterbridge* and Du Coté de Chez Swann (the relation between pride, independence and the old economic order; the relation between emotional dependence, memory and artistic creation) though we may feel that any previous formulation these ideas had received is so remote from what the novelist does with them, that such an approach will tell us nothing important about the book. This is at any rate debatable; but even if it is true, we would be left with the perfectly acceptable view that ideas are directly responsible for some kinds of work, and less and less responsible as we travel along a scale of cynicism, or complexity, or Romanticism, or anti-intellectualism.

As a test case, I would like to look at one of the most impressive examples we have of the attempt to treat ideas as determinants of literature: this is M. H. Abrams' study of the Romantic movement, *Natural Supernaturalism*.

Abrams traces a vast intellectual evolution, that of Platonic, Christian and Hermetic thought, to the point where it issues in Romantic poetry. Thus in discussing *The Prelude* he points to the central and familiar contrast between the tranquil influence of natural beauty, and the 'severer interventions, ministry More palpable' of Nature in her wilder aspects, both of which Wordsworth claims had a profound influence on him.

> I grew up
> Fostered alike a beauty and by fear.

Behind this contrast lies the contrast of eighteenth-century aesthetics, between the sublime and the beautiful. And what lies behind that?

> Centuries of speculation about the natural world — speculation whose concerns were not aesthetic but theological and moral, and which in fact constituted a systematic theodicy of the landscape.

13

This theodicy is concerned with the problem of justifying the goodness of an omnipotent Creator who has created an earth that is wild, waste, ugly, perilous and terrifying. The train of causation, for Abrams, is clear: a moral and theological problem leads to an aesthetic doctrine which leads to an actual poem. He is therefore able to claim [he actually passes on the claim of one Paul Reiff] that the key figure to the understanding of Romanticism is — well, who do you think? Shakespeare? Spenser? Homer? No, it is Plotinus.

This is one rather Hegelian way of seeing poetry, and Hegel looms large in Abrams' scheme. The enormous attraction of Hegel for him is that he sees thought as a motion, not static like the Neoplatonic One, and represents the development of spirit as a circuitous journey homeward, 'from its "moment of departure from its own alienated self," around and up and back, until it finds itself "at home with itself in its otherness"'.

Romantic poetry is full of circular and spiral quests, just as it is full of Neoplatonism and of German idealism; and Abrams' book has many insights to offer into what lies behind Romanticism. But to move from philosophy to poetry as if the second in some way derives from the first has its dangers, and to illustrate them I will look at Abrams' account of *Dejection: an Ode*. He calls it 'the most impressive instance of another circuitous form which Coleridge ... perfected.' It opens with the poet revealing himself 'to be static and self-enclosed (like the Ancient Mariner becalmed at the equator) for he lacks any natural outlet.' The poet is in a state of alienation from the outside world, and the necessary condition for overcoming this is joy. 'Joy is a central and recurrent term in the Romantic vocabulary, which often has a specialised meaning.' In Coleridge it refers to the 'conscious accompaniment of the activity of a fully living and integrative mind', an interpretation that Abrams supports from the Philosophical Lectures. *Dejection* concludes with the poet's triumph over his exclusive self-concern and his achievement of 'interchange' with the outside world. 'This interchange is expressed in a Neoplatonic figure for the circulation of emanation and return:

> To her [joy] may all things live, from pole to pole,
> Their life the eddying of her living soul.'

14

The fact that Abrams has had to force the poem a little to fit it into his pattern should not perhaps be held against his approach: the critic with a general pattern to offer requires almost superhuman restraint if he is never to force his examples, and the polysemous nature of literature enables one often to push a poem into the required direction without actually distorting it. All the same, I must say he has done a little distorting of *Dejection*. To call the state of alienation described at the beginning 'static' suggests overeagerness to make a parallel with *The Ancient Mariner*; and to attribute such careful structure to a poem which we know to have been a botched abridgement of a more autobiographical statement is certainly a case of forcing. All this however merely reminds us that Abrams is a man with a case. The tendency to see literature as determined by ideas has led him to say that 'joy' is a term with a specialised meaning, and to describe the image of the eddy as 'a Neoplatonic figure'. I believe that to regard 'joy' as a technical term here would eviscerate the poem: there is no reason to believe that it has any connexion with *intellectual* activity, and the pain which the ode is expressing is not at the lack of a special philosophical talent but at the joylessness of his existence; just as the image for the return of joy — 'their life the eddying of her living soul' — has as much to do with the feel of excited contact with the outside world as it has with Plotinus. What disappears when the poem is seen as an offshoot of the Neoplatonic tradition or part of the Hegelian working out of an implicit design in systematic thought, is the *cri de coeur* emerging — in this poem more than is usual even among the Romantics — out of the poet's personal agonies. However certain we may be that Coleridge is a Neoplatonist and an idealist, a poem like *Dejection* has a very different relation to personal experience from that of his philosophic speculations. And it is with some satisfaction that I can quote, in support of this point, none other than Hegel:

> This most variegated material is not made poetic simply by being harboured in our ideas, for after all a commonplace mind can shape exactly the same subject-matter into ideas... without achieving anything poetic.... It is not ideas *as such* but the artistic imagination which makes some material poetic.

Finally, there is a methodological objection to this fourth

determinant, which is simply Occam's razor. If we take the trouble, we can subsume it under the other three. Let us turn back to Spenser's letter to Raleigh. The claim that he has portrayed in Arthur 'a brave knight, perfected in the twelve private moral virtues' is preceded by the claim that he has 'followed all the antique poets historical, Homer, Vergil, Ariosto and Tasso'. It is 'by the ensample of which excellent poets' that he has designed his twelve-book/twelve virtue structure. The ideas that lie behind the *Faerie Queene*, in other words, had already been incorporated into literary conventions, and no doubt that is where Spenser got them. It is conceivable that he read Aristotle, decided that his ethical system could be made the basis of an allegorical poem, and only then realised (or pretended) that all the antique poets historical had already done this, but the likelihood of this being true is almost nil, since poets are far more influenced by previous poetry than by philosophy. Ideas reach them direct less often than they reach them immanent in literary traditions.

Ideas can also be subsumed under personal involvement, insofar as the author was in the habit of formulating his view of life. Any explanation of *Women in Love* in terms of Lawrence's personal history, emotional involvement and obsessions, would almost certainly find itself using such terms as phallic consciousness, whole man alive, mental knowledge and knowledge in the blood, sex in the head — a vocabulary devised by Lawrence himself. At this point the critic who looks to the personal factor finds himself with an impossible dilemma. On the one hand is the view that the most important parts of an author's life will be precisely those which he does not formulate as ideas. What makes a poet or novelist? Is it not precisely the ability to turn experience into imaginative expression in a way that goes beyond intellectual formulation — perhaps especially an intellectual formulation by the author himself. One of the most famous statements of this view is, as it happens, by Lawrence: 'It is such a bore that nearly all great novelists have a didactic purpose, otherwise a philosophy, directly opposite to their passional inspiration. In their passional inspiration they are all phallic worshippers.' The assertion can be applied to Lawrence himself. It is precisely the inadequacy of his opinions on blood-consciousness and modern lifelessness that make his novels so much profounder than the turgid theorising of *The Lion and the Unicorn* or the *Study of Thomas Hardy*. But if we then look for those aspects of Lawrence's experience that escape his empty phrase-making, where will we find them? Biographical facts are of little use: what can the scholar, working from documents, find out about the quick of the emotional life? Most of the first hand material will either be coloured by the 'dribbling lies' of the author, or it will have found literary expression that makes it, essentially, part of the creative achievement we are trying to explain. Hence the circularity of most literary biography: the work is explained by the author's development, for which the main evidence is the work.

This dilemma — that personal material is either coloured by ideas or incorporated into the literary work — is exactly paralleled by a similar problem with the social material. It is now a commonplace among sociologists that there is no pure or unmediated social perception: what we see is governed by our expectations, and the act of looking is ideological. This will mean that the study of social pressures and of intellectual influences cannot be kept distinct. We may want to move from the study of utilitarianism, political economy and laissez faire, to the study of the social conflicts and interests articulated by such doctrines, but our evidence for such conflict will come to us largely through those who were thinking in terms of the doctrines. Once again, there will be critics for whom this perhaps impossible task will be the most important of all, for whom what really matters in society will be precisely that which is not formulated in an intellectual schema. A useful recent statement of this position is that of Lucien Goldmann, who sees parallels between the structure of the novel and economic life in bourgeois society, claiming that such homologies emerge without there being any conscious formulation of these structures by the social groups that produce the literary works. What then would be the criterion for claiming that the novelist had succeeded in capturing the equivalent of the 'structure d'échange dans une économie de marché'? If we are dealing with contemporary novelists, we may say that social relationships of which, in our own experience, we were gropingly aware, have been more truly revealed by the writer than they had been by ideological formulation. But what of the past? Even if the critic turns social historian and soaks himself in the material from Restoration France or early Victorian England, how will be perceive their social relationships in a way that is freed from ideology and invites to a sense of the complexities to which Stendhal or Dickens were responding? If he claims that these novelists show a profounder understanding of, or at least response to, their society than do Michelet or Harriet Martineau (and we very often do wish to claim this), how can this be based on some independent access to social realities?

I therefore conclude that the ideas which lie behind a work of literature may already have been incorporated in literary practice, as a set of conventions; may derive from the personal philosophy of the writer, in which case they will be the result of his personal concerns, and will be part of his biography; and may be a formulation of forces in the society in which the work was produced, in which case to study them is to study the society. In all three fields there may be elements that are not explicitly formulated as ideas: these will be fairly easily observable in the first, much less so in the second, and perhaps undiscoverable in principle — though abundantly observable in practice, one feels — in the third. When we try to talk about these elements in a literary work that derive from what is not intellectually formulated, we find it very difficult to escape from the actual words of the text we are trying to explain.

§

I turn now to the opposite objection to my schema, that three factors is too many. This is of far greater theoretical importance. Such a threefold scheme can obviously be called pluralist, and so like all pluralism is subject to the attack of the monist; in the case of literature all three monisms are ready and waiting with powerful and time-honoured arguments. The monism of the individual maintains that nothing really matters except the creative act, that poems are the work not of traditions, subcultures, committees or doctrines, but of poets. It is orthodox Romantic doctrine from Wordsworth through Carlyle to Lawrence, and its vulgar manifestations, turning every discussion of a Yeats poem into anecdotes about Maud

Gonne, need not destroy the seriousness of the view that the poet is a man speaking to men, who makes poetry out of the struggle with himself.

The monism of tradition can be represented by such literary historians as Leo Spitzer or E. R. Curtius. It maintains that to understand a poem you must first read it *as a poem*, subordinating biographical data to literary conventions, which have a life-cycle of their own, largely independent of individual talents and social change. The method for arriving at such understanding is philology (this is to transliterate the German word: the nearest English equivalent would be 'literary history'). As an example of this position, I will take Spitzer's discussion of Milton's sonnet on his dead wife:

> Methought I saw my late espoused saint
> Brought to me like Alcestis from the grave,
> Whom Jove's great son to her glad husband gave,
> Rescued from Death by force, though pale and faint.
> Mine, as whom washed from spot of childbed taint
> Purification in the Old Law did save,
> And such as yet once more I trust to have
> Full sight of her in Heav'n without restraint,
> Came vested all in white, pure as her mind.
> Her face was veiled; yet to my fancied sight
> Love, sweetness, goodness, in her person shined
> So clear as in no face with more delight.
> But, O! as to embrace me she inclined,
> I waked, she fled, and day brought back my night.

This poem, Spitzer claims, is primarily about the nocturnal vision of a bereaved husband, and the consequent paradoxical relation of night and day. The poet's blindness is a secondary theme, which would be clear to the reader ignorant of the poet's biography only if he read the poem in the context of the surrounding poems ('When I consider how my light is spent', 'To Mr. Cyriack Skinner, upon his blindness'). To understand the structure of the poem, its movement from the pagan tradition (Alcestis) through the Jewish ('purification in the old law') to the Christian (reunion in Heaven) we need only understand the traditional significance of the references. Spitzer's aim is to insulate the poem from 'biographical data or parallel personal experience' and so assert the objectivity of philology. But it is possible to accept the substance of his case without

19

going to such lengths of austerity. Milton would, I am sure, have agreed that his poem was clear without biographical knowledge, but not, surely, that his own situation had nothing to do with writing it; and if we had asked him whether a blind and widowed reader would find the poem especially moving, how could he have answered anything but Yes?

Can the meaning of a poem be distinguished from its emotional impact (or from its artistic value)? To Leavis, the answer is no; to R. S. Crane, yes; to the critic who questions whether literature is in any important way different from other discourse it is a question about language in general (and such a critic may reject the very concept of artistic value). I am trying in this essay to address as wide a range of critical opinion as possible, including all three of these positions; so this paragraph must be regarded merely as a parenthesis. I believe that Crane is more nearly right than Leavis, and that understanding is not the same as emotional involvement. Rejecting the third view, I believe that the artistic value of poetry is proved on the pulses, and that this makes the personal experience of the reader relevant — and that of the poet, insofar as an act of emotional communication has taken place. Insofar as philology is a matter of understanding, Spitzer is right to consider it impersonal, and to grant it priority over the personal. To those who believe that the reading of literature is a matter of personal urgency as well as objective study he is quite wrong.

The third factor, society, seems at a first glance quite irrelevant in this case. Bereavement and blindness, surely are intensely personal and also universal: it makes no difference whether they are endured by a medieval aristocrat, a solicitor's son in seventeenth-century London, or a modern factory worker. It is certainly worth observing that social factors loom less prominent in the personal lyric than in any other literary form: this is obvious, and like all truisms it needs saying insofar as it is being denied (as by certain kinds of rather crude Marxism it sometimes is). But like most truisms, it turns out on reflexion not to be all that true, as we can see if we compare the two themes. Blindness is as widespread today as ever, and as incurable; bereavement is far less common. Death in childbirth, from being a normal risk, has become exceptional, and widowhood is something men do not expect. Surely this must have profoundly altered the experience of reading the poem. Whether or not the contemporary reader was himself widowed, he would have regarded it as a normal experience, and though this may not mean that the meaning of the poem has changed, it must once more affect the quality, and the urgency, of the response.

I have represented the monism of tradition by means of literary historians; it is at least arguable that most forms of structuralism belong here too. The attempt to define literature through the competence and activity of the reader, rather than through the intent of the author or its representation of the world, is a claim that literature must be understood in terms of its conventions. The structuralist does not of course look for the same conventions as the philologist: much further removed from Renaissance genre-theory, he is likely to look for deep structures of which neither author nor reader was aware, and he is likely to break down and rearrange some of the traditional literary distinctions. All the same, he too is treating literature as an institution, and trying to understand its internal rules.

But the most widespread monism nowadays is of course the third, the monism of society, and its strategy will necessarily be the opposite to that of literary history: instead of emphasising the separateness of one factor it will emphasise inclusiveness. Neither the individual nor literary conventions, it will insist, have any existence apart from society. If this essay has any Marxist readers, they have probably been saying this to themselves from the first paragraph; but I must point out that you do not have to be a Marxist to say it (it can for instance be stated just as strongly in Durkheimian terms). Individual poets are not self-sufficient, literary conventions are themselves the result of social needs and pressures. Man is a social being, and the determinants of literature are all social.

As a representative of this position I will choose Raymond Williams. In his *Marxism and Literature* there is a section on conventions and a section on the author, in both of which we are told that these can only be understood as social phenomena. Conventions 'can be identified by formal analysis but can be understood only by social analysis'; 'no man is the author of himself' and the individual is only specific 'within the social

21

forms of his time and place.' Inclusive monism ('it's all society, *really*') is never likely to do much harm, since it can become a kind of tautology: as long as you make that obeisance, you can go on talking about other factors. Even Williams is not wholly free of this: thus when discussing genres, and maintaining that the traditional division into three 'stances', narrative, dramatic and lyrical, will no longer serve, he concedes that it does 'indicate the dimension that is in question: a mode of basic (social) organisation which determines a particular kind of presentation — the telling of a story, the presentation of an action through characters, univocal expression, and so on.' This seems to me to say that the division *will* still serve, but that to be fully understood it must be placed in a wider context — the same point that was made about conventions (conventions and genres are both, of course, elements in what I have been calling tradition). Until the point is spelt out, the word 'social' in the quotation above is merely redundant.

Williams does not do much spelling out in *Marxism and Literature*, but would no doubt claim that his previous work provides that. In the chapter cited, he mentions the difference between 'the final "settlement" chapter in early Victorian English novels — e.g. Gaskell's *Mary Barton* — and the final 'breakaway' chapter in English novels between 1910 and 1940 — e.g. Lawrence's *Sons and Lovers*.' This is suggestive, as it is meant to be, but gives us pause when we consider it in detail. The last act of romantic comedy is traditionally a 'settlement', and it is hard to trace that to a particular time and place; and Elizabeth Gaskell surely thought she was following a very old pattern when she married her lovers off and sent them to start a new life in Canada. Most societies have narrative patterns that culminate in settlement, and perhaps they also have impulses towards openness. To articulate such differences is what genres are for. To understand the ending we must look for the interaction of literary tradition and early Victorian England, and to say this is to deny that the former can be understood *only* by social analysis — except in the tautological sense that everything is ultimately social.

At this point I shall have to disappoint the reader who is hoping for a clear statement that will either choose and defend one of these monist positions, or offer a pluralist refutation of them all. Such a discussion has its value — even, for certain purposes, its urgency — but it is not literary criticism nor even, I believe, a necessary prolegomena to literary criticism. It was not for nothing that I began by offering a working hypothesis, even a rule of thumb.

Since I have no wish to be evasive I would like to satisfy this reader by telling him where I stand; but as an agnostic by temperament, I do not find it easy to know. I am prepared to entertain all three monisms, especially the third (though less in its Marxist than in its Durkheimian form); but what I find it far more important to assert is that the practice of literary discussion can and must continue, and that it need not take the form of three uncommunicating universes. The interest of literature and even of literary criticism consists precisely in the fact that the different monists can agree so much on particulars. The Carlylean must admit that sonnets or anti-Utopias or epistolary novels have a good deal in common whoever wrote them, and even that two sonnets may have more in common than a love sonnet and a satire by the same man. The philologist must admit that literary conventions did not drop from heaven but can often be seen as formulations of social norms or the hopes, fears and interests of particular groups (though he may go on to point out how obstinately they survive the disintegration of those groups). And the Marxist will have to admit that there was a man called Dickens, whose novels have a good deal in common — to the extent that a sentence by him can be instantly recognisable — and who had a real father about whom he felt strongly.

2

Where does Alceste go?

(The Satirist as Misanthrope)

Molière's Alceste, the misanthrope, is the man who is never
satisfied. From the beginning of the action, he affirms his total
rejection of politeness, flattery and accommodation to the
weaknesses of others, and drops dark hints that he would like
to walk out of it all:

> Et parfois il me prend des mouvements soudains
> De fuir dans un désert l'approche des humains (143-4)

So it is not surprising that when he is finally disillusioned with
Célimène and convinced (though it is not at all clear that he has
any fresh evidence for this) that she is trifling with him, he
announces that he is going to carry out his threat:

> — Et je veux me tirer du commerce des hommes. (1486)
> — La raison, pour mon bien, veut que je me retire (1573)
> — Au dessein que je fais de fuir tous les humains (1762)

His final declaration to Célimène consists of a reiteration of
this intention and an appeal to her to come with him. She
declares her love, but cannot make such a sacrifice:

> La solitude effraye une âme de vingt ans (1774)

Alceste walks out, and his last words reaffirm his intention:

> Et chercher sur la terre un endroit écarté
> Où d'être homme d'honneur on ait la liberté. (1805-6)

Where does he go? It is clear from the lines already quoted

that we are not told. His intention is announced in such general terms that we are not invited to imagine the life he is going to lead. If we turn to the commentators for help on this point, we find them totally unhelpful. The Larousse editor glosses *désert* as 'un endroit isolé, loin du monde: quelque château à la campagne.' This is ridiculous because what matters about Alceste's retreat is not whether it's going to be in a 'château' (are we being reassured that he's not actually going to starve?) but what mode of life he is proposing. The same editor's remark in the introduction ('proposer la vie solitaire de Tristan et Iseut a Célimène') does address the right point, but with an answer that shows utter incomprehension. Alceste is certainly not proposing an existence in the Cave of Love, where the couple will pass a time of idyllic happiness, thinking only of one another; and Tristan and Iseut were certainly not driven into solitude by their hatred of human wickedness.

The first problem is to decide what sort of question we are asking. It is certainly not a biographical question, concerned with where Molière spent his weekends; and it is not, ultimately, a linguistic question either. A linguistic approach is clearly possible, and some commentators invoke *Le français classique*, by Gaston Cayron, and behind that the *Dictionnaire universelle* of Furetière (1690): 'ainsi on appelle la Grande-Chartreuse un beau désert' (s.v. 'désert'). Is this a linguistic or a social observation? Is Furetière recording without judgement part of the meaning of *désert*, or is he making a critical comment on how pretentiously people use the word? I find it impossible to accept the first view, and to believe that '*désert*' *means* 'un Château a la campagne'. The term lacks any such specificity, and its very vagueness is what enables us to realise that the question I have posed is one of *genre*. It is a question about literary convention: what kind of play is Molière writing?

There are two well-known and traditional answers to the question, where does Alceste go? — the pastoral and the Christian. He could be leaving the world for the solitary retreat of hermit or monk, and he could be leaving the court for a rustic Arcadia. Either destination would be appropriate for a satirist. Denunciation of one's fellow men can have a religious basis, attacking human vice and folly as the product of man's fallen state, implying as alternative the reunciation of the world and

25

aspiration to higher things. Sir Walter Raleigh's poem *The Lie*, written in the 1590s, will illustrate this:

> Go soul, the body's guest,
> Upon a thankless errand:
> Fear not to touch the best;
> The truth shall be thy warrant.
> Go, since I needs must die
> And give the world the lie.

'Since I needs must die.' This can mean that denunciation of this sort is dangerous but, since I needs must die, why not risk one's life by speaking out? But it can also be a gesture to a higher criterion, to the fact that in attacking the world you need not take your values from the world. The first meaning is that which the stanza most obviously uses, but the second would not escape any well-informed reader. It must however remain a hint, since satire must not be too openly religious. A simple denunciation of the world from an explicitly Christian standpoint would not be satire but preaching: the transformation into satiric irony is beautifully done at the end of the same poem of Raleigh's:

> So when thou hast, as I
> Commanded thee, done blabbing
> — Although to give the lie
> Deserves no less than stabbing —
> Stab at thee he that will,
> No stab the soul can kill.

This stanza feigns to accept the vocabulary of the world it is denouncing. 'Blabbing' is an offence against worldly honour, and can lead to 'stabbing': I take it this could either be in a duel or the result of a cloak and dagger attack, in either case the vengeance of a worldly courtier or egoistic defence of honour, for whom such tactless truthtelling 'deserves' such punishment, as Alceste, to Oronte, 'deserves' to be arraigned for his frankness. Out of this terminology emerges the final couplet, with its mocking repetitions of stab and its calm, at last unironic, assertion of the criterion of judgement that has been used

> No stab the soul can kill.

Only at the very end does satire directly assert its basis, and even then the directness has to emerge from a highly skilful indirection.

Alceste, then, could be bound for some monastery, hermit's cave or Stylites pillar from which to indulge his *contemptus mundi*. The other possibility is that he could go into an idyllic rustic retreat from which to contemplate the corruptions of sophisticated man, and say to his companions (for in this kind of 'solitude' one always has companions):

> Are not these woods
> More free from peril than the envious court?

There is a necessary relationship between satire and pastoral. When the pastoralist goes to court he automatically becomes a satirist. A simple effect in *As You Like It* is based on this. It takes a good while for Rosalind and Celia to get to the Forest of Arden: and all theatre-goers are familiar with the feeling of delighted relief that their arrival brings. Once in Arden, we stay there — except for one brief scene. The return to Duke Frederick's Court in III.i. is startlingly effective theatrically, for it is a reminder of what we have escaped from.

Duke F: ...Thy lands and all things that thou dost call thine
       Worth seizure, do we seize into our hands
       Till thou canst quit thee by thy brother's mouth
       Of what we think against thee.

Oliver: O that your highness knew my heart in this.
       I never loved my brother in my life.

Duke F: More villain thou. Well, push him out of doors.

The last line never fails to draw a laugh — or, better still a gasp. Villainy has at any rate this usefulness, that it can smell villainy out, and destroy it in others. The brevity of this scene is part of its sharp, cutting effect. Just for a moment, we need a reminder of what the court is like: then we can be taken to Arden. I have seen a production in which this scene was transposed, and given earlier, before Rosalind, Celia and Orlando, are safely in Arden. The dramatic loss was enormous: we need to breathe the liberating air of the pastoral in order to gasp at this reminder of corruption.

If the renouncing hermit or the happy countrymen are implicit satirists, the satirist has locked up in him a pastoralist or a preacher, waiting for a breath of country air or a glimpse of the waiting congregation in order to step out and announce himself. It may not always be easy to decide which of these is implied, and to seek for the answer will tell us something about the quality of the satire.

The Revenger's Tragedy, perhaps the most brilliantly narrow of all Jacobean plays, is almost entirely set at court. Only in the opening speech, in which Vindice establishes himself as a malcontent chorus and then deliberately decides to enter the corrupt world, and in the two scenes with his mother and sister, are we allowed to escape from the oppressive atmosphere of sophisticated vice.

Since Vindice's initial entry into the play was his decision to come to court, it is natural for him to say 'let blushes dwell i' th' country'. A pastoral standard is automatically implied. When he is later introduced to Lussurioso under his real name, he greets him in dialect: 'How don you? Gi ye good den.' Lussurioso is amused:

> We thank thee.
> How strange such a coarse homely salute
> Shows in the palace where we greet in fire,
> Nimble and desperate tongues! Should we name
> God in a salutation, 'twould ne'er be stood on.
>
> IV.ii.44

The amusement remarks, first that the court is not coarse and homely; then, that it is not religious. There can be no doubt that Tourneur was more interested in the second of these: his rejection of sophistication is more that of *contemptus mundi*, than that of the simple rural swain. But it seems almost inevitable that he should swing from one to the other. Employed by the Duke to seduce his own sister, Vindice escapes from court to a world of simpler virtues. When Castiza resists his overtures, he drops his disguise to praise her and to threaten his mother (who had not resisted). Pastoral and religious implications mingle almost inextricably in his speeches. His praise of honesty, for instance, is cast in social terms:

> And't has a good report, prettily commended,
> But pray, by whom? Poor people, ignorant people;
> The better sort, I'm sure, cannot abide it.

And by what rule should we square out our lives,
But by our better's actions.

II.i.146

This is Touchstone's use of the term when he refers to himself
as 'thy better, sirrah', speaking to the rustic clown. But
though the immediate undertone of moral rejection is pastoral
(country folk, says the irony, are morally better than their
'betters'), the ultimate scheme of values is religious. 'Poor
people, ignorant people,' is not simply a social irony, it is an
echo of New Testament language.

I have cited *As You Like It* as an example of a pastoral that
automatically takes on a satiric face when it looks back to
court; so it is incumbent on me to add that to leave it at that
would be to oversimplify the play. There is, first, the fact that
the play's pastoralism is regularly undercut by a vein of
mockery: not a point that undermines the use made of it in our
argument, and not anyway strong enough to amount to a real
rejection of pastoral. More important is the fact that this play,
too, contains its misanthrope:

Duke: Come, shall we go and kill us venison?
          And yet it irks me the poor dappled fools,
          Being native burghers of this desert city,
          Should in their own confines with forked heads
          Have their round haunches gored.

First Lord: Indeed, my lord,
          The melancholy Jaques grieves at that
          And, in that kind, swears you do more usurp
          Than doth your brother that hath banished you.

II.1.21.

What is Jacques' point (apart from his pleasure in his own
eloquence)? It is that the pastoralist, escaping from court to
Arden, brings his world with him. He is a unsurper too, and
finds in Arden all the vices he has left behind. It is not clear, as
Jacques 'moralises' the spectacle of the stricken deer 'into a
thousand similes' whether the world of Arden is as full of
pathos and greed as the court, or whether that is the only way
Jacques can see it:

          Anon a careless herd,
          Full of the pasture, jumps along by him
          And never stays to greet him: 'Ay,' quoth Jacques,

29

'Sweep on, you fat and greasy citizens,
'Tis just the fashion! Wherefore do you look
Upon that poor and broken bankrupt there?'
Thus most invectively he pierceth through
The body of country, city, court,
Yea, and of this our life, swearing that we
Are mere usurpers, tyrants, and what's worse
To fright the animals and to kill them up
In their assigned and native dwelling place.
                                                11 52-63

It is impossible to take Jacques wholly seriously, for it is impossible to know just what he is saying. The Arden where the Duke usurps is not uninhabited wilderness but rural society: the countrymen kill venison too, so that is no proof of 'usurpation'. Perhaps the true usurpation is the inability to see anything but the court, and in that respect the greatest culprit is Jacques himself: his 'moralising' consists of an insistence that Arden is not Arden, and he is at least as insensitive to pastoral simplicity as he accuses the Duke of being. So it is not surprising that Jacques ends by giving up the pastoral retreat. When the Duke does this, and shows the hollowness of his pastoralism by eagerly returning to court, Jacques renounces both court and country. He will join the repentant villain, Duke Frederick, in the company of the old religious man, and will try — no doubt with continued self-consciousness — to be the other kind of satirist.

It is by now, I hope, clear what one learns by asking where Alceste goes — or, since it would take us beyond the edge of the play, 'goes'. If he would tell us, we would know whether he has been attacking the sophisticated life for lacking rural simplicity and the purity of an earlier time, or the sinful nature of fallen men. His nearest hint is when he contrasts Oronte's polished sonnet with the plain lyricism of an honest popular song; but in the end he never tells us, and Molière is careful to keep it dark. The words used to describe his retreat — *solitude*, *desert* — remain abstract and general (the best translation is surely the abstract, polyvalent and slightly archaic 'wilderness'). The horror felt by Célimène at joining him is purely negative:

Moi, renoncer au monde avant que de vieillir,
Et dans votre désert aller m'ensevelir!   (1769)

It is not where she's going that distresses her, but what she'll have to leave behind.

Anthony Hecht's brilliant poem *Alceste in the Wilderness* derives much of its shock effect from the fact that it sends Alceste off to a perfectly real desert:

> One day he found, topped with a smutty grin,
> The small corpse of a monkey, partly eaten.
> Force of the sun had split the bluish skin,
> Which, by their questioning and entering in,
> A swarm of bees had been concerned to sweeten.
>
> He could distill no essence out of this.
> That yellow majesty and molten light
> Should bless this carcass with a sticky kiss
> Argued a brute and filthy emphasis.

Here Alceste is really acting out his rejection. Not for this Alceste the *lâche methode* of those who stay in the 'world': he sets off to find out what that world is based on, what screaming birds are needed to devise the abstractions of ornament:

> Evening is clogged with gnats as the light fails,
> And branches bloom with gold and copper screams
> Of birds with figured and sought-after tails
> To plume a lady's gear.

Why could he 'distill no essence out of this'? The line surely has a stylistic as well as a moral/psychological meaning. Of course it means that he could not draw a significant moral from it, it was just disturbing raw experience. But also it contrasts the vivid particularity of the monkey's corpse, the stickiness, the white fingernails, with the distilled essence of Alceste's usual reflections, in which

> J'ai pour moi la procès, and je perds justice

or in which

> C'est que jamais, morbleu? les hommes n'ont raison.

It is in order to get back to the distilled essence of that abstract language that Hecht's Alceste must return from his all too real wilderness, 'peruked and stately for the final Act'.

Alceste's refusal to specify where he is going is not the only thing we are not told in *Le Misanthrope*. What, for instance, is his *procès* all about? Who is suing whom about what? He knows how much he has lost ('ce sont vingt mille francs qu'il 'en pourra coûter') but does that ruin him or not? (If it does, no *chateau à la campagne* for him, and his flight may be dictated by necessity!) There is even a mention that Célimène has a *procès* too: are all these edgy people constantly fighting one another at law?

This may seem trivial: but the vagueness is found at the centre of things too. The celebrated slanging-match between Célimène and Arsinoé, for instance, contains few particular accusations:

> Qu'il n'est conte fâcheux que partout on n'en fasse,
> Et que, si vous vouliez, tous vos déportements
> Pourraient moins donner prise aux mauvais jugements.
> Non, que j'y croie, au fond, l'honnêteté blessée,
> Me preserve le Ciel d'en avoir la pensée!   (902-6)

General terminology like this can be of two kinds. It may be elegant variation on a particular accusation whose meaning is perfectly plain. This is probably the case with *honnêteté blessée*, and is quite certainly the case with 11.1001-24, in which Arsinoé sets forth her view on what price Célimène has doubtless been paying for her hordes of suitors.

> Qu'aucun pour nos beaux yeux n'est nôtre soupirant
> Et qu'il faut acheter tous les soins qu'on nous rend.

Here the trick with language is simply that of obviously meaning what you do not say. That, however, is not characteristic of Molière's language, in which normally we do not know what the accusation is. What for instance is the relationship between Alceste and Célimène? When he explodes in jealousy, does he suspect her of sleeping with his rivals, or can he just not bear to think of her smiling on them? Hecht seems to have no doubt that Alceste sleeps with her but I am not at all sure that the elegant metaphors of love —*flamme, coeur, bénédiction* — cover so clear-cut a meaning.

Molière creates for us a world where the style is unbelievably precise and the content never clear, where the tone with which people handle one another is polished with great care, but what exactly is going on is not mentioned — a world in which a musician would be completely at home, and a lawyer would go mad with frustration. The lack of action that critics have

commented on since the seventeenth century is appropriate to
this world: we are following the nuances of a set of relationships, not on account of what is really going on. The language
does not contain experience, and is not in itself very witty: the
wit comes from the clash between language and situation —
the way Oronte can't bear to get on and read his sonnet, the
extravagant compliments that Oronte and Alceste make each
other when seething with fury, and which verbally do not
differ from ordinary compliments. In a sense, it's even
important that they should not be witty. The demolition of
Cléonte, the bore, is quite unlike Horace's bore, or Donne's.
Whereas Donne's description is restless in its hydroptic desire
for linguistic ingenuity and far-fetched analogies, Molière
keeps decorum to the point of dullness. Here are representative details from Donne's account:

> He asks, 'What news?' I tell him of new plays.
> He takes my hand, and as a still, which says
> A sembrief, twixt each drop, he niggardly,
> As loath t'enrich me, so tells many a lie ...
> He knows who loves; whom; and who by poison
> Hastes to an office's reversion.
>
> (Satire IV,1.93ff.)

Célimène says of Cléonte:

> C'est un parleur étrange, et qui trouve toujours
> L'art de ne vous rien dire avec de grands discours,
> Dans les propos qu'il tient on ne voit jamais goutte,
> Et ce n'est que du bruit que tout ce qu'on écoute. (579-82)

This is a description of what she herself is doing, so it must not
display wit. Donne does not care about point of view, or an
irony that circles back on itself, so he can let himself go
linguistically; Molière's passage is all structure, all situation,
and linguistically blank.

If Anthony Hecht developed the feelings of Alceste in a way
that went beyond anything Molière would say, the same is even
more true of Shakespeare. To compare Molière's misanthrope
with Shakespeare's will be to discover an enormous stylistic
contrast, representative of the difference between the two
writers, even of that between the Elizabethan and the neo-
classical, even perhaps of that between English literature and
French.

The contrast is so striking because the situations are so similar. Shakespeare's most famous misanthrope, like Molière's, announces his rejection of mankind:

> — mon dessein
> Est de rompre en visière à tout le genre humain   (95)

> — Henceforth hated be
> Of Timon man and all humanity
>   III.vi.114

And where does he go? We have far more evidence to answer the question in his case, since he walks out halfway through the play, not at the end. We see him in his 'desert' or, as he more often calls it, in the woods:

> Timon will to the woods, where he shall find
> The 'unkindest beast more kinder than mankind.

These woods are not the woods of Arcady. Instead of the soft primitivism of pastoral they offer (to use the valuable contrast proposed by Lovejoy and Boas) the hard primitivism of unyielding Nature:

> Your greatest want is you want much of meat.
> Why should you want? Behold, the earth hath roots.
> Within this mile break forth a hundred springs.
> The oaks bear mast, the briers scarlet hips.
> The bounteous housewife, Nature, on each bush
> Lays her full mess before you. Want! Why want?
>   IV.iii 418-23

The first bandit reveals his corruption when he says 'We cannot live on grass, on berries, water', for grass and berries teach you to despise Athens. The relation of this to satire is the same as that of pastoral, locating the norm in a simple life, against which periwigs, money-making and meat-eating are all condemned.

Yet Timon does not really draw moral strength from his 'woods': his life there involves no superiority. His *saeva indignatio* is not on the whole that of the primitivist: he despises the world because 'all's obloquy', because nothing is level. Under the rough Athenian garments the Christian moraliser with his *contemptus mundi* is scarcely concealed:

> O thou wall,
> That girdlest in those wolves, dive in the earth,

And fence not Athens! Matrons, turn incontinent!
Obedience fail in children! Slaves and fools,
Pluck the grave wrinkled Senate from the bench,
And minister in their steads! To general filths
Convert o' the instant, green virginity!
Do 't in your parents' eyes! Bankrupts, hold fast.
Rather than render back, out with your knives,
And cut your trusters' throats! Bound servants,
    steal!
Large-handed robbers your grave masters are,
And pill by law. Maid, to thy master's bed!
Thy mistress is o' the brothel. Son of sixteen
Pluck the lined crutch from thy old limping sire,
With it beat out his brains!

                                          IV.iii.1-15

The nearest thing to this in Alceste is probably the following:

Non, vous avez beau faire et beau me raisonner,
Rien de ce que je dis ne me peut détourner;
Trop de perversité règne au siècle où nous sommes.
Et je veux me tirer du commerce des hommes. (1483-6)

To the ear trained on Shakespeare, Alceste's couplets sound like a preliminary throat-clearing, a balanced introduction, before he starts on his real complaint. In Shakespeare's blank verse, every sentence overspills its line, and every thought seems to overspill its sentence. Actions are stated with a blunt vividness ('maid to thy master's bed') that is immediately reinforced with an equally blunt cynicism; and the acting of them is imagined with a particularity to which Molière's verse offers no parallel ('Pluck the lined crutch...'). Shakespeare's monosyllabic verbs ('dive' 'fence' 'pluck' 'pill' 'beat') fill the verse with power and force: besides the rugged genius of this, Molière's conceptual dance is so shadowy as to become almost invisible. So specific is Shakespeare's writing that even his abstractions sound concrete:

Je ne trouve partout que lâche flatterie,
Qu'injustice, intérêt, trahison, fourberie.
J n'y puis plus tenir, j'enrage, et mon dessein
Est de rompre en visière à tout le genre humain. (93-6)

This is probably the strongest opportunity for the actor to 'rage' which the part of Alceste offers: the second line can be

35

spoken as a mounting series of steps as indignation grows. But compared with Timon, it is tame in its symmetry:

> Piety and fear,
> Religion to the gods, peace, justice, truth,
> Domestic awe, night rest and neighborhood,
> Instruction, manners, mysteries and trades,
> Degrees, observances, customs and laws,
> Decline to your confounding contraries,
> And let confusion live!
>
> IV.iii.15-21.

Once symmetry has ceased to be a virtue, complexity like this is unleashed: the interplay of meaning, sound and positioning, the shift between Anglo-Saxon monosyllables and Latinate terms, the slight touches of alliteration and wordplay, fill this list with a vitality one would have thought hardly possible in a list of abstract nouns.

These lines of Alceste are also, probably, the most self-conscious he utters, the nearest he comes to explicit awareness of playing the role of misanthrope. Timon, in contrast, has that constant awareness of role-playing that so often characterises the Elizabethan hero: Vindice *plays the part* of the Malcontent, as Tamburlaine does of the tyrant and Lear of the wronged Monarch. Molière's audience develops, from the total structure of the play, an awareness of Alceste's role which is not played against an equivalent (or even stronger) degree of self-awareness in the character. Of course we may feel that Timon's role-playing goes with — even rationalises — a lack of true self-knowledge, but at least he raises the issue of seeing his whole conduct as a dramatisation. It is therefore Timon and not Alceste who says 'I am Misanthropos, and hate mankind.'

Hence Apemantus. Timon is given, as Alceste is not, a competitor in misanthropy. The Apemantus parallel is puzzling in many ways. It is not clear whether one is meant to be more or less sincere, more or less bitter, than the other; nor is it clear what provokes their quarrel. All that is clear is that two misanthropes must inevitably quarrel, like two rabbis; and that we are being invited to observe Timon playing his role by comparing his version with another.

Hence too the error of some of the comparisons with Lear. George Hibbard for instance, in the Introduction to the Penguin edition, asserts that whereas Lear grows in stature,

Timon does not, but 'remains immobilised, as it were, in the fixed posture of the much wronged man' and for this reason 'in the last analysis he is, as a tragic hero, inadequate.' As a contrast between the two plays this is sound enough: there are similarities, and *Lear* is the greater play. All the same, it is not certain that *Timon* is trying to be like *Lear* and failing: Lear goes through a misanthropic phase, Timon is a misanthrope, and he is not intended as a tragic hero. The strengths of both *Le Misanthrope* and *Timon of Athens* are that they offer a central figure who is in a fixed posture, and though this does not vive the same opportunities for development as tragedy does, we would impoverish our literary experience if we wanted to turn all satires into tragedies.

They are of course satires of a particular kind: dramas, in which the satirist is the central figure, and in which consequently, we are invited to see his satiric power as a consequence of an almost crippling misanthropy. We identify with and we judge the misanthrope at the same time: such a tension is the natural experience of responding to great literature. And if in order to judge we need to understand, it is natural for us to ask what they reject the world *for*: which means, where do they go? Neither Molière, who writes with so much generality, nor Shakespeare, who writes with such particularity, quite tells us this. This need not weaken their work: but it does mean that our understanding will be shaped by our asking the question and not being quite sure of the answer.

§

Since this essay has compared two plays in terms of genre and contrasting stylistic tradition, I shall conclude with a brief note on a critic who moves beyond literary history to explanations in terms of the society from which the work emerged. The view of French classical drama I am advancing owes much to the brilliant chapter of Erich Auerbach's *Mimesis*. To confess this debt is made difficult by the fact that Auerbach's view of Molière seems to me much less true than his view of Racine and in particular not true of *Le Misanthrope*. According to Auerbach (though it is risky to try and simplify his complex argument), Molière differs from the majority of the moralists of his century in being less concerned with character types and more with rendering individual reality. This individualism however is only for the purpose of creating grotesque extremes: the moral and aesthetic norm is the typical and not the individual. Auerbach's main example is Tartuffe, and on this his interpretation is at any rate tenable; but I am quite sure that Alceste is neither grotesquely particularised nor ridiculous. Perhaps the most striking thing about *Le Misanthrope* is that critics and audience have so much latitude in their judgement of Alceste: some see him as a tragic hero, some as extravagant to the point of absurdity, and the truth obviously is that he stands somewhere between these two extremes, the meeting-point of forces in tension.

Auerbach concludes his discussion of Molière by saying:

> He consistently avoids any realistic concretising of the political and economic aspects of the milieu in which is characters move,

and he goes on to contrast the detail which Balzac supplies on how Eugénie Grandet accumulated his fortune with 'the absolute generality and ahistoricity' of Harpagon's economic situation. If the argument of this essay is sound, Auerbach does not go far enough: it is not only the political and economic aspects of the milieu that are left abstract (that would apply to Timon as well): it is the very nature of the experience that is not concretised.

For Auerbach, this abstraction reflects the social situation of seventeenth-century court drama: the lack of any real social function for the aristocracy who saw the plays finds expression in the treatment of kingship: 'being a prince is much rather a posture, an "attitude", than a practical function.' This leads to a brilliant interpretation of Racine, but Molière does not write about princes, nor solely for the aristocracy. To explain the whole extent of his abstract style by means of the social situation of one class may be tempting, but it would lead to a rigidity of social determinism that so subtle a critic as Auerbach ought never to allow.

3

Literature and Money

Let us begin with a famous old tale about money, that of the three young men who went in search of Death, and found a pile of gold — and so found Death. It is known to us of course as the story of *The Pardoner's Tale*, but it is older than Chaucer. The earliest known version is in one of the birthtales of Buddha, and there are several late medieval versions, always as an illustration of the evils of avarice. In *Novella* 83 of a collection published in 1525 (*Le ciento novelle antike*) but whose material is thought to go back to the thirteenth century, Jesus, out walking with his disciples, sees a treasure and warns them not to take any because it will rob them of their souls — as they'll see if they watch what happens to the robbers who find it (which they do). In an *exemplum de avaricia* from a manuscript written at Prague in 1406, a hermit finds a treasure and runs off crying in a loud voice 'Death, death, death!' In the fifteenth-century play *Representazione di Sant' Antonio*, the spirit of Avarice actually appears rejoicing at the end, and a moral points out how much evil comes from this cursed she-wolf. The story caught the medieval imagination, as it had caught the oriental imagination long since, and for much the same reason: it was a warning against the lure of worldly wealth.

Chaucer's version is slightly unusual, in that it does not begin with the heap of gold: so it is only on turning to other versions that we see clearly that this is the most important detail in the story. The fighting and the poisoning are consequences of the money; the quest for Death with which Chaucer begins makes a brilliant ironic setting, but the story is centrally not about boasting but about greed. This is said explicitly by the Pardoner when he explains that he always preaches on the same subject, *radix malorum est cupiditas*; and the fact that he is himself totally dominated by greed simply adds, of course, a characteristically Chaucerian irony.

The view of money conveyed by this story is overwhelmingly moral. There is no suggestion that money is an ordinary thing, needed for the continuance of everyday social life: it is a temptation and a threat, offering dreams of unearned opulence, or bringing conflict and lurid death. There is one moment in Hans Sachs' sixteenth-century version of the story when the hermit, after fleeing the sight of the treasure, comes back, reflecting that it may be useful to the poor, but finally decides to shun it after all. This might look at first like a different attitude to wealth, but it isn't really: for even this good use suggested for it is something exceptional. Against wealth as a form of corruption is set the possibility of wealth as a way of rectifying the injustices of society: in neither case is it seen as part of normal social activity. It is there to test our moral worth: usually to corrupt, possibly to help, but always as a moral test.

There is little in common between Chaucer's tragically ironic narrative and Shakespeare's Plautine farce, *The Comedy of Errors*: so it will be all the more striking if we can find a resemblance in their view of money. What sort of society does the play depict? The opening scene makes it clear that Ephesus and Syracuse are both trading towns: their enmity sprang from unfair treatment of each others' merchants. Egeon, father of the twins, is a merchant, and so (we must presume) is Antipholus of Ephesus, who keeps a large establishment, lives in comfort, and is a friend of the Duke. Certainly he can hardly live on inherited wealth, since he arrived in Ephesus a foundling; but all we see of his life suggests a gentleman of leisure. No doubt there is good literary reason for this: Shakespeare wants us to see Ephesus through the bewildered eyes of the Syracusans, for whom the town is full of cozenage, is Fairyland where you talk with goblins, so he naturally peoples it with a sense of danger and a leisured class, not with sober industry.

Whatever the reason, there can be no doubt of the result. We see Antipholus as master of his time whose only duty is to get home for dinner. His sister-in-law refers briefly to his meeting merchants in the mart, but she seems to think of this activity as an assertion of male independence of the home ('A man is master of his liberty') rather than as a way of earning a living. The only transaction we see him indulging in is ordering a gold chain for his wife; and the only person who handles money is the other Antipholus, who has brought it with him — and even that money is never spent, it is merely the occasion for a comic beating and a series of misunderstandings. The chain does change hands, but to the wront Antipholus, who in a world of common sense would not accept it, but who takes it as a sign of the magical wealth, the 'golden gifts' of Ephesus.

All mention of the practical functions of money has been carefully removed. We neither know nor care how Antipholus of Ephesus keeps his establishment going, and it is only the foils and social inferiors, like Angelo and Balthazar, who have the worry of paying their debts. Yet money is prominent in the Antipholus-Dromio situations, as an occasion for confusion, or as a test of good intention. The reason Angelo does not get his money for the chain is not because chains are expensive and Antipholus was extravagant, but because of the confusions of the comic plot. If we compare this with *The Pardoner's Tale* we can see that we have moved from tragedy to farce, but are still in a world unconcerned with the practical purpose of money.

What would an alternative view of money be like? It would see it not in moral but in functional terms: as something we take trouble to acquire, and spend with care and judgement. As something we earn in reasonable and variable amounts, over time, not suddenly and unexpectedly; and as something we need for everyday wants. Even the poisoned drink that the youngest rioter bought had to be paid for: as the ordinary, unpoisoned drink and bread that we buy every day.

To see this other view, as an extreme contrast, let us turn to *Middlemarch*. When Tertius Lydgate arrives in the town as an ambitious young medical practitioner, he knows it will be unwise to marry too soon. Not yet established in practice, determined to pursue his scientific researches, he has neither time nor money for domestic life: chatting to Mayor Vincy's accomplished daughter is all very well — mild flirtatious chat, laced with sexual tension but perfectly proper and (most important) non-committal. But marriage is an arrangement that changes one's way of life, and which presupposes capital and/or a regular income.

Lydgate, as we know, was caught by his own sexual susceptibility. Why did his marriage ruin his career? The obvious answer is, because his wife had neither the imaginative sympathy to share poverty with him, nor the economic sense to manage their money matters. Rosamund clearly does not understand money. When her mother is chattering to her, in a very down-to-earth way, about where to buy linen, and how to furnish a house, she remarks that Mr Vincy is not going to give any money. 'Do you think Mr Lydgate expects it?' To this Rosamund answers: 'You cannot imagine that I should ask him, mamma. Of course he understands his own affairs.' All Rosamund's education is implied in this supremely self-satisfied remark. Her bland lack of interest in Lydgate's affairs suggests feminine submission, but in a way it is feminine dominance as well: for it is this refusal to be involved with his problems that breaks Lydgate. And although Rosamund would consider it unladylike to interest herself in financial details, it would equally be unladylike not to expect the results. As George Eliot has already told us, earlier in the book, 'There was nothing financial, still less sordid, in her previsions: she cared about what were considered refinements, and not about the money that was to pay for them.'

Here is one of the central insights of George Eliot's realism: that in order to be above money, you need to have it. Rosamund is a very expensive plant; and the very fact that she has been trained not to think about expense, makes her more expensive still. In both Rosamund and her brother Fred we can see this contempt for anything 'sordid', and we can see how their upbringing caused it; yet it would be quite wrong to blame Lydgate's troubles entirely on her. Just as he would not have married her if he had looked for strength of character rather than charm and accomplishment in a wife, so he would not have allowed himself to get into such difficulties if he too had not been above such sordid matters as financial calculation. These are the famous 'spots of commonness' in Lydgate's character: the fact that he did not apply to human and social matters the high qualities of mind that he showed as a scientist:

> Lydgate entered into treaty for old Mrs Bretton's house in an episodic way, very much as he gave orders to his tailor for every requisite of perfect dress, without any notion of being extravagant. On the contrary, he would have despised any ostentation of expense; his profession had familiarised him with all grades of poverty, and he cared much for those who suffered hardships. He would have behaved perfectly at a table where the sauce was served in a jug with the handle off, and he would have remembered nothing about a grand dinner except that a man was there who talked well. But it had never occurred to him that he should live in any other than what he would have called an ordinary way, with green glasses for hock, and excellent waiting at table.
>
> (Chapter 36)

How well George Eliot knew Lydgate: the perfection of his behaviour as a doctor, combined with his assumption that none of these difficulties he knew how to make allowances for would ever apply to *him*. There is a good deal more about Lydgate's preparations for marriage, all imbued with George Eliot's marvellous insight that the sensitive taste which does not calculate is in fact insensitive:

> Happening the next day to accompany a patient to Brassing, he saw a dinner-service there which struck him as so exactly the right thing that he bought it at once. It saved time to do these things just when you thought of them, and Lydgate hated ugly crockery. The dinner-service in question was expensive, but that might be in the nature of dinner-services.

'Lydgate hated ugly crockery': how the short, blunt sentence reveals the curtness with which he shuts out the nicely calculated less or more. And when Mrs Vincy says she hopes it won't be broken, Lydgate's reply is once more revealing: '"One must hire servants who will not break things," said Lydgate.' What it would be vulgar to inquire into is treated with the magic word 'must'. It is the same shedding of responsibility Lydgate has already shown over marriage: one must marry a wife who will make one's home gracious. Lydgate does not know about the material basis of domestic affection, he takes it for granted; so it is not surprising that he finds a wife who does the same.

43

There is one character in *Middlemarch* who does understand
the material basis: that is Mr Farebrother, the clergyman, who
understands so much. Lydgate is a little shocked to find Mr
Farebrother playing cards for money; and since he usually has
more insight into other people's situation than his own,
realises that Farebrother needs the money, and relies on his
winnings. When — partly through Lydgate's help — Farebrother finds himself better off financially, he remarks:

> It's rather a strong check to one's self-complacency to find how much
> of one's right doing depends on not being in want of money. A man
> will not be tempted to say the Lord's Prayer backwards to please the
> devil, if he doesn't want the devil's services.
>
> (Chapter 35)

The details of domestic economy — details which old-
fashioned readers might feel beneath their consideration — are
for George Eliot the true meaning of money: something a
professional man has to earn bit by bit, and a family man has to
spend with care. That is what I suggest we should call the
functional not the moral view of money. This terminology is, I
admit, tendentious: is not George Eliot renowned as one of
the most deeply moral of novelists? But though a moralist, she
is also a realist: her first concern is to render the quality of
social experience, to show us what taking a decision is like, by
making sure we understand fully what the choice is between;
only then are we led to ask what was the right decision. The
traditional view of money, however, is moral at the expense of
realism: the categories of social perception are themselves
formed by the moral scheme. It is to emphasise this difference
that I suggest a terminology by which our great novelist of
moral concern is not placed among the moralists.

Yet the traditional view of money is found in *Middlemarch*
too. The one story that uses a very old comic formula is that of
Featherstone, the bed-ridden miser, whose greatest delight is
in tormenting the relatives who hope to inherit his wealth. He
uses money as a lure and a threat — as an assault on human
emotions, not as a practical necessity for living. Greedy himself, he arranges and gloats over a satiric comedy in which *radix
malorum est cupiditas*. And so when Featherstone is dead and
the relatives gather for the reading of the will, George Eliot
prints as epigraph a few lines from *Le légataire Universel* of

Regnard, a follower of Molière, describing the discomfiture of
the legacy-hunters who get nothing but *un bonsoir avec un pied
de nez*. These conventional lines about the corrupting effect of
greed, in a comic form that goes back through Molière to
Terence and Juvenal, now commend themselves to her as
appropriate for her own satire. Yet as we read the chapter, we
soon discover that it is not traditional satire after all.

> Poor Mrs Cranch being half moved with the consolation of getting
> any hundreds at all without working for them, and half aware that her
> share was scanty; whereas Mrs Waule's mind was entirely flooded
> with the sense of being an own sister and getting little, while some-
> body else was to have much.
>
> (Chapter 35)

The situation is that of Regnard or Juvenal; but the treatment
is that of George Eliot. These women have families and
comprehensions of their own: they lack the sharpness (and
also the simplicity) of a Voltore or a Tartuffe.

This mingling of convention and realism is seen perfectly in
the story of Fred Vincy and Stone Court, old Featherstone's
home. Fred had always hoped, and sometimes thought, that
the property would be left to him; and is naturally disappointed when it isn't. But in the end Fred, because he is the
hero and has come through his trials successfully, does get the
property, and there lives happily with wife and children. To
tell the story in summary like this is to make it sound like a
fairy tale; but how different when we look at what actually
happens. For Fred does not earn Stone Court by passing magic
tests in the manner of the youngest son who helps the fairy
disguised as an old woman, or of Bassanio, the spendthrift who
knows how to moralise and choose the leaden casket while he
makes a speech against money. Fred's triumph lies in accepting
his disappointment and living through its consequences. Because he has lost his expectations he has to work; he still has
the same careless character, and he has to learn to do small
uncomfortable things, like giving up billiards and learning to
write legibly, not large symbolic things like making speeches or
choosing caskets. Fred gets a real, not a symbolic Stone Court:
and he gets it because he has shown himself competent to
manage it. His response to his disappointment is not the fine

moral gesture of learning to despise riches, but the practical measure of learning to work instead of living in hopes.

I have so far discussed money in terms of its effect on men's lives, that is, in functional terms; but we can add a word on the form of its existence as object. For here too there is a clear contrast between the moral and the functional treatment. In the medieval stories money is gold coins, glinting with temptation and chinking the tune of corruption. Chaucer's rogues found

> Of floryns fyne of goldy-coyned rounde
> Wel ny an eighte busshels, as hem thoughte.

Hans Sachs' hermit saw the treasure in an old tree-stump, and ran away with it. Wealth in this tale is a physical object. But for Lydgate, money is represented by those abstractions that the economy finds convenient: banknotes, bills and cheques. In order to find that he is in difficulties, he does not count coins, he performs calculations. The only moment in Middlemarch at which money takes on a vivid physical existence is when old Featherstone is dying, and wants Mary to burn a will for him. As he grows desperate at her refusal he opens the tin box in which he keeps his money, and offers it all to her, the notes and the gold;

> Mary, standing by the fire, saw its red light falling on the old man, propped up on his pillows and bed-rest, with his bony hand holding out the key, and the money lying on the quilt before him. She never forgot that vision of a man wanting to do as he liked at the last.
>
> (Chapter 33)

Here the novel has taken on a different kind of power from usual — something more traditional and less realistic, more in terms of vivid symbolic moments and less of the slow pressure of actuality; and it is wholly appropriate that at this moment we *see* money as nowhere else in the book.

Georg Simmel points out, in his essay on Secrecy, that money enables transactions to be carried on in 'otherwise unattainable secrecy'. Three characteristics of money make this possible: its compressibility (which permits one to make somebody rich by slipping a cheque into his hand without anybody's noticing it'), its abstractness, and its effect-at-a-distance. This possibility is a sign of the large impersonal group. The literary point I have been making confirms Simmel's view: in our society, the more important the money, the more abstract its form. The child spending his pocket money feels the coins in his hand, and knows by physical contact how much he has. Wages come in the somehow less tangible form of banknotes, that were once mere promises, like cheques, and have now come to seem to us like real money as they have grown less important. It is cheques that really matter now, or share certificates, or other statements of transactions that take place only through ledgers or computers. Gold coins chink only in antique shops, where they are 'paid for' with paper.

§

George Eliot is not the only novelist (though she is perhaps the most brilliant) to offer us the functional treatment of money: indeed, it could be claimed that every great nineteenth-century novelist uses it, since they are all analysts of the workings of their society. For two briefer examples, I turn to Trollope and Balzac.

Trollope's interest in the traditional landed aristocracy is respectful but shrewd: he is aware that it is infiltrated from commerce and the professions, and he is concerned to study the response. He is concerned too with the further infiltration of foreigners into commerce and finance. His picture, as is natural in a writer more voluminous than subtle, is detailed and elaborate. He is concerned with the difference between the great families, often active in politics, wealthy and needing even more wealth, and the squirearchy, more conservative, more detached from the centre of power, and to Trollope's mind more truly representative of traditional English virtue. He is concerned too with the upstarts and the immigrants, and how English society adjusts itself to receive them. His finest study of this situation — perhaps his finest novel — is *The Way We Live Now*, the story of the rise and fall of the Jewish financier Melmotte. Trollope does not care for Melmotte: he shows him as dishonest, blustering and coarse, and he considers his success a symptom of the decline of English society — hence the novel's title. Yet the book is not a simple piece of xenophobia. Not only is Trollope careful to have a good Jewish financier to contrast with the corrupt ones; he keeps his most savage satire for the young English noblemen who do nothing except drink, hunt, gamble, and quarrel with their fathers, and who are perfectly prepared to use Melmotte for their own convenience while continuing to despise him.

What we have here is a hierarchical society which is having to change: the landed interest can only survive if it comes to terms with the moneyed interest. Of course this has always happened in English society: Pitt actually suggested that every man with a thousand a year should be raised to the peerage. So when Plantagenet Pallister, rising politician and heir to a duke-dom, marries Glencora for her vast wealth, he is only doing what dukes and landed politicians have always done. But because the process is now happening faster, it is more notice-able: the traditional classes have no longer time to absorb the new and make them like themselves. Trollope has a very simple way of showing his change: what ought not to be bought or sold can now be had for money.

The squirearchy's attitude to money is revealed by that heart-of-oak Englishman Roger Carbury. He has a Roman Catholic priest staying with him, whom he describes as follows:

> Certainly he is a gentleman. He took his degree at Oxford, and then became what we call a pervert, and what I suppose they call a convert. He has not got a shilling in the world beyond what they pay him as a priest, which I take it amounts to about as much as the wages of a day labourer. He told me the other day that he was absolutely forced to buy second-hand clothes.
>
> (Chapter 15)

Why does the priest's lack of money not make him socially unacceptable? Because it is not a sign of class distinction. There is a distinction in Roger's mind between a gentleman and an inferior, that does not appear to depend on money. Of course all such distinctions *are* based on property: a gentleman is someone who belongs to the possessing class. But on the individual level, property is expendable: Father Barham is a gentleman because he has the attributes of his class — manners, speech, interests. No doubt this makes him accept-able because it is seen as a kind of guarantee that he will not threaten the class interest. Roger Carbury is perfectly pre-pared to make friends with a poor priest; whereas to make friends with a poor labourer would have been socially subversive.

Into this world, where there are things money can't buy, and lack of money can't forfeit, comes Melmotte and buys everything. He simply tramples the unwritten rules and uses his vast wealth to buy what ought not to be for sale, but that a corrupt aristocracy is all too willing to sell:

> The ball was opened by a quadrille in which Lord Buntingford, the eldest son of the Duchess, stood up with Marie. Various arrangements had been made, and this among them. We may say that it had been a part of the bargain...
> 'Of course they are vulgar,' the Duchess had said, — 'so much so as to be no longer distasteful because of the absurdity of the thing. I dare say he hasn't been very honest. When men make so much money, I don't know how they can have been honest. Of course it's done for a purpose. It's all very well saying that it isn't right, but what are we to do about Alfred's children? Miles is to have £500 a-year...
> 'Of course they expect something in return; do dance with the girl once.' Lord Buntingford disapproved — mildly, and did as his mother asked him.
>
> (Chapter 4)

For a popular Victorian novelist, Trollope can be remarkably cynical; and the main effect of *The Way We Live Now*, for all its sentimentality and leisurely pace, is of a cynical bluntness. There are even blunter passages than this one, but this is fierce enough. If the Duchess had been asked what 'vulgar' meant, she would no doubt have said it meant doing anything for money, just what she is doing. All that is left of her breeding is the habit of despising those sho do openly what she barely conceals. English society, Trollope seems to be saying, consists of those who can make money, and use it to buy rank, and those who have rank, and sell it for money.

§

For all the obvious differences, Balzac shares many of Trollope's concerns. He has the same interest in buying and selling, the same reliance on utterly conventional plots, the same concerns with what is happening to traditional society. Balzac seems to me more like Trollope than Dickens, with whom he is usually compared. The main difference is that (like Dickens) he can be furiously melodramatic, and at his worst he is a far worse novelist than Trollope ever is; but at the same time he is a shrewder and profounder historian, and at his best he shows a complexity of social understanding far beyond the range of Trollope.

One of Balzac's central interests is the contrast between provincial society and Paris. Perhaps *Illusions Perdues* is the best example of this. While Lucien Chardon is being sucked into the world of actresses, adultery and journalism, his sister Eve and her husband David Séchard back home in Angoulême are struggling against the meanness of a miserly father and the unscrupulousness of business rivals, trying to survive financially while David perfects his new method of paper-making. This is not simple Horatian praise of rural simplicity against urban corruption. Paris is corrupt, certainly; but the most explicit praise of rural content probably comes from old Séchard, the totally callous miser who refuses to do anything for his son — and is approved by the locals for his firmness. Balzac is concerned to show two complicated and callous worlds, and how they contrast, and his preference for the provincial is only intermittent.

There are many ways to show the contrast; and none better than their attitude to money. We must of course realise that this is not the extreme contrast between the subsistence economy that doesn't use money, and the abstractions of city finance. Angoulême is a town, with trade and industry, and its commercial life is an utterly unscrupulous war of each against all. David is an inventor, and cannot survive without backing; but his potential backers are all creditors. His main problem is to find enough to live on, and to keep his family, while he is perfecting his process (and allowing his printing firm to go to ruin); only later does he encounter the even more serious problem of the capital needed to develop the invention. In the end (Balzac for once resisting the really melodramatic outcome) he attains modest success, while the unscrupulous Cointet grows rich on him.

Provincial society is neither virtuous nor idyllic, but it is still very different from Paris. For the getting and spending of money in Angoulême is more or less rational: the struggle is ruthless but not mad. In Paris however it comes and goes unpredictably: the same person may move from affluence to poverty and back in a very short time. Lucien spends most of his money on clothes as soon as he arrives — and half of those are useless because he went to the wrong tailor. Prices are arbitrary: a dinner can cost 18 sous chez Flicoteaux (22 with wine), but when Lucien tries to cheer himself up by having a good dinner (to initiate himself into the pleasures of Paris) he is startled to find that the bill removes the 50 francs he had been relying on to go a long way in Paris. That dinner, says Balzac, cost a month's living in Angoulême. The extreme example of this arbitrariness of money is gambling. Lucien's friend Lonsteau is a gambler, and his financial irresponsibility corresponds to the intellectual irresponsibility that leads writers into journalism. Lucien follows his friend down both these slopes.

Where does the money come from that is spent so recklessly by the fast set in Paris? There are three main sources. Some they earn themselves, by their journalism. For this one needs a prostituted talent. The man of genius and integrity, represented by Lucien's friend d'Arthez, will go on eating chez Flicoteau; but Lucien, though he can't write as memorably as d'Arthez, has a ready talent that makes him far more successful than those who initiate him into his new life.

No journalist earns enough: the very talent that earns drives them to spend excessively. For their second source of income, they rely on their mistresses, who all have sugar-daddies. We're never really told how these pompous infatuated self-deceiving old gentlemen get their money (Trollope would have told us: but then he wouldn't have written about kept women in the first place); but we can see that the sugar-daddy is a crucial institution for diverting the wealth of the bourgeoisie into the parasitic society that so fascinated Balzac. And the third source is also such a device. Some of Lucien's money comes from his devoted mother and sisters back home. Lucien is that characteristic Balzac character, the ambitious young man who bleeds his womenfolk. They are the leak through which provincial money runs into the sewer of the metropolis.

Le Père Goriot has many parallels with *Illusions Perdues*. Rastignac, its ambitious young man, is a Lucien (also, as it happens, from Angoulême) whose social aspirations are even more naked. Instead of prostituting his talent (he is a law student) he simply gives it up, relying on impudence, ambition and sexual charm for his social rise. In what is perhaps the most memorable conversation in the book, the cynical Vautrin describes how Rastignac appeared when he returned to the boarding house after his first evening of luxury:

> Ce jour-là vous êtes revenu avec un mot écrit sur votre front, et que j'ai bien su lire: *Parvenir!* parvenir à tout prix.

Arrive: but to arrive you need money; and getting there is the way to get the money. It is on that paradox that the climber gambles.

One particularly interesting paragraph of *Le Père Goriot* describes how the fashionable world regards its debts:

> Ils n'ont d'argent pour les nécessités de la vie, tandis qu'ils en trouvent toujours pour leurs caprices. Prodigues de tout ce qui s'obtient à crédit, ils sont avares de tout ce qui se paye à l'instant même, et semblent se venger de ce qu'ils n'ont pas, en dissipant tout ce qu'ils peuvent avoir.

Never satisfied with a general sociological observation, however acute, Balzac goes on to illustrate: the tailor or the boarding-house keeper has to give credit, because of the size of the sums involved, whereas the hatter demands cash. As a result (it is such consequences in consciousness that render sociological observations interesting to the novelist) the young man develops two different awarenesses of money. Moving from the provinces to Paris entails learning to distinguish cash from credit as two kinds of activity in yourself.

§

Both Trollope and Balzac, then, take a functional view of money: but not Dickens. It is a commonplace to remark that Dickens is the one great nineteenth-century novelist whose roots are still in earlier traditions that antedate the novel, above all in the humour-tradition of comedy. There is no doubt of his fascination with money, and at least three of his masterpieces (*Dombey and Son, Little Dorritt, Our Mutual Friend*) give it a central place — and a very traditional treatment.

The central symbol of *Our Mutual Friend* is the dustheap. Dickens knew a good deal about dustheaps, for he had published an article in *Household Words* ('Dust, or Ugliness Redeemed') in 1850, describing their contents in detail — the chemicals and soot found in them, as well as the rags, 'tin things,' broken glass, and even occasional jewels and (once) a cheque. There is a perfectly sound factual basis to the way old Mr Harman grows rich as a contractor in dustheaps, but on this basis Dickens has erected something more like a fairy tale. Noddy Boffin's comic name, the Golden Dustman, invites us away from realism; and this money corrupts him as money traditionally corrupts — *radix malorum est cupiditas*. It does not matter in the slightest that Mr Boffin tells us, in the end, that he was only pretending, in order to test Bella. He is a humour-figure who consists only of what he says and does in front of our eyes, with none of the individualising depth that makes it meaningful to ask whether he is sincere. The colourfulness of his corruption brings him to a comic (not a novelist's) life that is worthy of Ben Jonson.

Dombey and Son is very similar. Money is Mr Dombey's idol, and his devotion to its service has dried up his understanding of human emotion. We learn very little about how he made his money: it is not easy to be sure just what the house of Dombey does, and in a book in which the growth of the railway is so prominent it is notable that Dickens makes no attempt (surely George Eliot and Balzac would have) to connect the firm with the railway boom, or even to tell us that they had nothing to do with it. It is not easy to find economic reasons for the firm's collapse: it collapses because Mr Dombey has to be taught a lesson, even because in stories like this the character who starts rich has to lose money. Dickens turns away from this kind of interest in what George Eliot called 'the medium' to depict what he is most brilliant at, the dehumanising effect of living for business. When Mr Dombey hires a wet-nurse for his son, he explains 'I desire to make it a question of wages, altogether... It is not at all in this bargain that you need become attached to my child, or that my child need become attached to you.' He even buys her name: to remove all element of human relationship he stipulates that she should be 'always known as — say as Richards — an ordinary name, and convenient.'

Now if money corrupts what is the remedy? What positive

can be set against its evil power? the answer, scattered through almost all his novels, is clear: money. The social force that can undo the harm that comes from the temptation of money is also money — rightly used. This is clearest in *Nicholas Nickleby*, where almost all the help that is proffered comes from the Cheeryble brothers, wealthy and benevolent merchants. They embody the Dickensian ideal of benevolence — a helping hand, given with kindly understanding by individual to individual. It is hard to understand how the Cheerybles stay in business, just as it is hard to know how Mr Pickwick ever made his money: the greater art of the mature Dickens drew distinctions that never arise in the simple early books, such as that between Casby and Panks. Casby, the Cheeryble of *Little Dorrit*, is only able to walk the world with his air of benevolence because he employs the unprepossessing but good-hearted Panks to grind the faces of the poor. Things are more complex in the later Dickens, but all the same, social rescue, when performed, is done with the help of money. Magwitch's money ruined Pip's character; but it was the one bit of that money which Pip had put to good use that saved him in the end.

And there is a further complication. There are those who like to declare their trust in money, such as the pert, un-redeemed Bella Wilfer, whose self-confessed longing to be rich is the cause of Mr Boffin's demonstration of the evil of riches. Bella gets morally better as she learns her lesson, but artistically feebler: it is when she is declaring her indignation at being poor, or delighting in the power of money as she spoils her father, that she is most alive and most attractive. Even more compelling is the scene in *Dombey and Son* when Walter Gay and Captain Cuttle call on Mr Dombey in his Brighton hotel, hoping to persuade him to rescue the ruined Sol Gills. It is one of the most brilliant scenes in Dickens. Mr Dombey insists on involving six year old Paul in the discussion. 'If you had money now,' said mr Dombey; 'as much money as young Gay has talked about; what would you do?' Of course Paul says he would give it to Sol Gills; and Mr Dombey thereupon lends it, saying 'And you see Paul, how powerful money is, and how anxious people are to get it.' We are meant to contrast Paul's simple kindness with his stern, calculating father: but how can we fail to notice that Mr Dombey was perfectly right, that he has in fact shown how powerful money is?

It is not unusual for the artist in Dickens to show himself more profound than the moralist: but what is striking here is that the artist has asserted the functional view of money. If George Eliot had written this scene she would have set out to show what Dickens has shown despite himself, that the cynicism of Mr Dombey is truer than the naivety of Paul.

§

By concentrating on the nineteenth-century novel, I may seem to have weighted things unfairly in favour of the functional view: so I ought to conclude by showing briefly what sort of literary power the moral treatment was capable of. Perhaps its finest expression is *Volpone*.

The theme here is of course traditional. Legacy hunters were a common object of satire in ancient literature, and we have seen how even George Eliot touched on the theme. Jonson's profoundly traditional originality lies in the verbal richness with which he handles the theme of riches and the fact of gold. The morning hymn to gold which opens the play is a parody of a creation hymn, in which the literal gold of the coins is endowed with the quickening power of the metaphoric gold of sunlight:

> Hail the world's soul, and mine....
> That lying here among my other hoards,
> Shew'st like a flame by night, or like the day
> Struck out of chaos, when all darkness fled
> Unto the centre.

This is parody taken to the point of greatness: it contains the very abilities whose abuse it is satirising. Volpone's moral error is based on a misuse of metaphor; but poetry like this is impossible unless we take metaphor seriously.

The resulting tension reproduces perfectly Jonson's ambivalent attitude to the rogues he both identifies with and condemns. Even in the harsher, sourer poetry of Mosca

> —and, gentle sir,
> When you do come to swim in golden lard
> Up to the arms in honey, that your chin
> Is borne up stiff with fatness of the flood —

we cannot fail to be involved as well as disgusted (as is Mosca: and we share his complexity and add the irony of our distance from him).

The money which yields such brilliant poetry in *Volpone* is never earned: it is acquired through a battle of wits among the parasites. Volpone himself is very proud of the way he has got rich:

> I glory
> More in the cunning purchase of my wealth,
> Than in the glad possession, since I gain
> No common way; I use no trade, no venture;
> I wound no earth with plough-shares, fat no beasts,
> To feed the shambles; have no mills for iron,
> Oil, corn, or men, to grind them into powder:
> I blow no subtle glass, expose no ships
> To threat'nings of the furrow-faced sea;
> I turn no monies in the public bank,
> Nor usure private.
>
> (I.i.30)

Volpone is an artist, something like Jonson himself: thinking up his schemes shows the same talent that went to writing the play he is in, and this identification of author and rogue produces much of the complexity of our involvement in the play. But for our present discussion, what is even more interesting is Volpone's dismissal of all other ways of acquiring money. Simple-minded Marxist critics have seen Volpone here (and Jonson too) as a critic of capitalism, and certainly the reference to

> mills for iron,
> Oil, corn, *or men*, to grind them into powder

is a marvellously economical attack on exploitation, just as *turning* monies in the public bank makes financial dealings sound vaguely distasteful. But Volpone is not a social critic, he is a parasite: his distaste for capitalism does not imply a preference for any other form of economic organisation:

> I wound no earth with ploughshares, fat no beasts
> To feed the shambles.

Agriculture is made to sound as distasteful as usury: Volpone is not against capitalism, he is against productive work.

Jonson never invites us to think about ordinary uses of money, commercial, domestic or industrial, and it is hard to see how, in his almost total reliance on metaphor for his effects, he could have. *Volpone* (this is its greatness) makes no attempt to turn into a realistic novel; and instead of offering us the functional view of money it treats money as a fetish.

Jonson's creative fetishism develops a satire on the corruption of money that can lead us, in conclusion, to a brief comparison with the most famous modern doctrine of the fetishism of money: for Marx illustrates his doctrine by quoting not (as it happens) Jonson, but a satiric passage in very much the same tradition by his great contemporary. It is now necessary to commit the rash act of trying to summarise the Marxist view of money.

Money is the alienated ability of mankind: 'that which I am unable to do as a man, I am able to do by means of money.... Money transforms the real essential powers of man and nature into what are merely abstract conceits and therefore imperfections — into tormenting chimeras.' Thus the Economic & Philosophical Manuscripts. This process of abstraction produces the fetishism of commodities: the investing of objects with qualities that properly belong only to human activity and human relationships. 'Money is thus the general overturning of individualities which turns them into their contrary and adds contradictory attributes to their attributes.' Since money is the form under which commodities can be made to increase in value, capitalism must use money; and that means in turn that capitalism will lead to the fetishism of commodities, since money is the form in which the exchange-value of commodities most clearly supersedes their use-value.

When Marx attacks alienation in economic life, and fetishism in our attitudes to commodities, what he points to is the loss of the total human meaning of a situation, and money is the perfect symbol of this, since it reduces the actuality and variety of social life to the uniformity represented by price. Price ignores all particulars of a situation except those that can be stated in terms of money, i.e. of an abstraction.

Abstraction surround us everywhere. Science is not possible without the abstractions of mathematics; discussion is not possible without abstract nouns; and complex economic life may not be possible without money. Abstractions need not always be tormenting chimeras: they may be the only way of retaining control over complex systems. Yet equally we know that there are those who desire money for its own sake only, or who use abstract nouns without any awareness of what, in terms of experience, they are really talking about. We need therefore to distinguish between alienation as an inevitable process resulting from complexity, and alienation as fetishism, that is, as the distortion of values that results when a miser hoards money, the Dodson sisters hoard line, or a philosopher (Marxist or otherwise) plays with abstract nouns that have lost real meaning. It is precisely this distinction that Marx doesn't seem to me to draw adequately; perhaps to draw it fully we need not the economist or the philosopher, but the novelist or poet.

And Marx, as if admitting this (for he was a man of wide and deep culture), quotes Shakespeare, illustrating his theory of the power of money in bourgeois society from *Timon of Athens*:

> ... Why, this
> Will lug your priests and servants from your sides,
> Pluck stout men's pillows from below their heads:
> This yellow slave
> Will knit and break religions, bless the accursed;
> Make the hoar leprosy adored, place thieves
> And give them title, knee and approbation
> With senators on the bench.

Shakespeare, says Marx, 'excellently depicts the real nature of money.' Well, what he does depict is how money turns everything topsy-turvy, how it makes 'black white, foul fair', how it turns thieves into senators. But if money overturns order and degree, what set them up in the first place? How did the senators get on the bench? If money will 'lug your priests and servants from your sides', does that mean they weren't paid in the first place? We can see that for Shakespeare money is not the mechanism that keeps society functioning, it is what causes malfunctioning. Senators and servants have their rightful places by nature, and are displaced by gold.

Now of one thing we can be certain: that this is not a description of the power of money in bourgeois society. If we have to find a social analogy for this, it would be the intrusion of money into a subsistence economy. What we have in Shakespeare is a pure version of the moral view of money. Timon's speech is wholly traditional, and has nothing to do with capitalism.

I believe that Marx's mistake, in quoting this passage, is crucial. I believe, that is, that he was not simply swept away by his enthusiasm for Shakespeare into quoting a speech that does not really illustrate his point; but that the speech partly does illustrate the point, for the point is confused. Marx is himself hovering, in the Manuscripts, between a moral and a functional view of money. He shows very interestingly, in *Capital*, that money is part of the ideological language that distorts our perception of social realities, for it makes it seem as if the capitalist has some other source of wealth than the expropriation of unpaid labour. Even if this is true — even if money helps us to mis-describe social reality — that is not all it does. If production were treated as production by freely associated men, consciously regulated in accordance with a settled plan (as will happen in Marx's socialist society), something like money would no doubt still be used for convenience. I don't think Marx distinguishes, and I am quite sure most contemporary Marxists don't distinguish, between such necessary neutral abstractions, and those that ideology uses to distort social reality. It is gratifying to be able to suggest that a literary distinction can help us to criticise a social theory.

59

4

Psychoanalysis and Art

For the purposes of this essay, I assume the correctness of the following Freudian views. First, the mind is divided into three psychic functions — id, ego, and superego. The id consists both of primal instinctual drives and of repressed material; the ego is consciousness and the exercise of reason; and the superego is the unconscious mechanisms by which the id is controlled. Second, there are various unconscious mechanisms such as projection, displacement, rationalisation, and so on, which control behaviour. Third, material from the unconscious slips past the censor and reveals itself in behaviour such as dreams, free association, neurotic symptoms, jokes, folklore, and possibly art. Fourth, the significance of sexuality is wider than was believed in pre-Freudian psychology; there is a sexual element in much human activity traditionally considered 'innocent,' because sexuality often takes disguised and displaced forms. Finally, I assume that there is a language of symbols we can interpret by relating it to the unconscious material it represents.

For readers who have already decided that such assumptions betray enough gullibility to invalidate anything that follows, I hasten to add that I do not make the assumptions because I believe them to be true, but because they are sufficiently widely held to make it worth asking what theory of art can be built on them. I do not, of course, believe them to be nonsense, or the whole ensuing discussion would be a barren academic exercise; so perhaps a preliminary word is in place on the kind of assent they will necessarily command from the literary reader.

Much psychoanalytic theory restates more systematically (and, Freud himself claimed, more scientifically), ideas which, traditionally, have guided accounts of the working of the mind. To believe in reason, in any but the most naive form, is to believe that there are other mental functions contrasted with it (if man is *homo rationis capax*, he is clearly capable of other, more Yahoo-like, functions), so that the idea of the ego as separated off from, and having to control, the rest of our mental processes is nothing new — nor is the view that it is not always successful. The superego is similar to the traditional idea of conscience; it inhibits socially destructive activity not by confronting us with a clear view of its consequences, but by accompanying the activity with a feeling of guilt that arises with immediate force, and which may prevent committing the offence. Conscience and the superego are identical in their mode of operation, and differ only in the explanation of their origins; but even there there is a resemblance, since both imply the existence of a moral order outside the self, and therefore both are the internal or — to use the Freudian term — the introjected spokesmen of that order. In the one case, of course, the order is God's, in the other it is society's, conveyed mainly through parental prohibition. The often surprising strength of the inhibiting guilt is explained in the one case in theological terms, and in the other it is explained by the ingenious theory that the inhibited aggression is itself used in the service of the inhibiting superego in that it is turned against the self.[1] This can then be used to explain the startling drive toward self-punishment of which the superego is capable.

The id, which is the largest area of the mind, has a greater variety of names in traditional theories. Phrases such as the old Adam suggest that the unreflecting drives to self-gratification are somehow primary and basic, that the moral life is attained by the imposition on them of other levels of mental activity. Even what seems most distinctively characteristic of the Freudian id, the view (though this is a point sometimes glossed over by Freud himself) that it has two distinct kinds of content, the primal and instinctive, and the repressed, corresponds in a way to the distinction between sin as natural and

61

sin as perversion. Man has arisen from nature and has fallen from grace; the sinner is seen as a worm, a fox, a tiger, subject to all the natural passions and incapacities. The sinner is corrupted; sin draws upon what makes us human ('Aux objets repugnants nous trouvons des appas'[2]).

Whether or not we accept the scientific status of psychoanalysis, and whether or not we accept the more specific and elaborated elements in its theories, such as the details of dream interpretation or the amazingly complicated boundary lines drawn between pre-conscious and unconscious, let alone the elaborations of an actual analysis, the Freudian view of the mind is difficult for the student of literature to refuse, since he has so often met it before. This is my excuse for proceeding as if psychoanalytic theory were in some sense true. I now move on to discuss the consequent theories of art.

The classic statements by Freud himself are well-known. His discussion of fantasy in the *Introductory Lectures* concludes with the ingenious suggestion that there is one path from fantasy back to reality, and this path is art. The artist is a person of clamorous instinctual needs which cannot be satisfied; the artist therefore turns away from reality to satisfy the needs in fantasy, but because of the ability 'to elaborate his day dreams so that they lose that personal note which grates upon strange ears, and become enjoyable to others,' the artist avoids neurotic escapism. He possesses the 'mysterious ability' to disguise his fantasies and render them acceptable to others, and he is able, too, 'to attach to this reflection of his fantasy-life so strong a stream of pleasure that, for a time at least, the repressions are out-balanced and dispelled by it'. The successful artist is highly esteemed, and the result of this (described no doubt with something of a malicious chuckle by Freud) is that 'he has won — through his fantasy — what before he could only win in fantasy: honour, power and the love of women'.[3]

This theory is further elaborated in the essay entitled 'The Relation of the Poet to Day-Dreaming'. Once again art is seen as wish fulfilment, as the vicarious gratification, in fantasy, of desires that are denied in reality. Do we dare, asks Freud, compare an imaginative writer with a daydreamer?

Let us not choose for our comparison those writers who are most highly esteemed by critics. We will choose the less pretentious writers of romances, novels and stories, who are read all the same by the widest circles of men and women. There is one very marked characteristic in the productions of these writers which must strike us all: they all have a hero who is the centre of interest, for whom the author tries to win our sympathy by every possible means, and whom he places under the protection of a special providence.[4]

The reader identifies with that hero and thus experiences the pleasure of feeling invulnerable, of being the centre of attraction and the chosen of women, and of being invariably successful. Kingsley Amis' poem 'A Dream of Fair Women' is a succinct and witty statement of this view — a poem that could hardly, I suppose, have been written in pre-Freudian times:

> Feigning aplomb, perhaps for half an hour,
> I hover, and am shown by each princess
>   The entrance to her tower;
> Open, in that its tenant throws the key
> At once to anyone, but not unless
>   The anyone is me
>
> ...But honesty compels me to confess
> That this is 'all a dream,' which was, indeed,
>   Not difficult to guess.[5]

At the end of the essay, Freud returns to the question of what distinguishes the artist from other people. The ordinary daydreamer, ashamed of his fantasies, conceals them:

But when a man of literary talent presents his plays, or relates what we take to be his personal day-dreams, we experience great pleasure arising probably from many sources. How the writer accomplishes this is his innermost secret; the essential *ars poetica* lies in the technique by which our feeling of repulsion is overcome, and this has certainly to do with those barriers erected between every individual being and all others. We can guess at two methods used in this technique. The writer softens the egotistical character of the daydream by changes and disguises, and he bribes us by the offer of a purely formal, that is, aesthetic, pleasure in the presentation of his phantasies. The increment of pleasure which is offered us in order to release yet greater pleasure arising from deeper sources in the mind is called an "incitement premium" or technically, "fore-pleasure". I am of [the] opinion that all the aesthetic pleasure we gain from the works of imaginative writers is of the same type as this "fore-pleasure", and that the true enjoyment of literature proceeds from the release of tensions in our minds. Perhaps much that brings about this result consists in the writer's putting us into a position in which we can enjoy our own day-dreams without reproach or shame.[6]

This then is the famous theory of art as secondary gratification, or wish fulfilment. Let us look for a simple example. Everyone who admires the work of Toulouse-Lautrec values it for its easy, nervous line, its effortless but vigorous elegance, its ability to render energy and graceful movement. Turn from his pictures to a picture of the man himself; we see a stunted dwarf, grotesque and clumsy; but he was descended from an aristocratic line of warriors and horsemen, his father in particular was a colourful anachronistic character who lived with panache and self-assertion. The longing to be able to ride, dance, and fulfil himself physically must have been peculiarly intense, and it must have been responsible for the nervous intensity of Toulouse-Lautrec's drawing and the obsessive interest he showed in cyclists, dancers, and circus performers. Few artists offer so clear an illustrtion of art as wish fulfilment.

But this is a limited illustration, because it takes place at the conscious level. Toulouse-Lautrec must have been well aware of his own frustration, and in his painting he is symbolising what he could — and doubtless often did — give direct verbal expression to. There was no need for the material of his art to evade the censor, and it is therefore not possible to explain its intense power by claiming that it is expressed with the violent force of what was, otherwise, unable to find expression. It is not, however, possible to give a simple example of art as the secondary gratification of *unconscious* wishes. A theory of the various defence mechanisms at work and the displacements and condensations that conceal the forbidden material and thus allow it to be expressed would have to be incorporated into our example. In any example chosen, it is necessary to steer a course between implausibility and obviousness. If the work is interpreted as being 'about' unconscious material utterly unlike the manifest content (and there is no shortage of Freudian criticism that does just this), the interpretation appears arbitrary, but if plausible interpretations are offered, the natural corollary seems to be that the author was himself aware of them, so that his symbols do not disguise, and therefore contain none of the psychic power associated, in psychoanalysis, with displacement mechanisms.

The example I have chosen is not altogether orthodox, but is perhaps more interesting because of that; it is the interpretation of Baudelaire offered by Michel Butor under the title *Histoire extraordinaire*. Butor begins from an extraordinary letter by Baudelaire to Charles Asselineau,[7] describing a dream in which he visited a brothel, in order to present to the madam a copy of a book he had just published, which he observes to be an obscene book. The usual embarrassing experiences of dreams happen to him, including discovering that his trousers are indecently torn, and that he has no shoes on; and he has a conversation with a monster who has a long black rubbery projection attached to his head. Butor offers an ingenious interpretation of this dream, involving Baudelaire's relationship with his mother (who is identified with the madam) and his stepfather, General Aupick, on whom he felt humiliatingly dependent and who had reproached him for wearing indecent clothes. From this he moves to a discussion of Baudelaire's ideas on art and on sex, and the relationship between the two ('le jour où le jeune écrivain corrige sa première épreuve il est fier comme un écolier qui vient de gagner sa première vérole'). Since the dream took place on the very day on which Baudelaire's translation of Poe's *Tales* was published, it is related to his ideas on Poe, and by means of the process of substitution so common in dream interpretation Butor recognises (his word) without difficulty elements from Poe's life and stories in the details of the dream. A certain amount of punning too is used in the interpretation, and in his conclusion Butor observes: 'la plaque tournant du rêve donne sur tant de voies.'[8]

A few brief comments on this study may help our ensuing discussion. First, the distinction between what is and what is not a work of art is more or less ignored: Butor moves from Baudelaire's poems and essays into the details of his emotional life in much the same way as he moves from the actual dream. In one way, the distinction is unimportant here, for the dream is described at such length, and with such vivid elaboration, that it could easily pass for one of the prose poems of *Le Spleen de Paris*. Yet this is no answer: the offence, if offence it is, consists not in treating the actual dream as a work of literature, but in treating works of literature like biographical material, and its most questionable result consists in a trick of vocabulary that one soon learns to recognise in Freudian criticism. I have already singled out the way Butor 'recognises' elements from Poe's life in the details of the dream; later in the essay he claims that the rope which figures in the 'Balloon Hoax' 'becomes' the murderous rope of 'The Black Cat'. Verbs like 'becomes,' 'is,' or 'really is' have a single real meaning, taken from the unconscious of the author, which underlies the apparent meaning of his work. I shall return to the point, and will simply remark now that they are clearly reductivist in their effect.

Second, we can notice that although Butor's method is Freudian, his interpretation is not. He detects substitution, overdetermination, and displacement in orthodox psycho-analytic fashion, but the material is not necessarily sexual. He does sometimes find that a sexual element symbolises a literary concern, but he seems to believe that Baudelaire's writing is at least as important to Baudelaire as his relationship with his mother. The complete independence of a theory and a method that were developed in conjunction could hardly be better illustrated. In developing the example I have moved to the edge of criticising Freud's theory of art, but before doing this I want to ask what kind of theory it is. I suggest that it is a theory of content, not of form.

A vivid and apt example of the theory can be found in Dostoevsky. The frustrated narrator of *Notes from Underground*, living alone in his cellar, consumed with envy and bitterness, is nursing elaborate plans to humiliate an officer whose name he does not even know, but whom he hates for being handsome, confident, at ease in the world. He follows the officer about, trying — with indifferent success — to learn something about him:

> One morning, though I had never tried my hand with the pen, it suddenly occurred to me to write a satire on this officer in the form of a novel which would unmask his villainy. I wrote the novel with relish. I did unmask his villainy, I even exaggerated it; at first I so altered his surname that it could easily be recognized, but on second thought I changed it, and sent the story to the *Otetchestvenniya Zapiski*. But at that time such attacks were not the fashion and my story was not printed. That was a great vexation to me.[9]

A few pages later he describes his dreams. At the lowest point of frustration and dissipation, he is visited by dreams of the good and the beautiful, in which he is 'triumphant over every one'.

> Every one, of course, was in dust and ashes, and was forced spontaneously to recognize my superiority, and I forgave them all. I was a poet and a grand gentleman, I fell in love; I came in for countless millions and immediately devoted them to humanity.... Every one would kiss me and weep (what idiots they would be if they did not), while I should go barefoot and hungry preaching new ideas and fighting a victorious Austerlitz against the obscurantists. Then the band would play a march, an amnesty would be declared, the Pope would agree to retire from Rome to Brazil; then there would be a ball for the whole of Italy at the Villa Borghese on the shores of Lake Como, Lake Como being for that purpose transferred to the neighbourhood of Rome.[10]

Neither Dostoevsky nor his narrator would have had much time for Freud. Since the main point of *Notes from Underground* is to use human perversity and irrationality as a refutation of scientific theories of man, the most infuriating response possible must surely be an attempt to offer scientific explanations of irrationality and perversity. Yet this radical rejection of Freud's basic enterprise is combined, in Dostoevsky, with considerable anticipations of Freudian theory — as can be seen here. For these passages clearly state the view that art, like dreaming, is wish fulfilment.

The dreams of the good and the beautiful are obviously wish fulfilment: they offer the dreamer exactly those roles of which life deprives him, and his fantasies of being a grand gentleman and fighting a victorious Austerlitz have the the same function as Toulouse-Lautrec's displaced fantasies of horse riding and dancing. There is even a quite explicit admission that the function of these fantasies in waking life is to enable him to endure the lack of such achievement: 'Anything but the foremost place I could not conceive for myself, and for that very reason I quite contentedly occupied the lowest in reality.' The connection of these dreams with art is also quite explicit: 'and I can assure you that some of these fancies were by no means badly composed,' and the parallelism between the account of his dreams and the satire he wrote on the officer is quite clear. He does not appear to have figured as a character in that satire, but this need not invalidate its function as gratification, since the work as a whole fulfilled his longing to put down the officer, so that the implied narrator fulfils the role that the hero of his dreams played explicitly.

Now it is clear that what his own personal involvement contributed to the story he wrote is the emotional content: the events insofar as they express the needs of the writer, or offer a parallel emotional satisfaction to the reader. The same is true of Freud's own example: the elements of a story which are relevant to his theory are those which can be reproduced in paraphrase. He admits this quite openly by his confessed inability to deal with form. When he asks how a work of art *differs* from other forms of fantasy, he has no answer: Freud calls how the writer achieves these differences an 'innermost secret' in the daydreaming essay, and a 'mysterious ability' in the *Introductory Lectures*. This does not in itself make the theory valueless: if there are significant resemblances between art and daydreaming, then to point these out without being able to explain the differences is to offer not a false but a partial theory.

The next question then is obvious. Is there a Freudian theory of form? I believe there is, and to find it we must turn to the book on jokes. The main distinction made in this book is that between innocent and tendentious jokes. An innocent joke is an aim in itself, but a tendentious joke serves one of two purposes: 'it is either a hostile joke (serving the purpose of aggressiveness, satire or defence) or an obscene joke (serving the purpose of exposure).' The discussion of tendentious jokes is a clear parallel to the discussion of art:

> We can see that the case of tendentious jokes is a special case of the "principle of assistance". A possibility of generating pleasure supervenes in a situation in which another possibility of pleasure is obstructed so that, as far as the latter alone is concerned, no pleasure would arise. The result is a generation of pleasure far greater than that offered by the supervening possibility. This has acted, as it were, as an *incentive bonus*; with the assistance of the offer of a small amount of pleasure, a much greater one, which would otherwise have been hard to achieve, has been gained. I have good reason to suspect that this principle corresponds with an arrangement that holds good in many widely separated departments of mental life and it will, I think, be expedient to describe the pleasure that serves to initiate the large

release of pleasure as "fore-pleasure", and the principle as the "fore-pleasure principle".[11]

The 'greater pleasure' which is thus rendered possible consists in the release of repressed material (hostile or obscene urges, as we have seen), in a way closely analogous to the vicarious indulgence provided by the fantasy element in art. But in this book Freud does what he does not attempt in the essay; he discusses the nature of the 'fore-pleasure'. Innocent and tendentious jokes both offer this, but the innocent joke offers nothing else: it is , we may say, pure form. And though Freud considers its psychological role to be less profound than that of tendentious jokes, he does not dismiss it as unimportant. The pleasure offered by the act of joking itself consists in 'an economy of psychical expenditure or a relief from the compulsion of criticism,'[12] and the basic activity which the act licenses is that of regression. As the infant grows up, it has to forgo the pleasue of playing freely with words and thoughts, for it learns that this produces nonsense; a joke is an opportunity to go on with such play, and the meaning of the joke is a licence to indulge in its true attraction, the word play and free play of ideas: it is an opportunity to escape the tyranny of having to make sense — the tyranny of the ego. Freud points out that the techniques of jokes are not proper to jokes only, but so far from finding this an objection to his theory, he claims 'there is nothing strange in othe procedures drawing from the same sources for the same end'.[13]

Although poets in the 1970s seem to have largely given up rhyme, there is no doubt that rhyme has traditionally provided one of the main sources of formal pleasure in poetry; unless a really radical change in the nature of poetry is setting in, the poets may well come back to it. I choose rhyme as a conveniently limited example of fore-pleasure, and the suggestion that its attraction is really an occasion for regression is startling but interesting. There is no doubt of the infant's delight — and our own in certain uninhibited moods — in the arranging of echoing sounds, the grouping of words purely by sound and not by meaning; and a nursery rhyme without sound patterns is inconceivable. The obvious objection — that rhyme in poetry is not usually random but arranged in strict patterns — is no objection at all: the tension between the (adult) imposition of order and the (regressive) grouping of words that have nothing in common except their sound is a tension on which art thrives; it thwarts and indulges a not altogether permissible impulse in a rhythm of alternation.

§

I turn now to the criticisms of the theory I have tried to set forth and illustrate. It is clear that Freud treats art as a function of the pleasure principle; but there is at least one literary movement that has insisted on relating it to the reality principle:

> I had read of thieves by scores; seductive fellows (amiable for the most part), faultless in dress, plump in pocket, choice in horseflesh, bold in bearing, fortunate on gallantry, great at a song, a bottle, pack of cards or dice-box, and fit companions for the bravest; but I had never met (except in Hogarth) with the miserable reality. It appeared to me that to draw a knot of such associates in crime as really did exist; to paint them in all their deformity, in all their wretchedness, in all the squalid misery of their lives... would be to attempt a something which was needed, and which would be a service to society.[14]

Freud's theory compels us to say that Dickens is here renouncing art for science, giving up the kind of book in which identification with the thief offers vicarious adventure, in order to write an objective study that will provide the basis for social action. But Dickens thought he was giving up false art for true, and he is certainly maintaining that Hogarth is a better artist than those who paint thieves as fit companions for the bravest.

This is the orthodoxy of realism. The fact that Dickens is not nearly such a good realist as he believed need not detain us here. There is a rich irony in the fact that the description of the gallant thieves of tradition (derived no doubt in part from *The Beggars Opera*) resembles in spirit, though not in detail, the Artful Didger, in whom hostility and identification are held in ironic tension. It would have been possible to quote from Stendhal or Zola, George Eliot or Lewes, similar statements of the realist creed that see the rejection of the stereotypes of gratification (invulnerable heroes, poetic justice) as a *literary* movement. Nor is realism an isolated or eccentric movement in the history of literature: it is rather the making explicit of elements that had always been present in the enterprise of literature, whether it was described as the imitation of an action or as holding the mirror up to nature.

We can bring together two points in Freud's theory that he does not himself connect. The first is his selection of inferior and popular writers. He is unblushing about this, and after admitting that 'many imaginative productions have travelled far from the original naïve day-dream,' he adds, 'but I cannot suppress the surmise that even the most extreme variations could be brought into relationship with this model by an uninterrupted series of transitions'.[15] Could they? there is just such a series of transitions in *Notes from Underground*. I have already quoted the narrator's remark that some of his fancies were by no means badly composed; if we read it as part of its paragraph we find ourselves confronted with an ironic and brilliant discussion:

> You will say that it is vulgar and contemptible to drag all this into public after all the tears and transports which I have myself confessed. But why is it contemptible? Can you imagine that I am ashamed of it all, and that it was stupider than anything in your life, gentlemen? and I can assure you that some of these fancies were by no means badly composed.... It did not all happen on the shores of Lake Como. And yet you are right — it really is vulgar and contemptible.[16]

Freud was of course told that it was vulgar and contemptible to drag into public the underlying psychic mechanisms of apparently normal behaviour. The underground man's reply to the charge is very like Freud's: neurotic mechanisms are not distinct and unusual states, to be contrasted with healthy mental life, but simply intensified forms of the patterns of all psychic life. We are all ill, says Freud: it was no stupider than anything in anyone's life, says Dostoevsky's narrator. And so it is natural to go on to assert a continuity between such mechanisms and the creation of art, which Dostoevsky then does. But he does not stop there. There is good art, and there is less good — and what is the difference? 'It did not all happen on the shores of Lake Como.' Lake Como is the happy refuge where all dreams are fulfilled (perhaps the idyllic scenes in *La Chartreuse de Parme* which are set on the lake play a part in the choice of this image); it is the symbol of wish fulfilment, and the artistic success of the daydream ('by no means badly

71

composed') consists in the reduction of this element. Since Lake Como was transferred to the neighbourhood of Rome in the service of the fantasy, it is no doubt the reality principle too which is glad to see that it is not always the setting. The doubt expressed in the last sentence is not, I take it, a doubt whether such wish fulfilment is the basis of literary composition, but a revulsion from self-display, literary or not, well-composed or not. Poetry is full of such revulsions, of such surges of distaste for even the most beautiful compositions because of their basis in ostentatious egoism. Yet how little the emphasis needs to be changed for revulsion to turn into boasting, for the underlying egoism of art to be, paradoxically a source of its glory:

> I must lie down where all the ladders start
> In the foul rag and bone shop of the heart.[17]

The other point in Freud's theory is the central one: the relationship between the work of art and the wish is simply one of gratification. To identify the presence of wishes in the artistic impulse was an invaluable insight; but if we consider the complexity of our emotional life, and the complexity of a great work of art, it seems a ridiculous oversimplification to say that the function of art is merely to allow us to yield to the wish. The next point is obvious: it is clearly the inferior work of art that simply gratifies the wish. Freud's pious hope that he could reduce even the finest works to the same pattern is nothing more than a hope; it is a cavalier assertion impossible to demonstrate.

When Freud is concentrating on patterns of human development he often turns to literature for examples. Unable to go into details of actual case histories, because of the confidentiality of the material, he never hesitates to take his examples from Shakespeare, Schiller or Ibsen, often adding a remark on the intuitive understanding shown by the dramatist, which psychoanalysis has now confirmed.[18] This is not a theory of literature as substitute gratification; literature is a kind of knowledge offering insights that are less systematic and less explicitly discussed than psychology. But it is just as possible to ask if the insights are true. The reality principle plays its part in literature after all.

There is no reason for psychoanalytic theory to yield a reductivist account of art, or to deny complexity to the way in which art is related to emotional needs. I will therefore look briefly at another psychoanalytic theory of art, which involves a richer awareness of art nature, that of Simon O. Lesser.

The culmination of Lesser's study *Fiction and the Unconscious* is found in his theory of tragedy. Tragedy offers the supreme example of an aesthetic experience, which he describes in a way similar to Dewey's. In *Art as Experience*, Dewey sees actual living as a more or less indeterminate succession of what can in general be called experience. Only rarely do elements in it sufficiently cohere to form the shaped and satisfying whole Dewey calls 'an experience'. When this does happen, we are on the road to art, for a work of art, though built of the same materials as actual living, differs by structuring them into a coherent whole. In the same way, Lesser maintains that everyday experience may very occasionally offer us the consummate satisfaction of an aesthetic experience, but that on the whole we need art for this. To describe the aesthetic experience in its highest form, he turns to tragedy. The first striking characteristic of tragedy is its seriousness: by this Lesser appears to mean something very like an awareness of the reality principle. Tragic seriousness shows the most intense and painful experiences as they truly are: tragedy's realism is faithful not to the external world but to the internal enacting of crisis. Turning then to the nature of the tragic hero and of tragic action, Lesser develops many traditional points with great insight. He does not really introduce psychoanalytic concepts until he turns to his central point, which is that tragedy satisfies all three areas of mental life — id, ego, and superego:

> It is obvious that tragedy richly gratifies the instincts. It not only permits the vicarious fulfillment of some of our most urgent and stubborn — and *therefore* most strongly resisted — desires; it permits the satisfaction of those desires under conditions which momentarily re-establish their authority and invest them with a grandeur commensurate with their outrageousness. The satisfaction the events of tragedy offer the superego is equally obvious and equally prodigal. Tragedy is as relentless as the superego itself in punishing wrongdoing and in discovering appropriate punishments.... Though it is less apparent, I believe that the events of tragedy are also richly satisfying

to the ego. It benefits from having the claims of the instincts specified and brought into the open. It benefits from having them symbolically gratified and made more amenable to its control. Above all, it benefits from letting desire and inhibition, id and superego, engage in a mock but violent battle under the strict terms which tragedy proposes.[19]

What is satisfying about this view is that it does full justice to the complexity of artistic experience. We need not feel that in its eagerness to use art in order to exemplify a view of the functioning of the psyche it is brushing aside some of the elements of the poem, as Freud so clearly was doing. Indeed, our suspicion is more like to be the opposite: that in respecting the work of art, it is not doing a great deal to turn the account of it from the terms of literary criticism into those of psychology. This is not true of Lesser's book as a whole, which elsewhere uses quite specifically Freudian interpretations; but what really matters is the terminology and concepts he uses when developing his final and most general insight. I have of course given a misleading picture on this point by quoting the very passage in which Lesser does use psychoanalytical terminology, but to balance this I deliberately began by comparing his theory with that of Dewey.

Two things distinguish this view of tragedy from traditional views. The first is that it is completely internalised. Tragedy is no longer concerned with Eternal Justice, Providence, or man's relationship with the universe, but is seen entirely in terms of an inner psychic harmony in the spectator or reader. The second is that this inner harmony is stated in Freudian terms. Now the first is not new to Lesser; as he himself admits it is anticipated, in similar terms, by I. A. Richards. Richards sees tragedy as an experience in which the mind does not shy away from anything, but contemplates reality, even at its most painful, without any of the usual suppressions and sublimations. 'When we succeed we find, as usual, that there is no difficulty: the difficulty came from the suppressions and sublimations. The joy which is so strangely the heart of the experience is not an indication that "all's right with the world," or that "somewhere, somehow, there is Justice"; it is an indication that all is right here and now in the nervous system.'[20] There is a striking parallel here to the process of being psychoanalysed, but it is presented by Richards in wholly general terms. His concept of inner psychic harmony is compatible with almost any theory of mental dynamics, since he does not closely specify the nature of the conflict that is transcended or the forces that maintain the harmony. Has Lesser, by spelling out the nature of that harmony as one between id, ego, and superego, made it a more valuable critical tool than it was in the more general formulation of Richards?

I have space for only one example, and I choose *Antony and Cleopatra.*

> His legs bestrid the ocean, his rear'd arm
> Crested the world: his voice was propertied
> As all the tuned spheres, and that to friends:
> But when he meant to quail, and shake the orb,
> He was as rattling thunder. For his bounty,
> There was no winter in 't; an autumn 'twas
> That grew the more by reaping: his delights
> Were dolphin-like, they show'd his back above
> The element they lived in: in his livery
> Walk'd crowns and crownets: realms and islands were
> As plates dropp'd from his pocket.
>
> (V.ii 82-92)

This is the apotheosis of Antony, as delivered by Cleopatra after his death. It is undoubtedly the finest and most eloquent account of what so irresistibly appeals to us in that magnificent but unreliable leader. The fact that it can be delivered only after his death can be attributed to the superego without difficulty. Antony's irresponsibility has been so palpable that while he is alive we can identify with him only if we feel guilt at the same time; the need to punish him having now been fulfilled, we can at last indulge in the magnificence of this description without qualifications. The fact that the description is introduced as a dream and defended as reality fits very neatly into the theory. Cleopatra is indulging in her wish (and ours) to believe in a perfect Antony who does not cause the suffering that, as we have seen, too often follows after the exhilarations of the real Antony. Such wishes are indulged as dream, as she tells Dolabella, projecting on to him the cold role of ego ('you laugh when boys and women tell their dreams'); but she is playing a trick on Dolabella so that she can triumph over the ego by asserting that there *was* such a man. What she could never say, however, is that there *is* such a man. Ego can only be persuaded the wish is true when there is no reality to disprove it.

But are we justified in describing the wish as the id? What Antony stands for in this play is certainly not the direct gratification of instinctual drives. The fact that he is a middle-aged man introduces a great deal of secondary elaboration, and less urgent clamour of instinct, into his sexual life. The magic of Antony is not the appeal of uninhibited aggression or sheer sexual drive, but a more complex human attraction that wins the devoted loyalty of his followers and makes it impossible for Enobarbus to reject him without destroying himself. We do not need to describe that magic, since Shakespeare has done it in this very passage. What we are shown there is an alternation of impulses: first he has a God-like benevolence, then aggression that is once again underwritten by being identified with natural processes. Bounty, similarly, is followed by delight, and then again by bounty.

There is a strong element of instinctual gratification in all this. The image of the dolphin clearly has sexual overtones, and we are tantalised into thinking for a moment that Antony is himself the dolphin, that it threshes about in the waves as a simile for sexual activity, only to realise on rereading that the dolphins show *his* back not their own. The image has something of that incoherent confusion so marvellously used in this play, and it plays the sexual suggestion against a suggestion that Antony somehow emerges from, even transcends, his delights. It would be a travesty of the richness of this poetry to say that the gratification of our wish to see Antony triumphant is a gratification of the instincts.

The only way to do this would be to regard the poetry as a disguise, and to address ourselves to the task of stripping it away in order to reveal its latent meaning exactly as one does in dream interpretation. I do not suggest that Lesser wishes to do this; he is too scrupulous and sensitive a critic. But unless it is done, I do not see what is gained by speaking of the id. To allow to the impulse of assertion in the play the kind of complexity that this poetry holds, is to refrain from making any real use of the splendid simplifications of the psychoanalytic vocabulary, and to say no more than Richards had already said so well in his more general terminology.

§

I conclude this chapter with two observations. One simply sums up where it has been leading; the second is more far reaching and perhaps incompatible with the first. First, there are better Freudian theories of art that Freud's. I have space only for Lesser's, but would have liked to discuss Kubie and Kris as well.[21] Second, the value of a psychoanalytically oriented theory of art may diminish as it begins to occupy itself with the specifics of psychoanalytic theory, looking in the literary work for examples of the various defence mechanisms that analysis and dream interpretation strip away. If that is so, we must wonder about the dream interpretation too, but to pursue that line of thought would lead to questioning the assumption with which this essay began.

Notes

1   See *Civilisation and its Discontents*, ch. 7.
2   Baudelaire, 'Au Lecteur' (proem to *Les Fleurs du Mal*).
3   *Introductory Lectures*, 23, 'The Paths of Symptom-Formation.'
4   'The Relation of the Poet to Day-Dreaming,' *Collected Papers*, vol. 4, no. 9.
5   Amis, 'A Dream of Fair Women': conveniently available in A. Alvarez's anthology, *The New Poetry* (Penguin)
6   'The Relation of the Poet to Day-Dreaming.'
7   13 March 1856, *Corréspondence Générale*, vol. 1, no. 230.
8   *Une histoire extraordinarie: essai sur un rêve de Baudelaire*, 1961.
9   Trans. Constance Garnett, pt. 2, ch. 1.
10 Ibid., ch. 2.
11 *Jokes and their Relation to the Unconscious*, Vol. 4, Ch. 2.
12 Ibid., ch. 1.
13 Ibid., ch. 2.
14 Dickens, Preface to *Oliver Twist*.
15 'The Relation of the Poet to Day-Dreaming.'
16 Pt. 2, ch. 2.
17 William Butler Yeats, 'The Circus Animals' Desertion.'
18 See, for example, *The Interpretation of Dreams*, ch. 2 (Schiller on Poetic Creation) or ch. 5, section D (Sophocles and Shakespeare on Oedipus); or 'Some Character-Types met with in Psycho-Analytic Work,' *Collected Papers*, vol. 4, no. 18 (Shakespeare and Ibsen).
19 Ch. 9, para 2.
20 Richards, *Principles of Literary Criticism*, ch. 32.
21 Lawrence S. Kubie, *Neurotic Distortion of the Creative Process*, 1958; Ernst Kris, *Psychoanalytic Explorations in Art*, 1952.

5

Three Languages of Fiction

You the reader are about to do something important. In reading a discussion of the nature of imaginative literature, you will be forced to re-examine your relationship to your own moral life. Literature is the truest record of the moral sentiments: it is the placing and disciplining of attitudes that involve the personality at its most discriminating, and a fresh understanding of its mode of operation cannot be a trivial matter. Our deepest values are involved in the act of expression, and a more genuine insight into that act is an act of self-knowledge.

You open the book, hearing the faint whipcrack of the pages as you turn them to find the first chapter. The dull pressure of the chair-arm on your left wrist is intermittently present in attention. The book is a hardback, bound in dull blue-grey, smooth to the touch. You recognise the slight constriction in the jaw brought on by the possibility of encountering new ideas. Your breathing is perfectly regular; your eye begins its little leaps along the line of type.

You have been standing in misty landscape, fields stretching in three directions, a rockface on your right. As you open the volume, it is as if a door in the rockface swings slowly back: beyond is a light as bright as a scream. To step through it may be to walk over a conceptual precipice, and be torn to pieces by the ragged thoughts below; or it may be to walk on smooth rock in the clear sunshine of understanding.

§

I must begin to assuring the reader that I am not being vainglorious. In offering three different versions of the experience of sitting down to read this essay, I have found it best to assume that it is an important essay, and that the experience is going to be rewarding; but it is a purely tactical assumption, one that enables me to dramatise the contrast between the three versions more effectively than if I assumed it to be the drab experience it may well turn out to be.

It will be useful, clearly, to establish a terminology for the three versions. The first is the most traditional, and bears the closest relationship to the sort of language literary critics do in fact use. Of course I have taken the language from one particular school of criticism: instead of talking about a record of the moral sentiments, about the discriminating personality or about placing and disciplining, I could have talked of the semiotic, the proairetic and the hermeneutic code; or the ideology of a particular class; or the vicarious gratification of repressed wishes; or the pleasures of symmetry, irony and suspense. My choice of the Arnoldian critical tradition (more fully, of a vocabulary that draws on Arnold, Lawrence, Leavis, Trilling and others) rather than the structuralist, the Marxist, the psychoanalytic or the formalist was not accidental: for that is the tradition that uses the least specialised vocabulary, which borrows most of its concepts from ordinary moral discourse. It is humanistic (man is seen as social, as capable of benevolence and as rational) and it is moral (constantly concerned with discriminations between good and bad).

The second version I shall describe as behaviourist. It makes no value judgements, and attempts to describe as accurately as possible the physical acts and sensations that take place. It deals in a consciousness that can hear, see and feel, that can remember and recognise, but that does not judge, love, prefer or doubt. A rather moderate behaviourism is here used, since I have allowed myself access to the consciousness of the reader. A more rigorous form, which would almost certainly have to use the third person, would confine itself to the consciousness of an observer, and the second sentence would then say that a slight indentation was made in the reader's left forearm by the chair-arm, and that the arm was occasionally lifted and rubbed, or lifted and put back in the same position. The rigorously behaviourist version would not object in principle to mentioning the slight constriction in the jaw, though it would want to indicate whether this was perceptible or whether some kind of apparatus would be needed to detect it. It might not even object to saying that the reader *recognised* this, though it would regard the verb as a kind of shorthand for a hypothetical converstion: if you asked the reader whether this constriction had happened to him before he would say yes; further, he would be able to describe the circumstances under which it had happened. When it comes to the cause of the constriction, however, ('the possibility of encountering new or confused ideas') the rigorous behaviourist would be in real trouble, and however ingeniously he formulated his hypothetical conversation, it is doubtful if he would be able to convey the point.

The third version is characterised by its use of metaphor. The impending experience is designated not by abstract nouns but in terms of a door opening in a rockface. It is quite plain that these are not literal descriptions, but metaphors for bewilderment or insight — though many practictioners of this third language would object strongly to the way I have just glibly replaced the metaphors by abstract nouns: the argument for writing in metaphor is often that it enables you to convey experiences for which we have no abstract nouns. Metaphor is precise, abstraction is approximate. Of course abstract nouns are usually dead metaphors, but they lack the explanatory quality of the living metaphor, the sense that it is sending back reports from the actuality of experience. You can practise this language of metaphor because you believe that abstractions always lie and truth consists only in the particulars of fresh perception (that would be the most extreme position); or because you think that as well as the abstraction that enable us to classify and theorise we need metaphors, like auditors, to keep them up to the mark; or because, though you prefer abstractions you think readers are lazy and easily bored and need to be galvanised into attention by metaphor (this last, the most moderate position, is more or less that of classical rhetoric).

Three languages: or as Roland Barthes would say three codes (my distinctions are not the same as his but there are some connexions). It is now necessary to have examples of these three languages in narrative; and this time I will find them, and not make them up:

> J'avais contracté dans mes conversations avec la femme qui la première avait developpé mes idées une insurmontable aversion pour toutes les maximes communes et pour toutes les formules dogmatiques. Lors donc que j'entendais la mediocrité disserter avec complaisance sur des principes bien etablis, bien incontestables en fait de morale, de convenances ou de religion, choses qu'elle met assez volontiers sur la même ligne, je me sentais poussé à la contredire, non que j'eusse adopté des opinions opposées, mais parce que j'étais impatienté d'une conviction si ferme et si lourde. Je ne sais quel instinct m'avertissait, d'ailleurs, de me défier de ces axiomes generaux si exempts de toute restriction, si purs de toute nuance. Les sots font de leur morale une masse compacte et indivisible, pour qu'elle se mêle le moins possible avec leurs actions et les laisse libres dans tous les détails.

> (In my conversations with the woman who first encouraged my ideas, I had acquired an insurmountable aversion for all common maxims and all dogmatic formulae. So when I heard the self-satisfied discourses of the mediocre about well-established and indisputable principles in the realms of morality, propriety or religion (all of which they are happy to assimilate to one another), I felt driven to contradict, not because I inclined to the opposite opinions, but because I grew impatient at such rigid and clumsy certainty. Furthermore, some instinct warned me to mistrust general maxims so free of all qualification, so innocent of all subtlety. The morality of fools,is a compact and indivisible mass, designed to interfere as little as possible with their actions, and to leave them free in every particular.)

This passage is from the first chapter of Benjamin Constant's *Adolphe*; and I hope it will be immediately clear why it was chosen. It announces the author's impatience with the glib use of moral generalisations ('toutes les maximes communes, et...toutes les formules dogmatiques'). The way to understand any rejection is to look for a positive statement of what is preferred to it: for an example of what Constant prefers to say about our actions we can choose the following:

> Je cherchai enfin un raisonnement qui pût me tirer de cette lutte avec honneur à mes propres yeux. Je me dis qu'il ne fallait rien précipiter, qu'Ellénore était trop peu preparée à l'aveu que je méditais, et qu'il valait mieux attendre encore. Presque toujours, pour vivre en repos avec nous-mêmes, nous travestissons en calculs et en systèmes nos impuissances ou nos faiblesses: cela satisfait cette portion de nous qui est, pour ainsi dire, spectatrice de l'autre.

(Finally, I looked for an argument which could release me from this struggle in a way that would seem honourable to me. I said to myself that one ought not to be precipitate, that Ellénore was not sufficiently prepared for the confession I was considering, and that it was best to wait a bit longer. Almost always, to live at peace with ourselves, we disguise our powerlessness and our weakness as calculation or as a plan: this satisfies the part of ourselves which is, so to speak, the spectator of the rest.)

This is not a *maxime commune*, because of its cynicism; but it does not involve any rejection of the kind of language used. We see that it was the *content* of the *formules dogmatiques* that he mistrusted; he shows no objection to moral terminology, or to the use of abstract nouns to depict psychic states. He knows that his hesitations are *impuissances* and *faiblesses*: there is no scepticism about whether such words can embrace the complexity of action and motive. Indeed, the one apologetic phrase ('pour ainsi dire') is attached to an explanatory simile, and not to the abstract nouns.

For our second language we need a behaviourist novelist, and there is no doubt who is the best candidate for that:

The hills across the valley of the Ebro were long and white. On this side there was no shade and no trees and the station was between two lines of rails in the sun. Close against the side of the station there was the warm shadow of the building and a curtain, made of strings of bamboo beads, hung across the open door into the bar, to keep out flies. The American and the girl with him sat at a table in the shade, outside the building. It was very hot and the express from Barcelona would come in forty minutes. It stopped at this junction for two minutes and went on to Madrid...

He picked up the two heavy bags and carried them around the station to the other tracks. He looked up the tracks but could not see the train. Coming back, he walked through the bar-room, where people waiting for the train were drinking. He drank an Anis at the bar and looked at the people. They were all waiting reasonably for the train. He went out through the bead curtain. She was sitting at the table and smiled at him.

'Do you feel better?' he asked.

'I feel fine,' she said. 'There's nothing wrong with me. I feel fine.'

Ernest Hemingway: *Hills Like White Elephants*

What does this passage contain which cannot be subsumed under observation of behaviour? Very little surely — perhaps only the one word 'reasonably', and it would not be difficult to spell that out in behaviourist terms: they were not shouting or banging the table or (this brings us on to more sensitive ground) making the kind of remarks the girl was making.

Hills Like White Elephants is a story about two lovers quarrelling over whether the girl should have an abortion. The central concern of any such story will be their feelings, and there is little doubt about the man's feelings: he wants her to have the abortion, wants her to take this decision herself but also wants her to take the decision he wants; and he is being elaborately patient with her resentment. The girl is bitter and hostile, treats with coldness the solicitude he proffers, and wants only to stop talking about the matter. This is not explained to us in these terms: there are no words like 'haste' or 'solicitude' in the story, only dialogue like:

'Would you do something for me now?'
'I'd do anything for you.'
'Would you please, please, please, please, please, please, please stop talking.'

I have not yet raised the question whether these three are the *only* languages of fiction. It is clear that dialogue, if it is not to count as a separate mode, must fall under the behaviourist heading: to observe people will include to hear what they say. Certainly Hemingway's fiction makes us feel that this is where dialogue belongs: the cool eye that writes 'He drank an Anis at the bar and looked at the people' exactly matches the cool ear that puts down blunt dialogue without comment.

Now if the language of this story is behaviourist and its subject — inevitably — is feelings, there is an obvious sense in which method is inadequate to subject. This means either that the author is not *really* a behaviourist: he is trying to convey his effects with the minimum of means, he is showing us how much human content is implied by apparently superficial observation as long as it is accurate; or else he really is refraining from telling us important things. For most of the story we can say the first, though we would have to add that the behaviourist language is more than a *tour de force*: there really is a reductive view of the subtlety and complexity of human emotion in Hemingway's fiction. And at the end we have to say the second. The crucial question about the girl's final remark ('I feel fine . . .') is whether she is still being hostile, or whether the quarrel is now over and she is offering a reconciliation. The difference is instantly clear if we speak the sentences, but how do we know how to speak them? The only clue is that she 'smiled at him' — but what sort of smile was it? The limitation of the mode looks (here) like a limitation of subject matter. Deliberate, no doubt: but is the experience of being kept guessing as important as that of being offered insight? And is Hemingway the first step to the *nouveau roman*?

For the third language, I take a famous sentence from Virginia Woolf:

> It could not last she knew, but at the moment her eyes were so clear that they seemed to go round the table unveiling each of these people, and their thoughts and their feelings, without effort like a light stealing under water so that its ripples and the reeds in it and the minnows balancing themselves, and the sudden silent trout are all lit up hanging, trembling.
>
> *To the Lighthouse*, I.17

A passage like this is central to Virginia Woolf's conception of the novel, since it concerns the ability to penetrate beneath the surface of talk to discover deeper layers of consciousness and the possibility of non-verbal communication. And simply because this takes us into the inarticulate, it is clear that the third is the only form of language really appropriate to it. The second would be quite impossible, and the first would have to lean on abstractions for exactly those experiences that abstract nouns are not well fitted to encompass.

It is not very difficult to indicate what form of discourse each of our three languages points to: and thus what the novel would be assimilated to if dominated by any one of them — moral discourse in the first case, behaviourism in the second, poetry in the third.

Such a division into three languages is not intended as a way of classifying novelists: it would be crude to the point of uselessness if it were. To show that it cannot be so used, let us find all three in the same novel:

> Maman resta cette nuit-là dans ma chambre et, comme pour ne gâter d'aucun remords ces heures si differentes de ce que j'avais eu le droit d'espérer, quand Françoise, comprenant qu'il se passait quelque chose

d'extraordinaire en voyant maman assise pres de moi, qui me tenait la main et me laissait pleurer sans me gronder, lui demanda: "Mais Madame, qu'a donc Monsieur à pleurer ainsi?" maman lui répondit: "Mais il ne sait pas lui-même, Françoise, il est énervé; préparez-moi vite le grand lit et montez vous coucher." Ainsi, pour la première fois, ma tristesse n'était plus considérée comme une faute punissable mais comme un mal involontaire qu'on venait de reconnaître officiellement, comme un état nerveux dont je n'étais pas responsable...

Certes, le beau visage de ma mère brillait encore de jeunesse ce soir-la où elle me tenait si doucement les mains et cherchait à arrêter mes larmes; mais justement il me semblait que cela n'aurait pas dû être, sa colère eût été moins triste pour moi que cette douceur nouvelle que n'avait pas connue mon enfance; il me semblait que je venais d'une main impie et secrète de tracer dans son âme une première ride et d'y faire apparaître un premier cheveu blanc.

Mummy stayed in my room that night and, as if determined not to spoil by any touch of remorse those hours so different from what I was entitled to expect, when Françoise, who realised that something very unusual was taking place when she saw Mummy sitting next to me, holding my hand and letting me weep without rebuking me, asked her: But Madam, what is wrong with the young master that he's crying so? Mummy replied 'But he doesn't know himself, Françoise, his nerves are on edge; make haste and get the big bed ready for me, then go up to bed yourself.' So, for the first time, my grief was not regarded as a fault to be punished, but as an involuntary illness which had now received official recognition, a nervous condition which I wasn't responsible for.

To be sure, my mother's beautiful face still shone with youth that evening, when she held my hands so gently and tried to stem my tears; but that was exactly what seemed wrong to me, her anger would have been less distressing to me than this new gentleness, hitherto unknown to my childhood; it seemed to me that I had just traced the first wrinkle in her soul, and caused the first white hair to appear there.

If any novelist offers us moral analysis it must certainly be Proust, the great chronicler of egoism. In this passage, from early in *Du Coté de Chez Swann*, he is describing the struggles over his good-night kiss from his mother, how he waited only for that, till he grew disappointed when he heard her coming to his room to say good-night, because then it would soon be over. We have just been told of the episode when Marcel waits up to see his mother and is caught by his father, who is normally the more severe, and arbitrarily punishes him with a brusque, 'Allons, monte te coucher, pas d'explications'; but simply because he does not act on principle, his father can be arbitrarily indulgent too, and on this occasion, to Marcel's surprise, he tells his mother to stay and sleep there with him. This sends the child into fits of sobbing, and it is while his mother sits comforting him that this exchange takes place. It is clear that the narrator is crossing a threshold, his 'puberté de chagrin', and that this only makes his grief worse, for he has won a victory over his mother, the last thing he desires. Who, we are invited to reflects, is more severe — the punishing father or the scrupulous suffering mother or grandmother? It is because the mother's severity is the clear-eyed severity of love that the description of her *beau visage* is so moving, to the narrator and to us. It is crucial that he doesn't know why he is weeping: but the adult narrator knows exactly why, and from that knowledge comes the penetration of the analysis. He is learning through feeling the meaning of love and severity, egoism and vulnerability.

The final sentence is entirely concerned with the effect people have on one another; and the power of its images requires that they should not be given too much vividness. The mother *brillait de jeunesse*: the metaphor retains much of the abstraction of the tenor; and the touching glimpse of potential age — *une première ride, un premier cheveu blanc* — would lose its force it if took on the sprightliness of (say) 'till age snow white hairs on thee'. Moral language of this kind has only a limited tolerance of metaphor.

It is obvious that Proust is not a behaviourist in anything like the same sense as Hemingway; but there are frequent occasions when he — or his characters — display startling powers of sheer observation: the kind of observation in which moral concepts are suspended:

> Le désintéressement de leur pensée était tel, à l'égard de tout ce qui, de près ou de loin, semblait se rattacher à la vie mondaine, que leur sens auditif — ayant fini par comprendre son inutilité momentanée dès qu'a dîner la conversation prenait un ton frivole ou seulement terre à terre sans que ces deux vieilles demoiselles aient pu la ramener aux sujets qui leur étaient chers, — mettait alors au repos ses organes récepteurs et leur laissait subir un véritable commencement d'agrophie. Si alors mon grand-père avait besoin d'attirer l'attention des deux soeurs, il fallait qu'il eût recours à ces avertissements physiques dont usent les médecins alienistes à l'égard de certains

maniaques de la distraction; coups frappés à plusieurs reprises sur un verre avec la lame d'un couteau, coïncidant avec une brusque interpellation de la voix et du regard, moyens violents que ces psychiatres transportent souvent dans les rapports courants avec des gens bien portants, soit par habitude professionnelle, soit qu'ils croient tout le monde un peu fou.

Their thinking was so detached from fashionable or worldly life, and all that was linked to it, that their hearing (once it had realised that, from the moment when the conversation at dinner took on a frivolous or even matter of fact tone and these two elderly ladies had failed to bring it back to the subjects they preferred, it was no longer needed) turned off its receiving organs and imposed on them the beginning of a veritable atrophy. If after that my grandfather needed to attract the attention of the two sisters, it was necessary for him to have recourse to those physical warnings that psychiatrists use on certain catatonic cases: blows struck over and over on a glass with the blade of a knife, accompanied by a sharp challenge with voice and look, violent methods which these doctors often use in their everyday encounters with perfectly normal people, either through professional habit or because they think everyone a bit mad.

What has struck this observer is a purely physical resemblance, the tapping and the calling of the name. He is not interested in the rights and wrongs of his aunts' behaviour, but regards it with the eye of an anthropologist. The psychiatrists he mentions are not dangerous but amusing, the resemblance between the two situations is not frightening but interesting. We are not quite being told that the aunts are mad: rather that human beings are odd, if you only notice. Proust is reading meaning into the situation but only to a limited extent: too much interpretation would impede the observation.

Other examples of this language abound in Proust: overhearing the Baron de Charlus committing buggery, and realising that the frightful sounds he hears are the expression of (astonishingly) pleasure, or the grandmother's ability to distinguish Marcel's exact state of feeling by the way he taps on the partition between their rooms.

As for Proust the poet, I will take a sustained and rather formal simile:

Et comme dans ce jeu où les Japonais s'amusent à tremper dans un bol de porcelaine rempli d'eau, de petits morceaux de papier jusque-là indistincts qui, à peine y sont-ils plongés, s'étirent, se contournent, se colorent, se differencient, deviennent des fleurs, des maisons, des personnages consistants et reconnaissables, de même maintenant toutes les fleurs de notre jardin et celles du parc de M. Swann, et les nymphéas de la Vivonne, et les bonnes gens du village et leurs petits logis et l'église et tout Combray et ses environs, tout cela qui prend forme et solidité, est sorti, ville et jardins, de ma tasse de thé.

And just as in that game in which the Japanese entertain themselves by soaking in a porcelain bowl of water little bits of paper, apparently formless, which, once they are immersed, stretch, twist, take on colour, separate themselves, and turn into flowers, houses, solid and recognisable people; so all the flowers of our garden and of Mr Swann's park, the water-lilies of the Vivonne, the good people of the village, their small dwellings, the church, and all Combray and its surroundings, all that can take shape and grow solid now emerged, town and gardens, from my cup of tea.

This is the conclusion of the *petite madeleine* experience, the resurgence of forgotten memories into consciousness as the result of an accidental physical stimulus. The comparison of this resurgence with the opening of Japanese paper flowers is like an epic simile, the tenor of which (*mémoire involontaire*) is available only to introspection, and quite unobservable from the outside. On the scale suggested earlier, of how independent the meaning is of the imagery used to convey it, this passage falls somewhere in the middle: the simile is very much more than a mere decoration, but so formal and elaborate a comparison must imply the possibility of expressing the experience by other means, so that the dependence on imagery is less radical than in much poetry, or in the passage from *To the Lighthouse.*

§

To explain systematically the nature and use of the three languages of fiction requires not an essay but a book; and all I will now add to this brief exposition is an even briefer discussion of the two questions that must obviously suggest themselves. What happens when two or more of the languages combine (or, as the behaviourist might say, interfere with each other)? And, do these three exhaust the possibilities, or is there a fourth, even a fifth language?

However necessary the threefold scheme may be for analytic purposes, one would not often expect to find any of the languages in isolation: and the greater the novelist, the more complex we might expect their combination to be. But we might also expect that in a novelist of markedly individual style, this individuality might issue in a lopsided use of the three languages. I will take Dickens as an example, and from Dickens I choose the character of Uriah Heep, particularly interesting because it raises the question of how to depict hypocrisy, of behaviour intended (though in the case of the reader quite unsuccessfully) to deceive. Uriah is easy to recognise:

> I was hailed, through the dust, by somebody behind me. The shambling figure, and the scanty great coat, were not to be mistaken. I stopped, and Uriah Heep came up.

This act of recognition is presumably based purely on observation. It was not a difficult one, and the more striking the appearance the less acute the observation needs to be. So when, a few lines later, we see Uriah in all his grotesque vividness, the language of direct observation merges into poetry:

> Raising his great hands until they touched his chin, he rubbed them softly, and softly chuckled; looking as like a malevolent baboon, I thought, as anything human could look.

There is no real precision of observation in this brilliant descriptive sentence: its effect comes from the suggestions of the sinister, conveyed by rhythm and repetition in the first clause, and by the striking image in the second. Since Dickens never allows us to forget what an evil creature Uriah is, we can ask whether moral language is also present here. It may be the strength of the writing that it isn't: the one clearly moral word — 'malevolent' — is so transformed by its substantive that it sounds quaintly, even attractively, grotesque, as if a malevolent baboon was an interesting variety of baboon.

Let us turn now to a passage which quite clearly contains all three languages:

> As he sat on my sofa, with his long knees drawn up under his coffee-cup, his hat and gloves upon the ground close to him, his spoon going softly round and round, his shadowless red eyes, which looked as if they had scorched their lashes off, turned towards me without looking at me, the disagreeable dints I have formerly described in his nostrils coming and going with his breath, and a snaky undulation pervading

his frame from his chin to his boots, I decided in my own mind that I
disliked him intensely.

Here is Dickens at his finest: does the distinguishing of the
three languages enable us to say anything about his style? We
can, first of all, confirm that the language of external observation of behaviour can merge into imagery. As the passage
opens, the emphasis is on David's careful and precise observation, but for it to remain there we must be able to accept the
behaviour observed as normal: once we see Uriah as grotesque,
the emphasis will shift to what is observed. The first hint of the
sinister probably comes in 'softly' — a favourite word, we
notice, in descriptions of Uriah — and the sinister is very
powerfully present in the account of the 'shadowless red eyes'.
From then on image after image thrusts the figure of Uriah at
us in all its disturbing vividness.

And is there any moral language? 'Disagreeable dints',
though the alliteration gives it a certain sprightliness, is more
purely moral than was 'malevolent baboon', and correspond-
ingly is more conventional, the mere imposition of an adverse
judgement, like the last eleven words of the sentence. Insofar
as David is reporting a mental event this clause is neutrally
introspective (and a case for the possible fourth language to be
discussed shortly); but it seems probable that the emphatic
wording of 'I decided in my own mind' is intended to make the
dislike authoritative, and endorsed by the author, so that it is
not simply a feeling but a moral judgement.

If there is any doubt about the moral language in this
sentence, it is soon removed as we read on:

I recollect well how indignantly my heart beat, as I saw his crafty face,
with the appropriately red light of the fire upon it...

Here the moral is more prominent, and the moralising of the
firelight ('appropriately') removes almost all vividness from it.
And for virtually pure moral condemnation, we can go back to
Chapter 39:

I had never doubted his meanness, his craft and malice; but I fully
comprehended now, for the first time, what a base, unrelenting and
revengeful spirit, must have been engendered by this early and this
long suppression.

By now we have moved to Dickens at his most conventional: we learn nothing about Uriah here except that he is a bad man. The fact that he is a hypocrite exposes Dickens to a danger he cannot resist: that of simply announcing that his professions are not to be trusted because he is wicked — obviously the least effective way of conveying hypocrisy.

On the basis of these passages, if they are representative (as I believe they are) we can make a generalisation about Dickens' language. He does best to avoid moral language: when he uses it, it is in a crudely assertive way, and unfortunately he uses it quite often. There is a fair amount of direct observation of behaviour, which often moves imperceptibly into the richly vivid style of Dickens at his finest, which relies almost wholly on imagery for its effect.

George Eliot is my last example, and the discussion of her writing will lead us to the one significant language that may also exist, and has not yet been mentioned. Before coming to that, it will be best to deal with two other possibilities that, for the sake of thoroughness, need to be tidied away. First, it is clear that there is the language of plain narrative statement. 'She got up', 'he sat down': or to take details from the books already discussed, 'Maman resta cette nuit-là dans ma chambre', 'All the way down to the beach they had lagged behind together.' Strictly speaking, such language (of which most novels contain a great deal — though *To the Lighthouse* less than most) ought to be called narrative summary. A detailed account of the actions of the characters would tend to the behaviourist; but the mere assertion of 'got up' or 'stayed in my room that night' does not specify the behaviour in sufficient detail to count as real observation. Narrative summary should be regarded as the neutral norm from which our three languages diverge.

As for dialogue, there are clearly two ways one can handle that. Either dialogue is regarded as what a character says, and to write it down is to observe accurately, in which case it will count as direct observation of verbal behaviour; or else it is regarded as language, which can itself be divided into three kinds.

George Eliot, all her readers agree, is a profoundly moral writer. Does this mean that moral language will be dominant in her novels? It need not mean this, since language is manifested locally, and need not necessarily correspond to the overall purpose of a book. It is possible that a novel written mainly in the second and third languages should have a moral purpose: this will then be achieved mainly by juxtaposition and general design.

The second and third languages are found in George Eliot, and she uses them very effectively, but they do not seem central to her. After Mr Casaubon has informed his wife that his work has been praised in 'terms which it would not become me to repeat', he

> leaned over the elbow of his chair, and swayed his head up and down, apparently as a muscular outlet instead of that recapitulation which would not have been becoming.
>
> *Middlemarch*, chapter 37

The wit of this is very like that of Proust and his old ladies: the comical effect of what the mischievous eye might see as a substitute for boasting depends on the unexpected precision of the observation.

For the language of imagery, here is a typical example:

> A lady was obliged to respond to these things suitably; and even if she had not shrunk from quarrelling on other grounds, quarrelling with Grandcourt was impossible: she might as well have made angry remarks to a dangerous serpent ornamentally coiled in her cabin without invitation.
>
> *Daniel Deronda*, chapter 54

Where does the intense quiet power of this come from? First, from the cool tone, a tone of detached observation, clashing with the startling image, and most evident in the near-irony of 'ornamentally'; and second from the fact that the tenor of the image has nothing to do with Grandcourt's appearance: it is entirely an image for his relationship to Gwendolen. Elsewhere in the book Grandcourt is compared to a reptile with some reference to its appearance, but never solely so, and here not at all. There is almost always some moral implication, and even in this sentence, where the image dominates, there is some moral language; and a tellingly ironic example of it in the short next sentence: 'And what sort of dispute could a woman of any pride and dignity begin on a yacht?'

Clearly I cannot longer postpone looking at an example of George Eliot's moral language:

> In her first outleap of jealous indignation and disgust, when quitting the hateful room, she had flung away all the mercy with which she had undertaken that visit. She had enveloped both Will and Rosamond in her burning scorn, and it seemed to her as if Rosamond were burned out of her sight for ever. But that base prompting which makes a woman more cruel to a rival than to a faithless lover, could have no strength of recurrence in Dorothea when the dominant spirit of justice within her had once overcome the tumult and had once shown her the truer measure of things.
>
> *Middlemarch*, Chapter 80

Readers familiar with George Eliot would have little difficulty in attributing this passage to her. It bears her stamp, and in moments of honesty her admirers will feel that it is characteristic not only of her power but also of her limitations. Is she not too eagerly vindicating Dorothea, too insistently taking the opportunity of distinguishing right from wrong? The word which jars most surely 'base': the value of the generalisation about women and rivals does not require this underlining of what is right and wrong, and moral analysis has here given way to moralising. To a milder extent, the same could be said of 'justice' and 'truer': 'hateful', on the other hand, is necessary as a rendering of Dorothea's own feeling.

Does this suggest that moral language is best if not too moral? Another — and finer — passage may reinforce this:

> To Lydgate it seemed that he had been spending month after month in sacrificing more than half of his best intent and best power to his tenderness for Rosamond; bearing her little claims and interruptions without impatience, and above all, bearing without betrayal of bitterness to look through less and less of interfering illusion at the blank unreflecting surface her mind presented to his ardour for the more impersonal ends of his profession and his scientific study, an ardour which he had fancied that the ideal wife must somehow worship as sublime, though not in the least knowing why. But this endurance was mingled with a self-discontent which, if we know how to be candid, we shall confess to make more than half our bitterness under grievances, wife or husband included. It always remains true that if we had been greater, circumstances would have been less strong against us.
>
> (Chapter 58)

There is one striking touch of metaphor ('the blank unreflecting surface her mind presented'), but for the rest this is the language of moral discourse. Yet how little it is concerned to praise or blaime Lydgate: how much of it is concerned to understand. We know clearly that this 'ardour' is admirable and that Rosamond's 'little chains' are selfish, but if we could imagine a reader who thought Lydgate a mere bully, or regarded his medical researches as a black art which he ought not to have practised, there is nothing in the passage that such a reader could take exception to. 'If we know how to be candid' is an appeal to the reader, but not to take sides: rather to assent to the psychological insight.

If there is a fourth language of fiction, this is it: the language of insight. It will use much of the traditional vocabulary of moral discourse, but its concern will be less to approve and disapprove than to understand and explain. It is tempting, but would be too misleading, to call it the language of psychology: it would have to be a psychology which is prepared to deal with the full complexity of human consciousness, and which uses traditional terms for wishes, decisions, fears and motives. Psychoanalysis is excluded on the second ground, most other schools on the first.

My hesitation as postulating a fourth language is the suspicion that the language of insight is better seen as the result of the other three. When they interact, and each corrects the limitations of the others, insight is what results. To see from the outside, to enrich by metaphor, to understand a moral situation: some varying combination of these is perhaps the formula for any great novel.

6

Literature and Social Change

Once there was a Prince of Abbyssinia who grew up in a happy valley, cut off from the world. His discontent led him to escape, along with his sister Nekayah, and the poet Imlac; they roamed the world in order to make their choice of life but finally, having discovered that happiness is illusory, hopes vain and choice meaningless, they abandon their quest and return to the valley. You will have recognised the story of Dr Johnson's fable *Rasselas*. To understand the book's attitude to the human lot we can begin by observing how apt is the phrase 'the human lot'. Here is part of the discussion of marriage:

> I know not, said the princess, whether marriage be more than one of the innumerable modes of human misery. When I see and reckon the various forms of connubial infelicity, the unexpected causes of lasting discord, the diversities of temper, the oppositions of opinion, the rude collisions of contrary desire where both are urged by violent impulses, the obstinate contests of disagreeble virtues, where both are supported by consciousness of good intention; I am sometimes disposed to think with the severer casuists of most nations, that marriage is rather permitted than approved, and that none, but by the instigation of a passion too much indulged, entangle themselves with indissoluble compacts.

Imagine that pinned up on the wall of a Marriage Guidance Office. Nothing could be less appropriate: for it sees the causes of connubial infelicity as universal and undetermined. To control your own destiny by informed choice is here seen as a task suitable for gods, not for men; we do not possess that degree of control.

Just over a hundred years later a young man called Tertius Lydgate did make his choice of life; and the marvellous fifteenth chapter of *Middlemarch* tells the story of that choice. Lydgate was a quick fellow who, 'when hot from play, would toss himself in a corner, and in five minutes be deep in any sort of book that he could lay his hands on'. One day he took down one of

a dusty row of volumes with grey-paper backs and dingy labels — the volumes of an old Cyclopaedia which he had never disturbed. It would at least be a novelty to disturb them. They were on the highest shelf, and he stood on a chair to get them down. But he opened the volume which he first took from the shelf: somehow, one is apt to read in a makeshift attitude, just where it might seem inconvenient to do so. The page he opened on was under the head of Anatomy, and the first passage that drew his eyes was on the valves of the heart. He was not much acquainted with valves of any sort, but he knew that valvae were folding-doors, and through this crevice came a sudden light startling him with his first vivid notion of finely-adjusted mechanism in the human frame. A liberal education had of course left him free to read the indecent passages in the school classics, but beyond a general sense of secrecy and obscenity in connection with his internal structure, had left his imagination quite unbiased, so that for anything he knew his brains lay in small bags at his temples, and he had no more thought of representing to himself how his blood circulated than how paper served instead of gold. But the moment of vocation had come, and before he got down from his chair, the world was made new to him by a presentiment of endless processes filling the vast spaces planked out of his sight by that wordy ignorance which he had supposed to be knowledge. From that hour Lydgate felt the growth of an intellectual passion.

Let me point out a few things about Lydgate's decision. First, he made it for himself. He did not ask what was good for mankind, he asked what would suit him. He carried to his studies 'the conviction that the medical profession as it might be was the finest in the world; offering the most direct alliance between intellectual conquest and the social good'. The sequence of ideas is revealing: you don't start from the assumption that the social good is your aim, you start from your own particular aim, and the right profession for you is the one that contains just the right seasoning of social good. Here is a reasoning in particulars, quite unlike Johnsonian general views:

> Let Observation with extended view
> Survey mankind from China to Peru.

But social conditions, and medical education, in China might be quite different from Peru. Just as they might change with time: Lydgate's enthusiasm was for the medical profession 'as it might be' — i.e., he is not intending to accept it, but to tinker with it a bit.

Second Lydgate, like Rasselas, is young; but George Eliot has taken the fact far more seriously than Johnson. Young men think differently and talk differently from their elders and ancestors, and this difference has been inserted into the passage as a deliberate clash of styles.

> Something he must read, when he was not riding the pony, or running and hunting, or listening to the talk of men. All this was true of him at ten years of age; he had then read through, "Chrysal, or the Adventures of a Guinea", which was neither milk for babes, nor any chalky mixture meant to pass for milk, and it had already occurred to him that books were stuff, and that life was stupid.

Here is the youth's sensibility, modifying the style: the contemptuous surface of an impatient intelligence. Rasselas is always too close to the conclusions his author is drawing to be allowed to speak that way.

And third, Lydgate has a body:

> They were on the highest shelf, and he stood on a chair to get them down. But he opened the volume which he first took from the shelf: somehow one is apt to read in a makeshift attitude, just where it might seem inconvenient to do so.

By not leaping immediately to general conclusions, George Eliot retains the experience of thinking the ideas as well as the ideas thought, and of this experience the posture, standing on the chair, might be an important part.

What keeps all this out of *Rasselas* is in a sense the style: the weighty rational balancing of abstractions: 'the diversities of temper, the oppositions of opinion, the rude collisions of contrary desire.' Its tremendous rhetorical power depends on the universalising. The reach of these periods *is* from China to Peru. It is no accident that this kind of rhetoric goes with a universalised view of the futility of choice, and that the supple prose of realism explores the choices of particular men.

Clearly I am moving towards saying that the difference between Dr Johnson and George Eliot is a matter of social awareness. The conception of society that informs *Rasselas* is a static one. Because what is really important is fixed, we have no significant choice of life. Vast impersonal forces will impose our destiny on us as they have done to generations before us: and how magnificent is the rhetoric that shapes itself to such vastness.

> When first the College Rolls receive his Name,
> The young Enthusiast quits his Ease for Fame;
> Through all his Veins the Fever of Renown
> Burns from the strong Contagion of the Gown;
> O'er *Bodley's* Dome his future Labours spread,
> And *Bacon's* Mansion trembles o'er his Head;
> Are these thy Views? proceed, illustrious Youth,
> And Virtue guard thee to the Throne of Truth,
> Yet should thy Soul indulge the gen'rous Heat,
> Til captive Science yields her last Retreat;
> Should Reason guide thee with her brightest Ray,
> And Pour on misty Doubt resistless Day;
> Should no false Kindness lure to loose Delight,
> Nor Praise relax, nor Difficulty fright;
> Should tempting Novelty thy Cell refrain,
> And Sloth effuse her opiate Fumes in vain;
> Should Beauty blunt on Fops her fatal Dart,
> Nor claim the Triumph of a lettr'd Heart;
> Should no Disease thy torpid Veins invade,
> Nor Melancholy's Phantoms haunt thy Shade;
> Yet hope not Life from Grief or Danger free,
> Nor think the Doom of Man revers'd for thee;
> Deign on the passing World to turn thine Eyes,
> And pause awhile from Letters to be wise;
> There mark what Ills the Scholar's Life assail,
> Toil, Envy, Want, the Patron, and the Jail.

The effect of these lines is built on the syntax. '*Should* Reason, *should* Beauty, *should* no disease...': the mounting series of unlikely conditions is a cumulative reminder of the forces stacked against individual prowess — it's all happened before. The line that contains a series of nouns — 'Toil, envy, want, the patron and the jail' — draws its power from the familiarity of what they mean: we must feel how every item crushes the individual. The most crushing effect of all comes four lines earlier:

98

Yet hope not Life from Grief or Danger free
Nor think the Doom of Man revers'd for thee.

Every one of the accumulating conditional clauses comes
crashing down, with withering contempt, on those two helpless monosyllables. Individual freedom simply has no chance.

It does not matter what Johnson's young man is studying:
this series of difficulties imposes itself on medicine and on
classics alike. But Lydgate's choice of life is quite specifically
the choice of medicine: even the transition from the classics is
described in detail. And if we were to continue the quotation we
would see that what Lydgate is changing to is not static. The
attraction of his profession is that it wants reform and so gives
a man an opportunity 'for some indignant resolve to reject its
venal decorations'. True, Lydgate fails in the end, as Johnson's
young man will fail, but we are never meant to see Lydgate's
failure as inevitable. Who are you to think of changing the
world?, is Johnson's theme; but Lydgate does not intend to
change the world, merely to make limited changes in one
specific institution. The causes of his failure are plural and
particular: they can be explained, and might have been
avoided.

I have begun with this contrast to show some of the
aesthetic consequences of the static and the mobile ideas of
society, of the difference between a world where choice of life
is illusory and where it is a complicated, limited, difficult
actuality. It is not of course an accident that a hundred years of
European history have intervened between these writers: the
comparison is not between two individual temperaments, but
between the eighteenth and the nineteenth centuries. I have
now to admit that my gesture towards an interdisciplinary
approach is very limited. I am not going to pause — as I
perhaps should — to ask how much social mobility there
actually was in 1759, and how much more in 1872. Indeed, one
could even pause to ask how real the contrast is between a
static and a mobile society. No human situation is motionless;
but change has speeded up so much since the cavemen, and
even since the eighteenth century, that the contrast, though
one of degree, is large and real. And I feel justified in regarding
nineteenth-century society as mobile because that is how it

saw itself. 'We have shown the example of a nation', said Palmerston in 1860,

> in which every class of society accepts with cheerfulness the lot which providence has assigned to it; while at the same time each individual of each class is constantly trying to raise himself in the social scale, not by violence and illegality, but by perservering good conduct and by the steady and energetic exertion of the moral and intellectual faculties with which his creator has endowed him.

This is the ideal of equal opportunity and self-improvement associated above all with Samuel Smiles, prophet of self-help. Beatrice Webb's mother believed that 'it was the bounden duty of every citizen to better his social status; to ignore those beneath him, and to aim steadily at the top rung of the ladder'. No doubt the rise from penniless worker to successful mill-owner was less common in Victorian England than Smilesian apologists like to maintain, but the possibility was central to the contrast between an old world of deference and fixed hierarchy, of cap-doffing inferiors who knew (and kept to) their place, in which the drive to increasing wealth was simply absent; and the new open society of industrialism. In this new world of social change the main literary form was the novel, and within that form we can see a constant battle between inherited literary traditions, that assume an earlier stage of social evolution, and a responsiveness to the society around. One way of describing this battle is to see it as the struggle between convention and realism: another is to call it the attempt to kill off Dr Johnson. What I want to do for the remainder of this essay is glance at the form taken by this struggle in a few of the great nineteenth-century realistic novels. And first Balzac, from whom I have chosen *Les Paysans*.

Balzac has no hesitation in stating explicitly what his view of society is. It is profoundly materialist: 'Dis-moi ce que tu as, je te dirai ce que tu penses.' It believes the natural state of society is conflict, not harmony: 'qui terre a, guerre a.' And it is conservative, believing that the social order must be preserved. Riches are necessary for culture: 'Comment ne comprend-on pas que les merveilles de l'Art sont impossibles dans un pays sans grandes fortunes?' Great men will produce more enlightened government than assemblies: 'La loi émanera toujours d'un vaste cerveau, d'un homme de génie et non de neuf cents intelligences qui se rapetissent en se faisant foule.' The peasant is a danger to the institutions of society because of his un-scrupulous and boundless rapacity: there is no gainsaying 'la haine du proletaire et du paysan contre le maître et le riche'. The peasant is an 'infatigable sapeur, un rongeur qui morcelle et divise le sol'; he is egged on by the petit bourgeois, who makes of him 'tout à la fois son auxiliaire et sa proie'.

All of this could come from a political treatise or a work of social history. Balzac refuses to apologise for the length of his explanations, for, the 'historien des moeurs [which he sees himself as] obeit à des lois plus dures que celles qui régissent l'historien des faits: il doit rendre tout probable même le'vrai'. It was these long explanations that repelled early readers of the book , who found it tedious; and I wonder how much their interest revived if they read as far as the point (p. 157 in the Garnier edition) when Balzac at last says 'ce drame commence'. For the interest of *Les Paysans* is at least as close to that of social history as to that of a great novel. Its events are predictable, its pleas for sympathy laboured, but what it does most marvellously show is the complex interrelationships of the life of the community. A paragraph at the end of Chapter 9 states the theme of the book:

> Enfin, songez que cette ligue de tout un canton et d'une petite ville contre un vieux général échappé malgré son courage aux dangers de mille combats, s'est dressée en plus d'un départment contre des hommes qui voulaient y faire le bien. Cette coalition menace inces-sament l'homme de génie, le grand politique, le grand agronome, tous les novateurs.

> (Finally, reflect on the fact that this alliance of an entire canton and a small town against an old general, survivor, despite his courage, of the dangers of a thousand combats, has been formed in more than one department against men who wish to do good there. This coalition is a constant threat to the man of genius, the great politician, the great agriculturalist, all innovators.)

What sort of a novel can this come from? This sounds like a general maxim on the wickedness of democracy, not a living drama; it suggests the blind prejudice of a defender of property and privilege. Ever since Engels' famous letter to Margaret Harkness we have known the answer to this. Engels maintains that realism can break through a novel despite the author's opinions, so that Balzac's reactionary views did not prevent him giving an admirable account of French society — he *saw* the ever increasing advances of the bourgeoisie, he *saw* the economic revolution and its cultural consequences. And how does he show it to us? The answer lies in that paragraph: he shows the 'ligue de tout un canton', the 'coalition menaçante'. What informs every page of *Les Paysans* is its picture of the whole population conspiring against the law and against the landowner: 'dix paysans réunis dans un cabaret sont la monnaie d'un grand politique.' This combination makes it impossible to defeat them. The bourgeoisie control the district by their kin network and by their money; the people look after one another, make use of the letter of the law, and can't be caught by the handful of gamekeepers and servants loyal to authority. Balzac attributes this to their wickedness; but would a radical see it differently? When Montcornet succeeds in barring the gleaning to those without a certificate of pauperdom, the people refuse to accept the ruling: 'Eh! bien, nous glanerons! …dit Vaudoyer avec cet accent résolu qui distingue les Bourguignons.' Why should this not be the heroic resistance of the wronged people, saying indomitably, 'Nous glanerons et nous serons en force'. If the picture of the people were not by their enemy but by someone whose imagination was fired by their resistance, would it be different? When the old workman Laroche speaks about resistance, and using scythes on the legs of the horses, he says: 'Si les trois villages se soulevaient et qu'on tuait deux ou trois gendarmes, guillotinerait-on tout le monde?' Balzac has just told us what a good-for-nothing old Laroche is, but if we had just been told that he was the heroic organiser of the oppressed, teaching them to assert their rights, would he say anything different? Balzac wrote in hate, but this led him to such a careful scrutiny of the behaviour he was describing that the result is indistinguishable from love — indeed it is better, for the man of the people he *does* admire, the upright republican Niseron, the 'noble dupe,' 'dur comme le fer, pur comme l'or' is much less of a living, breathing person.

There is one limitation to Balzac's picture of social conflict. I have quoted his remark on how the bourgeois makes of the peasant 'son auxiliaire et sa proie' but there is no real conflict in the novel between bourgeoisie and people. It is announced in one of the brilliant speeches of le père Fourchon, who tells his son-in-law Tonsard that the bourgeoisie will be worse than the seigneurs, will make them dance to the tune of 'j'ai du bon tabac, tu n'en auras pas'. However, Tonsard doesn't believe him, and nothing in the book really confirms the prophecy. Rigou and Gaubertin, the self-made rich men, control the people through fear and a kind of deference. Balzac remarks bitterly that whereas the generous payments of Montcornet, the landowner, bring him only hatred, the exploitation by Rigou wins him respect. The cynicism may be justified: but this will surely be an unstable situation. There are innumerable opportunities for hostility between Rigou and his creditors, but none is allowed to develop. I can see that a Marxist might find this point attractive: it will show that Balzac is writing before the bourgeois revolution is accomplished, when bourgeoisie and people can both, as allies, invoke the populist rhetoric of 'down with the rich': only in the next phase will Gaubertin, who is already rich, seem so, because he will be the establishment. But the point I want to make is a different one. Balzac has oversimplified the situation because he sees the enemy as all-powerful: the intensity with which he conveys the 'coalition menaçante' has the vividness of fear, even of paranoia. And fear, in these matters, sees the same as hope. The war of all against the seigneur, in which he must lose, is a vision of inescapable conflict: no liberal will see things that way, but the frightened reactionary might, and so might the exhilarated revolutionary.

The reason why *Les Paysans* is among the most interesting of Balzac's novels is precisely the reason why contemporaries found it tedious: that it has no plot. For Balzac fits better than anyone into the model I would like to suggest for the nineteenth-century novel, of a set of narrative conventions that come down from the earlier age, and are being invaded by social awareness. The plots and narrative situations of Balzac seem to me to descend unchanged from the stereotypes of melodramatic fiction, whereas his depicting of the social context is full and rich. Crude power is juxtaposed with documented insight. In this novel we see the social historian more or less uninhibited, and though the pages do not turn rapidly the insights are fascinating.

Engels' interpretation of Balzac (which has become famous through its extension by Lukacs) sees such a contrast between the author's political opinions and the world created in the novel that it has to be called anti-intentionalist. It assumes the position that has become familiar to English critics under Lawrence's formula, never trust the teller, trust the tale. I think that position is in the last resort inevitable: but we are not always driven to it so directly as in the case of Balzac. Stendhal for instance seems to hold political opinions quite compatible with those implied in his novels. He is a progressive, who sees social change everywhere, and welcomes it. A glance at his letters and autobiographical writings shows how much he loved to see himself as a subversive, unacceptable to authority because of his delight in telling the truth without fuss. 'Montaigne doutant des dogmes de la sottise ancienne, voilà un grand mérite': such simple progressivism abounds in his writings. His hatred of cliché and pomposity, his insistence on 'petits faits', so central to his aesthetic, is important not only artistically but also socially; for (as he points out in *De l'Amour*) 'tout ce qui est cérémonie, par son essence d'être une chose affectée et prévue d'avance, dans laquelle il s'agit de se comporter *d'une manière convenable*, paralyse l'imagination'. Stendhal is so persistent in perceiving social movement, especially from below, and so inclined to attribute it to material conditions, that some of his observations sound as if they might come from Marx — this marginal comment to Montesquieu for instance: 'Adorer le Dieu des Chrétiens par l'intercession de la Vièrge, c'est s'accoutumer à faire la cour à un Despote, avec l'intercession du Ministre Sécrétaire d'Etat.' A more sustained example comes in a letter from London (15 September, 1826) which would not be out of place in the Marx-Engels reports on Britain thirty years later: sabbath breaking is the worst of sins, there is one law for the rich and one for the poor, poaching is the commonest crime because it is directed at the property of the landowning class. The materialism revealed here is important to Stendhal's whole vision of society. If there is any one quality central to the Stendhalien hero it is energy: and the connexion of this with his radicalism and his materialism emerges from a remark in the *Vie d'Henry Brulard* (Chapter 2): 'Donc suivant moi *l'énergie* ne se trouvait même à mes yeux (en 1811) que dans la classe qui est en lutte avec les vrais besoins.'

Such are Stendhal's opinions: but it is not opinions alone which make a novelist. It is not even necessary, in his case, to wait for the critic (Marxist or New Critic) who comes to rescue the tale from the teller, since Stendhal was himself aware of the tension in himself between opinion and taste. 'J'abhorre la canaille', he declares in the *Vie de Henry Brulard*, '...en même temps que sous le nom de *peuple* je désire passionnément son bonheur'. His ineradicable aristocratic tastes would make it more acceptable to him to pass half of every month in prison than to 'vivre avec les habitants des boutiques'. Prison is after all no loss of social status to the gentleman sent there for his opinions by a government run by (say) M. de Rênal. Stendhal's writings are full of confessions of this ambivalence — so much so that it is clear that he revelled in it, that the divided self of the aristocratic radical is one of the roles which this amateur of role playing most enjoyed. If then we look for ambivalence in the social meaning of his greatest novel, we can be said to follow only his own far-reaching suggestion.

There is no doubt that *Le Rouge et le Noir* is offered as a novel about social contrasts. Its subject is not the unchanging human heart, but the pressures brought to bear from without on the volatile heart of Julien. These pressures are complex, since they depend on interacting social forces and conflicts. I suggest these are of three kinds.

First, there is the cultural contrast between Paris and the Provinces. Verrières is full of provincial pettiness — the malice, the coolness and the ambitions of M. de Rênal and M. Valenod that look so ridiculous when seen from outside. The conversation which Julien overhears in the stage coach in the first chapter of Book II, which we know contains the nearest thing to a direct appearance in the novel by the author, is also the most direct attack on provincial life: it is confirmed by the hatred of Grenoble that burns in the *Vie de Henry Brulard*. Yet for all its anti-provincialism, the novel does not offer Paris as a norm; for Paris is the seat of boredom, to which vitality comes from the provinces. In the end, the cultural centre needs an infusion of provincial naivety. Mathilde needs Julien to overcome the emptiness of her sophisticated life; and the contrast between Julien's two women is the clearest illustration of the contrast between Paris and the Provinces. Stendhal's essay on the book, though factually wrong in its account of the affair with Mathilde, is profoundly right in its contrast between 'l'amour vrai, simple ne se regardant pas soi-même' of Mme de Rênal, and 'l'amour de tête' which, the author prides himself, has not yet been depicted in any book, and which is also 'l'amour parisien'. Stendhal's 'amour de tête' is more interesting, I suggest, than Lawrence's sex-in-the-head, to which it has some resemblance, largely because of the author's ambivalence. If Stendhal despised Mathilde with the directness of Lawrence's contempt for Hermione Roddice or Clifford Chatterley, *Le Rouge et le Noir* would be the worse for it.

More important than this cultural and geographical contrast is the class contrast: it is here that Stendhal's proto-Marxism will operate. A passage from *Promenades dans Rome* on the case of Lafforgue (one of the two originals of the plot of the novel) offers an explanation to delight the hearts of sociologists:

Tandis que les hautes classes de la société parisienne semblent perdre la faculté de sentir avec force et constance, les passions déploient une énergie effrayante dans la petite bourgeoisie, parmi ces jeunes gens qui, comme M. Lafforgue, ont reçu une bonne éducation, mais que l'absence de fortune oblige au travail et met en butte avec les vrais besoins.

(While the upper classes of Parisian Society seem to be losing the power of strong and steady feeling, the passions are releasing a terrifying energy among the petite bourgeoisie, among those young people who, like M. Lafforgue, have received a good education but, because of their lack of fortune, are obliged to work, and are exposed to real need.)

Work keeps them from becoming effete; and in the future it is probable that all great men will come from this class — as did Napoleon. Now this is just the kind of explanation that we find in the novel itself. From many possible examples I choose one: when Julien is in prison, M. de Frilair offers to Mathilde a version of his conduct that is clearly wrong, but which she believes and is miserable. Why did Julien shoot Mme de Rênal in church, instead of hiding in her garden like a sensible man? Because he was jealous of the priest: and Mathilde, being an aristocrat, is unable to understand the impulsive lack of prudence which is the correct explanation. Social class determines what we are capable of seeing.

Just as social class dominates our passions. Nowhere is this clearer than in the love between Julien and Mathilde, from which the tension of class hostility is never absent. Mathilde's passion for her father's secretary is so closely tied to her contempt for the upstart that the alternations between disdain and self-humiliating surrender become understandable; as does the unforgettable cry of delight of the happy lover — 'la voilà donc cette orgueilleuse, à mes pieds'.

Finally, there is *le moment*. Stendhal's third type of social explanation is in terms of chronological development, and often seems advanced as the most important of all. It provides the subtitle of the novel, *Chronique de 1830*, and it is stated explicitly in his essay on the book. Stendhal's view seems to be that there are three Frances. There is that of the ancien regime: 'gaie, amusante, un peu libertine, qui...faisait le modèle de l'Europe.' There is that of Napoleon, the era when a common man could become a general: Napoleon is seen as the perfect example of the bourgeois principle of social mobility. And there is that of the Restoration, when the way to rise is no longer through the army but through the church (hence the title, *Le Rouge et le Noire*): this is 'la France grave, morale, morose que nous ont léguée les jésuites, les congrégations et le gouvernement des Bourbons de 1814 à 1830'. This is the France under which Julien, the worshipper of Napoleon, has to live.

That is Stendhal's scheme. If we turn now to the novel as an imaginative creation, and ask how that scheme functions, we shall find that it explains some parts very well and misleads on others. It is obvious that *Le Rouge et le Noir* is about social mobility (Julien's first question, when engaged by the Rênal family to teach their children, is 'avec qui mangerai-je?'), and the most obvious manifestation of this is the plot. The rise of a young man is the natural form for a novel on this subject, and the development of Julien from 'petit paysan' to the lover of

Mlle de la Mole and the wearer of epaulettes implies much of Stendhal's social analysis. That needs saying, but it is so obvious that it need not be lingered on. As well as plot, there is an image that embodies the view: it is that of a young man trying to stay on his horse. Lucien Leuwen falls off his horse twice under the window of the woman whose lover he wishes to become. In a letter to Clementine Curial, Stendhal compares himself to a conscript, newly arrived in a regiment, trying to stay on the spirited horse he has been given ('le cheval, c'est le caractère'): and his own difficulties in riding are mentioned in the *Vie de Henry Brulard*. To stay dignified while controlling a natural force that would like to unseat you but also provides your power and energy: this is the social situation of the hero. It is clear in the brilliant eighteenth chapter of *Le Rouge et le Noir*, in which Julien is given a position in the guard of honour when a king visits Verrières. Envied by some, admired by others, he sees in the eyes of the women that he is being talked about: 'Ses épaulettes étaient plus brillantes, parce qu'elles étaient neuves. Son cheval se cabrait à chaque instant, il étaient au comble de la joie.' With consummate tact, Stendhal translates a social situation into a physical accomplishment, and the result is the perfect realistic presentation of the *arriviste*.

Does this mean that *Le Rouge et le Noir* is not of all times but for an age: that to understand it, we need to place ourselves in a very particular social situation? This is the position of the finest critic who has written on Stendhal (though not Stendhal's finest critic). In his memorable chapter in *Mimesis* 'In the hotel de la Mole', Eric Auerbach claims that the greatness of the novel lies in its ability to render 'the political situation, the social stratification, and the economic circumstances of a perfectly definite historical moment'. The boredom which reigns in the hotel de la Mole is 'no ordinary boredom' — it is that of 1830 France.

How can that be true? Greatness surely consists in shaking free of what is specific to 1830, perhaps even of what is specific to nineteenth-century France, to perceive forces of more universal significance: else where is the generalising power of literature? This brilliant account of Stendhal's kind of realism, as Auerbach states it, would limit the interest of the novel. To look at Stendhal's letters after reading *Le Rouge et le Noir* is to feel excluded: they are tied to particulars — particulars only available to the scholar — as the novel is not. It may be that for a full understanding of the novel we need to detach it from its specifics, even from its author's own threefold scheme of social interpretation. And we are certainly encouraged to do this by the complexity of Stendhal's irony.

What is the most famous social interpretation of the story? It is surely Julien's own, in his speech during his trial: 'Messieurs, je n'ai point l'honneur d'appartenir à votre classe, vous voyez en moi un paysan qui s'est revolté contre la bassesse de sa fortune....' He expects to be condemned because he sees among the jury some who want to take the opportunity to keep down those who, born in an inferior class, 'ont le bonheur de se procurer une bonne education, et l'audace de se mêler à ce que l'orgueil des gens riches appelle la société'. The old Barrault film of *Le Rouge et le Noir* began with this speech: an effectively theatrical idea, but one which seemed very wrong. For although those who use their talents and their education to rise in the world are the group whom Stendhal (or should we here say Beyle?) deeply identifies with, the author is not identified with Julien in this speech. It is too clear that he is putting on a performance. He wants to be found guilty, and is deliberately goading the jury; at the same time, he may be offering himself a convenient exoneration. After all, he is not being tried for *arrivisme* but for his most striking abandonment of it, the shooting of his old mistress in an impulsive abandonment of the schemes that had at last reached success. To find the feel of the speech, we can compare it with that of Felix Holt, also delivered at his trial, also defying the jury. After explaining how his unsuccessful attempt to control the riot resulted in the death of a police constable, Felix adds:

> I'm not prepared to say I never would assault a constable where I had more chance of deliberation. I certainly should assault him if I saw him doing anything that made my blood boil: I reverence the law, but not where it is a pretext for wrong, which it should be the very object of law to hinder....

This speech too goads the jury, and helps to procure Felix's conviction. It is intended to show us what a fine fellow Felix is, how his honesty compels him to state his views meticulously, even against his own interests. George Eliot's admiration for Felix is here unquestioning; and leads her to attribute to him a transparent sincerity that comes out, alas, as preaching. Why is Julien's speech so much more convincing, so much truer to the book? Because Stendhal is not swept into fulsomeness by admiration for his hero, because he has kept his distance — as he always does. Stendhal never identifies totally with his heroes, because of his awareness of their role-playing. In his love for Mathilde, Julien is able, at his most intense moments, to forget 'son triste rôle de plébeien revolté'. The crucial word here is 'rôle': it is the most important concept in Stendhal. It necessarily implies a detachment of author from character, of the kind that George Eliot unfortunately does not have from Felix (with the result that he is by far the least convincing character in an otherwise superb novel). Julien is playing a role when he declares that the class situation is the fundamental explanation of his 'crime', and the result is partly to undercut what might otherwise seem the message of the book.

And now returning to an earlier example, I must confess that (with a coolness borrowed from Stendhal) I offered a merely partial interpretation of M. de Frilair's views. I pointed out how wrong he was to offer a merely personal interpretation of Julien's actions, because he did not understand how the minds of the lower classes work. But was he altogether wrong? Certainly Julien did not calculate, as M. de Frilair assumes; but he was jealous. He was not interested in the abbé Marquinot, but he did find the church the right place to shoot her: this is not said explicitly, but nothing is quite explicit in the terse, resonant prose that ends Chapter 35 and narrates the climax so briefly. If we transfer M. de Frilair's views from the conscious to the unconscious, they are on the right lines: and Mathilde, though on one level misled, has on another rightly understood how deeply personal his motivation was.

In trying to interpret *Le Rouge et le Noir* with a full awareness of the resonant ironies, how much do we modify the interpretation that sees it as concerned with social conflict? I suggest that we need to drop 'le moment': the truth (almost the opposite of Auerbach's view) is surely that the boredom of the hotel de la Mole is not merely that of 1830, but also that which we can understand today. From the other two social issues we need to take the most general points, those that might apply to other, comparable social situations. To some extent the novel has already done this for us. I have, for instance, used the word 'class' in describing the tensions and misunderstandings between the bourgeoisie and the 'petit paysan', but the term is not strictly correct. Social classes identify themselves in opposition to one another, and for all that the edges may be blurred, must be thought of a discrete and contrasting. Stendhal often seems to think more in terms of a continuum, from high to low: a conception that can be applied to a variety of social situations and class contrasts. In any society where there are people at the top and others at the bottom (i.e. in any society) and where there is some mobility (and so the possibility of realistic fiction), his points will be understood.

The rise of a young man, I have suggeted, is the natural plot for a novel concerned with social mobility; and we have at least one other example in nineteenth-century fiction as apt and as well known as *Le Rouge et le Noir*. The central action — and the title — of *Great Expectations* tell of a village boy, apprenticed to the blacksmith, who is taken from his rustic obscurity, and sent to London to be made a gentleman. There he loses his natural affection, becomes the victim of snobbery and extravagance, is unjust to his old friends Joe and Biddy, and defends himself with the self-righteousness of the unconfessed guilty conscience.

The first thing to say of this fable of social mobility is that it is not easy to be sure which side it takes. For the Pip of the end of the book is a wiser and profounder man than he could ever have been if he had stayed at the forge. He has been able to help Herbert, and has got Miss Havisham to help Matthew; more significant, he understands the moral strength of Joe and Biddy in a way they hardly do themselves. We have of course the concepts to describe this: Pip has moved from once-born innocence, through the Fall, to the wisdom of experience. We must not oversimplify: the world of the marshes is not Eden, but contains cruelty, boastfulness and injustice. Yet it also contains Joe. Joe is the benevolent giant, the figure of pastoral innocence. He lives in the country and is ill at ease in London, and this is appropriate, but not essential. Dickens believed that innocence like that could turn up anywhere: Frederick Dorritt is a musician, Trooper George keeps a shooting gallery, both in London. But though the geography of pastoral is only accidentally appropriate, the psychological contrast is central: Dickens is showing that meanness and snobbery are the dark path to fuller consciousness, and that the Pip who has fallen and been redeemed, though he may not be better than Joe, understands better what goodness is like.

There are two traditional patterns for describing the contrast between innocence and experience: the pastoral, which sees a simple contrast between Arcadia and corruption, and the Christian, which has a three-fold pattern — innocence, the Fall, possible redemption. *Great Expectations* hesitates between the two. Pip actually takes the decision to give up his sophisticated insights and revert to the simple life, when he goes back to the village intending to marry Biddy and leave it to her whether he is to work at the forge with Joe or go off to a distant place. If he had done this he would have been a typical pastoral hero, for it is a rhetorical device of pastoral that the simple homely shepherd is often an ex-courtier who chose to return to Arcadia. He is only saved by Dickens' plotting, for he comes too late: Providence tells him that it is his role to be sadder and wiser than a blacksmith.

I have assumed so far that social mobility equals the Fall, that the static society can be the home of innocence, and that discontent (and consequent depravity) belong in a world of Gettin On. I do want to suggest that we should consider this, for it explains a good deal, but of course there are complications. There are, for instance, two kinds of social mobility, which it is crucial to distinguish. There is Getting On, and there are Great Expectations. Getting On is the great nineteenth-century gospel of success: the work ethic, the rewards due to talent and industry, the spirit that made the Industrial Revolution, which Samuel Smiles preached and Ruskin detested. It is not this which takes Pip to London, but the hand of a fairy godfather (or, as he thinks, godmother): his rise, so far from being the result of had work and virtue, is the beginning of idleness and new vices.

Now this I suggest is the concept of social rise appropriate to a static society. A fairy godmother chooses very few — in fact she really chooses *one* person, whose story is seen as unique; she chooses him (or her) for moral and psychological — for internal — reasons, not for qualities that society needs and rewards. Expectations of that sort are not seen as a process. Indeed, I should not be calling them expectations, since they are essentially *un*expected: they spring like a day-dream from the ashes of the grate or from a sinister gentleman biting his forefinger. Dickens' title shows that the old idea of social rising is touched by the new.

And more than touched: for Pip's fairy-godmother rise leads in fact to a Samuel Smiles rise. This is done through Herbert Pocket. That Pip even at his most selfish has an unselfish affection for Herbert, and uses his coming of age present to help him, is a moral point about Pip; at the same time, it conveys the social point, that Pip recognises that what Herbert needs is not a present but a career. Herbert's career is not a pure example of Smilesian success, for it contains the old-fashioned idea of a premium: to step on to the ladder you need not only hard work but enough property to pay the entrance fee. Pip does this behind Herbert's back so that Herbert thinks he has found the opening himself, and only learns the truth in the second-last chapter. I find the social implications of this ambivalent. On the one hand, it makes Pip himself like the fairy godmother and the whole thing smacks of Providence rather than social process; on the other hand, it means that for Herbert the experience is *more* Smilesian, for he is conscious of getting the post, and then the partnership, only through his own efforts. True, he is wrong; but Dickens takes some pains to show that Herbert does deserve his rise, and when he relationship is reversed, and Herbert is able to offer Pip a job, no money changes hands, and Pip rises entirely through his own efforts. Neither Pip nor Herbert is brilliant: they rise through the best Protestant virtues, steady industry and application:

> Many a year went round before I was a partner in the House; but I lived happily with Herbert and his wife, and lived frugally, and paid my debts, and maintained a constant correspondence with Biddy and Joe.

Perhaps it is hard to believe that the ineffectual Herbert would really have been all that competent, just as it is hard to credit that David Copperfield's friend Traddles (that very similar character) would have ended up a judge. But this too may be a subtle social point: that not individual character alone but the situation you are placed in enables you to work well, and that England's commercial greatness is not only the result but the cause of the steady labours of Traddles and Pocket.

Now the greatness of this novel does not consist in its portrayal of the successful career of Herbert Pocket, simply because such tame unimaginative success is not the stuff of great literature: imagination needs imagination, and Dickens' imagination feeds on the fact that the social system he depicts is fitful in its workings, and frequently dams up the outelts that certain kinds of energy need. Take Orlick, for instance. This melodramatic villain begins as Joe's journeyman. There are indications that as long as he holds this place, his malevolence can somehow be contained: thus after Joe has felt obliged, like a good husband, to knock him down for insulting Mrs Joe, a pot of beer appears from the Jolly Bargemen, and they share it by turns in a peaceable manner. There is a place for work relationships, and a place for family honour, and the two have achieved a *modus vivendi*. But this stable situation cannot last: Orlick's alienation is too great, and he leaves his place with Joe. He turns up as Miss Havisham's porter, and Pip gets him turned away because he's untrustworthy. Alienation and lack of fixed employment go together in Orlick, each one causing the other: he is a figure for the energies that could be turned to useful work (he has enormous strength) and in a completely harmonious society would be. His alienation is not wholly different from Magwitch's: the difference consists mainly in Dickens' insistence that society's unfairness caused Magwitch's villainy, whereas the causal link runs largely (not completely) the other way with Orlick.

As for Magwitch, he is the most marvellous example of an instability in the social system. His life story makes it plain that he never had a chance, and with more economy than Dickens usually manages:

What were you brought up to be?
A warmint, dear boy.

114

He answered quite seriously, and used the word as if it denoted some profession.

The constant interaction between a moral account of what Magwitch has become, and a social account of what situation lies behind it, comes out in his own vocabulary, in which Pip's social distaste is suddenly revealed for what it is by Magwitch's touching awareness of it ('I'm a heavy grubber'); or in which his own self-pity and aggression are characterised by a social term ('Look 'ee here, Pip', he says obsessively. 'Look over it, I ain't a going to be low'). To put the point at its crudest, the alienation of Orlick and Magwitch would not arise in a harmonious stable society; it would find useful outlets (like Herbert's milder alienation, his fecklessness) in a harmonious mobile one.

How much of the human material of this novel can be explained in social terms? You will realise I am trying to steer a judicious course between a dogmatic belief in universal insights (which says, None) and a dogmatic Marxism (which says, All). For a kind of answer, let us look at Pip's childhood. There are two overwhelming experiences of Pip the child, both wonderfully realised in the opening chapters — his fear, when taking the food to the convict, and his shame, when he meets Estella at Miss Havisham's. The fear seems to me a universal:

> The gates and dykes and banks came bursting at me through the mist, as if they cried as plainly as could be, "A boy with Somebody-else's pork pie! Stop him!" .... One black ox, with a white cravat on who even had to my awakened conscience something of a clerical air — fixed me so obstinately with his eyes, and moved his blunt head round in such an accusatory manner as I moved round, that I blubbered out to him, "I couldn't help it, sir! It wasn't for myself I took it!" Upon which he put down his head, blew a cloud of smoke out of his nose, and vanished with a kick-up of his hind-legs and a flourish of his tail.

The details of this are specific and concrete — not property, but the pork pie, not conscience but the black ox with a white cravat on — but the situation is timeless. In any society where there is theft and property, in any landscape where the mornings are misty and the animals large, in any world where children are imaginative, this experience would be the same. It does not need to be a convict, a victim of class oppression, an

115

orphan brought up by the blacksmith's sister, and this writing is not of an age but for all time.

The writing is just as powerful when Pip's shame is being described, but this time the context is different. Why should Pip be so upset at Estella's disdain — why, for that matter, should she bother to mention his coarse boots, or that he calls the knaves Jacks? She must have known that working boys were coarse, he must have known that fine ladies were elegant. In a wholly stable society, no class expects the other to be anything but different from it, and does not get upset about this. What we have here is a tendency on the part of each class to relate itself to the other, to feel disdainful because threatened, ashamed because of the possibility of being less coarse. You may say that it was Miss Havisham's whim, in bringing Pip to play, that caused this, but why does that whim have such consequences if it is not socially significant? Somewhere present in the consciousness of this episode is a new, more mobile relationship between the classes; so it seems appropriate that Estella should turn out not to have been born a lady, and it is with a great sense of something rising to the surface that we read the last paragraph of the chapter in which Pip is dismissed by Miss Havisham:

> Finally, I remember that when I got into my little bedroom, I was truly wretched, and had a long conviction on me that I should never like Joe's trade. I had liked it once, but once was not now.

What Pip has learnt, through his shame, is that a blacksmith can dream of rising in the world. If such dreams were not possible, he would not have minded his boots.

My final example is the latest in time yet, in one sense at least, the earliest in spirit. Theodore Fontane was born in the same year as George Eliot, but none of his important novels had been written by the time she died. In the restrained and dignified books of his old age, we can once more watch the contest between literary convention and social awareness. We know that Fontane the man did not lack social awareness, but it is clear that he did not automatically transfer this to his novels. Peter Demetz sees the bulk of Fontane's work (and all his best work) as the *Roman der guten Gesellschaft*, and has described the complicated defence mechanisms to keep history out of the material of these novels. 'Die gute Geschellschaft', though distinct from the dangerous brilliance of the court, is also distinct from the world of economic activity, which it treats with a contempt that Fontane did not share in real life. Demetz sees Fontane's literary mentor as Jane Austen, in whose world of good society decorum reigns and social change does not break through and steal; but times have changed, and it is no longer possible to keep history out.

Much of the power of Fontaine's novels lies in the depiction of the defence mechanisms of an apparently secure privileged group that will not let Botho marry his working-class mistress, that pays lip service to romance but insists that the Treibel family must marry money. The stratagems succeed, good society is safe, but-the existence of such powerful mechanisms must imply the reality of the threat. The care with which social change is just not present in the world of Fontane's novels is a kind of proof that it really could be present. The example I have chosen is perhaps the most delicately written of them all. *Unwiederbringlich* is the story of the failure of a marriage. Two careful and delicate character sketches show how Graf Holk and his wife, once so happy, have drifted apart: she does not take easily to his worldliness, his passion for building and for agriculture, his not always acceptable humour; he is less and less comfortable with her piety, and what he sees as a consciousness of superiority — she is too virtuous for him. The result is a subtle and moving personal tragedy.

Personal? Yes, all novels are personal: but are the persons seen as having an autonomous existence, or can we see social forces operating through them? Fontane has taken great trouble to place his couple in a social context. Relatives and neighbours, first in the Holks' home at Hokenäs in Schleswig-Holstein, then at the royal castle at Frederiksborg where Holk is taken as part of the court of the princess — above all in the contrasts between the three clergymen of the story, build up to a picture of two contrasting worlds. On the one hand there is the world of rural piety, family devotion and strict virtue, to which Christine belongs completely. On the other hand, there is the world of the Danish court, where marriage is not respected but wit and light-hearted sophistication are, a world rich in social graces and charm of manner, but shy of profound

117

emotional involvement — to which Holk belongs sufficiently for it to break up his marriage, but not sufficiently to set up a new relationship with one of the court ladies. The personal estrangement, it is clear, has a social basis: we see this from the moment Holk gets the letter summoning him to court, and Christine delivers her judgement on Kopenhagen life. The *Wahlverwandtschaft* between Holk and his wife is spoilt, more clearly than in Goethe's original, by the contrasting pull of two different milieux, acting through them. And the novel draws much of its strength from this: it is beautifully written on the personal level — 'Das Licht unseres Lebens heißt die Freude, und lischt es aus, so ist die Nacht da, and wenn diese Nacht der Tod ist, ist es noch am besten' — but the moving episodes with which it begins and ends take on their full substance through the steady filling out of the context, through Holk's rather slow realisation that he cannot easily capture the tone, or understand the implications, of sophisticated court conversation — not even of its imitation in the mouth of his landlady and her daughter.

Denmark emerges then as a society of two worlds that, when they cut across a marriage, can tear it asunder. But what we cannot possibly say, is which world is ousting which. We could put up a good case that Protestant piety is the new world, replacing the old aristocratic frivolity of the parasitic court, or that Protestant piety is the old, giving place to new, relaxed, secularised attitudes. Fontane sees society as intricate, composed of contrasting groups existing in a state of tension: he sees this much more clearly than Stendhal, and to that extent has a stronger claim to be a novelist of class conflict. But what Stendahl deals with and Fontane does not, is change: the question of what belongs to the past and what to the future.

It might be illuminating, at this point, to insert a theoretical statement. In his book *Marxism and Form*, Fredric Jameson offers the following explanation of the idea of a class:

> Each class implies the existence of all the others in its very being, for it defines itself against them, and survives and perpetuates itself only insofar as it succeeds in humiliating its adversaries.

This is the Marxist conception, contrasted with the 'purely sociological' in that it sees the function of classes in class struggle, not their existence as 'substances tranquilly persevering in their own essence'. I suggest that this formulation, though it is concerned with how to see society itself, is of great literary interest. For in a novel too one way of life defines itself most clearly in contention with another: Jameson could almost be describing why plot is necessary. One half of the Holk marriage becomes comprehensible through the clash with the other: and the fact that Helmuth and Christine preserve the humane graces and never try to humiliate each other cannot conceal that the relation of the two worlds is that of adversaries. Now Jameson sees this as class *struggle*, and to a Marxist, struggle will issue in the victory of one class, the defeat of the other. No doubt this is historically correct: the kind of tension here depicted is likely to be unstable, and the contesting social attitudes will spring from groups whose influence is growing or declining. But to say this is to add a theory of historical change to our interpretation of the novel. The book itself may have no concern with projecting the implications of its conflicts into the future.

In his *Nachwort* to the Goldman edition of *Unwiederbringlich*, Walter Muller-Seidel claims that Fontane's distinction lies in his reflexion of social life, that the 'Eheroman zum sozialen Roman wird'. This sounds so like the point I am making that it is worth looking at more closely. For Muller-Seidel, Holk represents the new and Christine the old: he's always thinking about novelties, he built a new house on the edge of the sea; she dislikes novelties, she dislikes 'diese moderne Götze der Nationalität', she sticks to the principles she was brought up in. Now this is to see old and new as personal, not social qualities. It may well be that a taste for building belongs to a class that is losing rather than gaining power, whereas sticking to the principles you were brought up in is just what gives many a rising class its strength. Only by relating their taste for the new or the old to the social group that lies behind the Weltanschauung can we begin to write a social novel.

As if to refute this criticism, Muller-Seidel asserts in his next paragraph that Holk's novelties are of a superficial kind. He too is really a relic of past times: hence his interest in genealogy, his taste for the medieval. The new nationalism he occasionally

119

speaks for is something he has picked up from others. So there is no real version of the new in this novel: a conclusion that seems to me correct, and shrewd. But in stating it, Muller-Seidel goes on to draw a corollary that pushes us towards a way of seeing fiction that the whole of this essay is a protest against.

> Weil as nirgends im Raume dieses Romans zu echter Erneuerung kommt, muß auch die Ehe ein tragisches Ende finden und zerbrechen.

> (Because there is no trace of genuine renewal anywhere in the course of this novel, the marriage too has to come to a tragic end, and break up.)

What is the relation of the personal story to the social background? There are always two possibilities in fiction, symbolic and representative. The realist is the man who makes it representative, and Fontane is nothing if he is not a realist. Now to a progressive writer for whom all that's good is new, the rescue of a marriage may well symbolise the possibility of renewing the society, but to the realist the success of a marriage depends on compatibility: that the pair should belong sufficiently to the same world, as Holk and Christine in the end don't. It does not matter which world is new, which old: marriage will hold up if between members of the same world; it will be threatened if two worlds meet in it. Fontane does explain the personal tragedy in social terms, and to that extent the tensions of society have invaded the 'gute Gesellschaft' and two worlds at war trample the patient flesh; but we can't be sure that *history* has invaded, since we do not know which, if either, is ousting the other.

The realistic novelist in the nineteenth century, a member of a society conscious of itself as changing as no society has ever changed before, possessed a double equipment. On the one hand, he inherited a series of literary techniques whose emotional impact was proved — rhetorical speech, the conventions of conversation, comic stereotypes (a way of never fully seeing those elements in society you want to keep at bay), melodramatic suspense, the conservative implications of the happy ending. No novelist could ignore these completely and still tell a shapely story. On the other hand are the new ambition of the panoramic novel, the new fidelity of realistic dialogue, the new belief that the personal can be explained in social terms. The struggle between these two modes, between literary tradition and social awareness, is fought in each novelist and in each novel, often with great complexity, and it is never (if the book is any good) a total victory for either.

7

Progress and Evil

In the fifth book of Spenser's *Faerie Queene* an encounter takes place between the hero, Artegall, who represents Justice, and a giant with a huge pair of scales in his hand, who boasts:

> That all the world he would weigh equally
> If aught he had the same to counterpoise.
> For want whereof he weighed vanity
> And filled his balance full of idle toys:
> Yet was admired much of fools, women and boys.

This giant has a number of ambitious technological projects: to rearrange land and sea, to supersede the weather, to 'balance heaven and hell together', to restore the earth to its pristine smoothness and reduce all things 'unto equality'. These projects earn him great popular esteem:

> Therefore the vulgar did about him flock...
> In hope by him great benefit to gain,
> And uncontrolled freedom to obtain.

Artegall disputes with the giant, telling him that he must first know what everything was like 'of yore'; all things were created 'in goodly measure', in a state of harmony, and all are in their place now in a well-ordered world which it is blasphemy to think of rearranging:

> All change is perilous, and all chance unsound.
> Therefore leave off to weigh them all again.

In reply, the giant maintains 'how badly all things present be', and insists that both protuberances and inequalities should be smoothed out:

> Therefore I will throw down these mountains high,
> And make them level with the lowly plain;

and, as a parallel activity, he will overthrow tyrants,

> And Lordings curb, that commons overawe;
> And all the wealth of rich men to the poor will draw.

Artegall replies that for all the apparent changes taking place, things stay essentially the same. Both kinds of inequality (geographical and political) are good because decreed by God:

> The hills do not the lowly dale disdain;
> The dales do not the lofty hills envy.
> He maketh kings to sit in sovereignty;
> He maketh subjects to their power obey;
> He pulleth down, he setteth up on high.

For the giant to seek to rearrange the world is not only wrong but futile: no one can withstand God's 'mighty will'. The giant's projects are vain because he does not know the causes of things.

The showdown comes when Artegall challenges the giant to weigh words, and to weigh right and wrong, which he cannot do, because, as Artegall explains, it must be done in the mind. Whereupon (*ultima regum ratio*!) he has the giant thrown into the sea and drowned. This produces an uprising among the common people ('that rascal rout'), which is suppressed through their being knocked down by Talus, Artegall's iron follower.

Spenser's prescience in this episode is uncanny, and would have astonished and distressed him. In the figure of the giant he has foretold a good deal of the history of modern thought. The giant's scientific world picture is set against Artegall's traditional theological view, based on order and degree and the acceptance of God's universe. The giant has read his Archimedes, who declared he would move the world if he had somewhere to place himself; his science is based on mathematics, and issues in technology, so that while Artegall is concerned with the place of everything in a prearranged plan, he is busy measuring — the truly revolutionary procedure.

123

Natural scientists at this time were still drawing up tax-
onomies, a procedure that offered little threat to the traditional world order; whereas it is as if Spenser's giant was aware
of Whitehead's observation that Aristotle had told scientists
to classify when he should have told them to measure. Like a
good positivist, too, the giant is unhistorical: it is Artegall
who maintains that to understand the world you must know
how it was of yore. Where philosophy is traditional, conservative and hierarchical, science is democratic, even socialist,
for it abolishes old distinctions: the quaint ambiguity of
'equality' is a shrewd insight. As for Artegall's way of winning
the argument — there is as much ambiguity and confusion in
his case as in the giant's, but he has him thrown into the
sea — it seems such an admission that new ideas can be kept
down only by force, that one could almost believe it was
smuggled into Spenser's text by some irreverent radical.

A later system of thought, that does not fully exist yet, is
here condemned as if it were a wicked misunderstanding of the
world; and a very similar point can be made about *King Lear*.
As all students know, two views of Nature are used in the play,
normative and neutral. Normative Nature is now familiar to
us as part of the Elizabethan world-picture: it is God's ordered
universe, which responds with shock when the basic moral law
is transgressed. Duncan's horses take leave of their share of
natural reason when Duncan is murdered; unnatural events
take place in the heavens when Julius Caesar is about to be
killed. The positive side of the doctrine is stated by the friar in
Romeo and Juliet who explains, as he gathers medicinal herbs,
that everything in Nature has its own virtue, and that there are
curative and harmful properties in plants corresponding to sin
and grace in mankind. In *Lear* it functions as a standard to
invoke against 'unnatural' behaviour:

> Hear, Nature, hear! dear Goddess, hear:
> Suspend thy purpose, if thou didst intend
> To make this creature fruitful:
> Into her womb convey sterility,
> Dry up in her the organs of increase,
> And from her derogate body never spring
> A babe to honour her. If she must teem,
> Create her child of spleen, that it may live
> And be a thwart disnatured torment to her.

Because Goneril was a thankless child, it is possible to appeal
to Nature, the dear goddess who has arranged for the bond of
love and gratitude to bind parents and children; and Nature
can answer the prayer either by the physical curse of sterility or
by the moral curse of giving her a thankless child: the two are
parallel and complementary, for physical and moral are not
independent of each other. To give birth, that holy act of
fruitful Nature, would in her case be degraded into 'teeming'.
Lear of course is not himself moved by natural piety: he is
dictating to Nature, and he has already transgressed against
the family bond by inviting love in return for financial reward.
But it is not difficult to distinguish the doctrine itself from
Lear's perversion of it; and my immediate concern is not the
dramatic action of the play but the implications of its conception of Nature. When Lear, recovering from his great
passion, is being tended by Cordelia, she is told that there are
simples designed to bring about the foster-nurse of Nature,
repose: the same doctrine as that stated by the friar. To this
she responds:

> All blest secrets,
> All you unpublished virtues of the earth
> Spring with my tears! be aidant and remediate
> In the good man's distress!

It is impossible to be sure if this is a conceit or the direct
statement of a doctrine. The hope that simples will flourish if
we water them with our tears sounds like a charming poetic
fancy, deriving from Shakespeare's craftsmanship or Cordelia's
intensity; but Nature, in the normative view, can and does
respond to the appeal of a loving heart, so that Cordelia's plea
('be aidant and remediate') is at least as much prayer as conceit.

In contrast to this is the Nature of instinctual drives and
natural law, the Nature that contrasts with society and what
Edmund calls 'the curiosity of nations'. Edmund the bastard is
the natural child, in the revealing phrase which implies that
wedlock is unnatural — as perhaps the word wed*lock* already
suggests. There is a complication here, in that to the Christian
wedlock is not natural either, but supernatural: marriage is a
sacrament to the Catholic, and even to the Protestant requires
the blessing of the Church. But since Nature is imbued with

the spirit of God, the natural, by the normative view, includes the supernatural; whereas Edmund's Nature is quite different from, even opposite to, Lear's 'dear goddess'. It is the nature of natural science.

Now as it happens a modern play provides us with the perfect contrast to all this. In Sartre's retelling of the Orestes story, *Les Mouches*, there is a confrontation between Oreste and Jupiter just before the climax, in which the hitherto shifty and undignified god manages, through rhetoric and sound effects, to impress and overawe. Speaking now in a grandiose manner, he describe the revolution of the planets and the cycle of generations in language that recalls the Elizabethan world picture:

> Par moi les espèces se perpétuent, j'ai ordonné qu'un homme engendre toujours un homme, et que le petit d'un chien soit un chien, par moi la douce langue des marées vient lécher le sable et se retire à heure fixe ...

> (It is through me that species perpetuate themselves, I commanded that a man should always beget a man, and that the offspring of a dog should always be a dog; it is through me that the gentle tongue of the tides comes regularly to lick the sands, and withdraws.)

This last detail restates exactly what Artegall said to the giant: that constant movement does not mean disorder. Then, having asserted that physical order involves a moral order, Jupiter points out to Oreste that his attempted defiance will be repudiated by the earth itself, which will crumble under his feet. Oreste replies by reasserting his rejection of Jupier's world:

> Qu'elle s'effrite! Que les rochers me condamnent, et que les plantes se fanent sur mon passage: tout ton univers ne suffira pas à me donner tort. Tu es le roi des Dieux, Jupiter, le roi des pierres et des étoiles, le roi des vagues de la mer. Mais tu ne's pas le roi des hommes.

> (Let it crumble! Let the rocks condemn me, and let the plants wither as I pass: the whole of your universe is not enough to tell me I'm in the wrong. You are the king of the Gods, Jupiter, the king of stones and stars, the king of the waves of the sea. But you are not the king of men.)

This defiance constitutes his freedom: 'je suis condanné de n'avoir d'autre loi que la mienne.' Jupiter pities the humans to whom Oreste will offer the 'obscène et fade existence' that will remain to them after refusing integration in his scheme of things. Oreste does not dispute that this is what awaits them, but 'pourquoi leur refuserais-je le désespoir qui est en moi, puisque c'est leur lot?' Liberty, for Sartre, is emancipation from the Great Chain of Being and the Elizabethan world picture.

It is as if Oreste is asserting a historical point: that a new world-view was perceived by the old, but perceived as evil, or despicable. In order to claim the future, all Oreste needs to do is reverse the moral judgement. Jupiter is not saying all this for the first time, as we've already seen: already in the fourteenth century, a preacher responded to social mobility by saying 'God made the clergy knights and labourers, but the devil made the burghers and usurers' — that is, the new classes. Nietzsche's aphorism on the subject is more openly cynical: 'History treats almost exclusively of bad men who have later been declared good men.'

So far, what we have seen rebuked is science and democracy; to these we can add individual self-reliance and social mobility. What Samuel Smiles admired, Langland deplored:

> Ac sythe bondesmen barnes han be made bisshopes
> And barnes bastardus han be erchedekens.

The opposite view — that social conflict results from discrepancies of wealth — is found in *Piers Plowman*, but placed in the mouth of one of the Deadly Sins: egalitarianism is preached by Wrath. The intellectual questioning of Spenser's giant is also found, and also rebuked, in *Piers Plowman*: the dreamer is reproached by Reason for wondering at the marvels of the world (how birds have the wit to build their nests), instead of drawing moral lessons from Nature, and for wanting to know why the world is in such a bad state.

Why should literature perceive the future as evil? The obvious answer is that the imagination is conservative, and cannot accept a radically new way of perceiving reality, either social or natural: and its way of handling the unacceptable is to fit it into existing (moral) categories, so that repudiation takes the form of moral disapproval. The tension that results when that future grows more and more actual can persist for a very long time — as we see from the case of social mobility. Langland's disapproval, in varying form, persisted throughout the sixteenth and seventeenth centuries, not only in asides and incidentals, but as a central element in Jacobean satire and comedy. The well-born rake, whose sexual and financial behaviour displays little more than direct self-interest, is almost invariably depicted sympathetically in the comedies of Middleton and Massinger; in contrast, the City merchant, set on financial gain and buying his way into a higher social level, is a monster (or, if he is depicted as sensible and knowing his place, then his wife and daughters are monsters). Massinger in particular turned such figures into brilliant grotesques, Overreach in the misleading titled *A New Way to Pay Old Debts* (it shows a very old way to handle new men), and Luke in *The City Madam*. Here is Luke enjoying the spectacle of the virtuous family he has ruined:

> Ha, ha, ha!
> This move me to compassion, or raise
> One sign of seeming pity in my face!
> You are deceived: it rather renders me
> More flinty and obdurate. A south wind
> Shall sooner soften marble, and the rain
> That slides down gently from his flaggy wings
> O'erflow the Alps, than knees, or tears, or groans
> Shall wrest compunction from me. Tis my glory
> That they are wretched, and by me made so;
> It sets my happiness off: I could not triumph
> If these were not my captives.

The motives of the banker or money-lender who forecloses and perhaps ruins his debtor involve a whole change of social ethos. He operates under a financial code in which debts are paid and contracts honoured because they are debts and contracts, not because he takes a gleeful delight in watching others suffer or cutting out a pound of flesh. His morality is that of contract, not of natural justice or divine authority, and his dealings are determined by questions of legal right and obligation, not by the total human situation: if his actions cause suffering, he may genuinely regret it, but the responsibility rests with the sufferer who entered on the contract. What Massinger sees, however, is not the morality of contract but the immorality of cruelty: Luke is presented as if his chief aim is to enjoy the suffering. When to this is added the self-dramatisation of the Elizabethan villain, we get the diabolic chuckling of a speech like this, imperceptive as social interpretation, but full of linguistic vitality.

An almost exact parallel to the view I am suggesting, that the future is first perceived as evil, is found in Durkheim's theory of crime. Durkheim shocked his contemporaries by asserting that crime is a normal phenomenon, for in all societies some individuals must diverge from the collective type, among which divergences some must be criminal. He then went on to defent this divergence as necessary for social change. If the *conscience collective* imposed itself on individual *consciences* with complete success, a situation would arise in which no change was possible: crime is therefore necessary, in general as a sign that the moral situation is not frozen, and in particular but rare cases the criminal may himself be an innovator, the precursor of a new morality.

If progress is seen as evil, does this mean the reverse is true? That what an age (including, no doubt, our own) sees as evil must represent the morality of the future? The thought is almost too alarming to contemplate, and (perhaps for that reason) it is not easy to formulate reasons for rejecting it. The crucial question will concern the social basis of values, the fact that the same position can be seen either in moral terms or in historical terms: either as a statement of what conforms to a general principle, or attributed to the particular social group which is likely to hold it. Take, for instance, happiness:

But the whim we have of Happiness is somewhat thus. By certain valuations, and averages, of our own striking, we come upon some sort of average, terrestrial lot; this we fancy belongs to us by nature, and of indefeasible right. It is simple payment of our wages, of our deserts; requires neither thanks nor complaint: only such overplus as there may be do we account Happiness; any deficit again is Misery. Now consider that we have the valuation of our own deserts ourselves, and what a fund of Self-conceit there is in each of us, — do you wonder that the balance should so often dip the wrong way, and many a Blockhead cry: See there, what a payment; was ever worthy gentleman so used! — I tell thee, Blockhead, it all comes of thy Vanity; of what thou fanciest those same deserts of thine to be. Fancy that thou deservest to be hanged (as is most likely), thou wilt feel it happiness to be only shot: fancy that thou deservest to be hanged in a hair-halter, it will be a luxury to die in hemp.

So true it is, what I then said, that the Fraction of Life can be increased in value not so much by increasing your Numerator as by lessening your Denominator. Nay, unless my Algebra deceive me, Unity itself divided by Zero will give Infinity. Make thy claim of wages a zero, then; thou hast the world under thy feet. Well did the Wisest of our time write: "It is only with Renunciation (Entsagen) that Life, properly speaking, can be said to begin."

So Thomas Carlyle, transcendentalist philosopher and poet manqué, in 1835; and here, in contrast, Daniel Lerner (no relation to the present writer!), sociologist, in 1963:

The spread of frustration in areas developing less rapidly than their people wish can be seen as the outcome of a deep imbalance between achievement and aspiration. In simple terms, this situation arises when many people in a society want far more than they can hope to get. This disparity in the want-get ratio has been studied intensively in the social science literature in terms of achievement and aspiration. The relationship we here propose for study can be expressed by the following equation (adapted from an ingenious formula of William James):

$$\text{Satisfaction} = \frac{\text{Achievement}}{\text{Aspiration}}$$

...It is a serious imbalance in this ratio that characterises areas beset by rising frustrations. Typically in these situations the denominator increases faster than the numerator...

How does such an imbalance in the want-get ratio occur? How can it be prevented or cured?... There are six institutions which function as the principal agencies of social change (or its inhibition): the economy, the police, the family, the community, the school, the media.

The differences between these two passages are important, and fascinating. The most important difference lies in their style. Each, as it happens, quotes from an authority he respects, but whereas Lerner names him without evasion, Carlyle coyly presents Goethe as 'the wisest of our time', with a brief indication that he wrote in German. Is he being ironic? The whole texture of Carlyle's prose suggests irony: the archaisms, the Germanisms, the exaggerated imperatives, all convey the feel of someone playing with the language. In this playfulness lies his individuality, but it is never allowed to conceal the fact that deep down he means what he is saying; and once we have arrived at Carlyle's deep earnestness through the medium of his linguistic oddity, we are left feeling that we have made his message our own, as we could not otherwise have done.

The only detail in Daniel Lerner's sober sociological prose that corresponds to all this is the liveliness of the phrase 'the want-get ratio'. No doubt he is proud of it (the two blunt Saxon verbs qualifying the very abstract noun), but he does not play with it: and for the rest, he uses his prose as a window, which is to say, he has no style.

This stylistic difference is far more important than what at a first glance might appear more fundamental, the fact that one author uses imperatives, the other indicatives — that is, one is writing moral exhortation, the other dispassionate analysis. For with a little ingenuity, we could remove this difference. Instead of 'consider', 'see there', 'make thy claim', we could cause Carlyle to write 'in the case of those whose claims are zero, we will observe...', or Lerner to write 'put thy trust in the following institutions...' (or at any rate, if we want to keep him in the same stylistic universe, 'I suggest to the reader that he try putting his trust in...'). The fact that we can make this change and make it so easily shows us how much these two passages have in common, and makes it easier to accept the clear fact that the content of what they are saying is identical.

The relation between value judgement and social reality can be plotted on a continuum, whose two extreme positions are first, that moral criteria are wholly independent of what happens, and, at the other end, that morality is derived from society and must be understood historically. The first is formulated in Hume's celebrated distinction between is and ought and, more recently and succinctly, by Wittgenstein:

> The sense of the world must lie outside the world.... If there is any value which is of value, it must lie outside all happening and being so. For all happening and being so is accidental.
>
> (*Tractatus* 6:41)

For a statement of the second in its full crudity we can turn to a practical politician — Lenin, for instance:

> Our morality is completely subordinated to the interests of the class struggle of the proletariat.... Morality is that which serves to destroy the old exploiting society. [Therefore] we deny all morality that is drawn from some conception beyond men, beyond class. We say that

it is a fraud and a deception ... a fraud and a stultification of the minds of the workers and peasants in the interests of the landowners and capitalists.

Social reality, to the Marxist, determines moral perception; and since it is constantly changing, so is morality. The change in the material base results from interactions between different elements of economic activity, which act on each other not like two billiard balls, but by interpenetrating and causing changes in each other. There are innumerable accounts of the Marxist theory of how value is determined by the dialectical activity of the social base, and I shall here choose Lukac's exposition in *History and Class Consciousness* (from which I have already taken the analogy in the previous sentence). He explains that the solution to every insoluble problem is to be found in history: it may be insoluble if the contending elements remain the same, but historical understanding will show that they don't. To those who perceive only immediate reality 'every true change must seem incomprehensible', and the undeniable fact of change, when it occurs, will appear to be a catastrophe, a sudden unexpected turn of events that comes from outside and eliminates all mediations. Hence Lukacs' attack on absolutist forms of thinking, which he contrasts with a true understanding of the dialectical nature of historical process. So the absolutist ethical standpoint from which Artegall condemns the giant, or Massinger Luke, is the sign of a failure in historical understanding. Unless ethical judgements are made with such understanding, they will be bound by the class limitations of whoever makes them. And the first class to be capable of a truly objective social understanding will be the proletariat: since they exploit no one, they don't need an ideology (that is, an understanding of the world with built-in distortions to protect their class interests). So Lukacs can assert that 'whether an action is functionally right or wrong is decided ultimately by the evolution of proletarian class-consciousness.'

To the Humean, Daniel Lerner is being reductivist; to the Marxist, Carlyle is wasting his time. Lerner's mistake consists in posing the question of the nature of happiness and then reducing it to a consequence of the situation of whoever asks it, without admitting that the *criteria* for happiness must be independent of the situation which is judged against them. Carlyle's contrary error consists in treating the happiness formula as if it was an absolute, as if mere exhortation could lead us to reduce the denominator; only the form is absolute, and the actual determining of the fraction results from the material situation of the individual.

The argument of this essay is clearly incompatible with the Humean extreme, for if value is independent of reality, it cannot make any real difference that the future has become the present; does that mean that I am driven to the other extreme, and that the claim that progress is initially perceived as evil necessarily implies the philosophical position of Lukacs?

All theories that see theory as a symptom are in danger of cutting off the branch they are sitting on. The Freudian claim that resistance to psychoanalytic interpretations is a rationalisation of our reluctance to admit the truth about ourselves, is subject to the reply that the offering of those interpretations can itself be explained as a rationalisation (say of some aggressive impulse). And if all moral judgement is a rationalisation of class interest, why is this not true of the theory that moral judgement is based on class interest? Can the Marxist, who does not believe it possible to emerge from history, claim to have done so himself? It is a powerful strength in Marxism that it admits this point. It would not have been possible for dialectical materialism to emerge at any earlier point in history: only when the bourgeois revolution had taken place, and the possibility of a proletarian revolution had been realistically formulated (i.e. its material basis perceived) did it become possible to understand not only that morality is class-based, but that a non-ideological morality might come into being, based on the one non-exploiting class. Marxism is not outside history, but this does not invalidate its insights, since it knows where it stands.

I must now explain why I do not regard progress-as-evil as necessarily a Marxist theory, though I doubt if I could have formulated it in this way had there been no Marxism. I believe it possible to make use of Marxist insights without accepting Marxism as a system. For first, Marxism is not the only theory that sees moral thinking as a function of society, for it is not necessary that such a theory be materialist. Suppose we took the formulation 'interactions between different elements of economic activity', and replaced the last phrase by 'economic and intellectual activity', or 'economic activity and social habit', or even 'intellectual activity and social habit', one would then have a theory of social change in which the fundamental elements were no longer classes; and the form of the dialectic could be preserved, despite this alteration. There is a good deal of sociological theory that does just this. Durkheim is as strong an instance as Marx of a thinker who derives consciousness from society, and discusses moral propositions by tracing them back to the situation that gives rise to them: to the extent that his critics directed at him what is essentially the same criticism as Popper makes of Marx, of sliding from social pressures to moral rules. Yet at the same time Durkheim is explicitly anti-materialist, since he regarded religion not economic activity as the most primitive of all social phenomena, from which other institutions derive. And among recent historians Keith Thomas offers an interesting parallel. His explanation of witchcraft treats it as the consequence of social change, in particular of the rise of economic individualism; and it has much in common with the progress-as-evil theory, in that a new individualist ethic appears in the consciousness of the accuser as guilt (which he projects on to the accused) before it is openly held and defended. This looks like an economic explanation but it leaves open the question of whether new economic activity caused a change of attitude, or vice versa; and when it comes to explaining the decline of witchcraft, Thomas is quite explicitly anti-materialist: 'the change which occurred in the seventeenth century was not so much technological as mental'. Since attacks on materialism have usually taken the form of statements of faith (that it is demeaning to human dignity, or to human liberty, to regard beliefs as determined by the substructure), it is important to realise that there are scrupulously documented theories which reject it on the grounds that the evidence points against it.

And second, despite the finesse that I have praised, there is no complete escape from the problem of sawing off one's branch. The Marxist claim that it does not suffer from the limitations of class morality is based, essentially, on the claim that the proletariat is the class of the future. There are great conveniences in locating one's material basis in the future: it leaves one more room for adaption and unconstrained thought, for a material reality that has not yet come about is not very different from idealism. But once that future starts arriving, it may take on a definite and not necessarily attractive form, and to regard it as unavoidable will then turn into a doctrine of might is right. On this point, the argument of Popper seems to me irrefutable.

It is not my aim, either in this essay or elsewhere in the book, to propose solutions to philosophic problems: but rather to indicate what the alternative philosophic positions are, and to suggest the implications of each for literary theory and practice. The particular problem posed in this essay I cannot even begin to solve; and I will conclude by setting against Lukacs the (Humean) point of Popper, that even if a particular future is inevitable, this need not make it desirable, or even acceptable.

> It is at least conceivable (I do not assert more, at present) that a man who to-day foresees with certainty that we are heading for a period of slavery, that we are going to return to the cage of the arrested society, or even that we are about to return to the beasts, may nevertheless decide not to adopt the moral standards of this impending period but to contribute as well as he can to the survival of his humanitarian ideals, hoping perhaps for a resurrection of his morality in some dim future.
>
> All that is, at least, conceivable. It may perhaps not be the "wisest" decision to make. But the fact that such a decision is excluded neither by foreknowledge nor by any sociological or psychological law shows that the first claim of historicist moral theory is untenable. Whether we should accept the morality of the future just because it is the morality of the future, this in itself is just a moral problem.

(*The Open Society and its Enemies*, chapter 22)

This is a common enough position in our time; and it has developed its own literary form, the anti-Utopia. It is clear that there is a natural connexion between millenarianism and Utopia, and when the millenarianism is religious the Utopia is called the Kingdom of God. A Utopia is a description of a society which has solved all our present problems; an anti-Utopia describes a society that has solved the problems by destroying what we most value. It is clearly the appropriate form for those who watch the Saints, the Party, the Fifth Monarchy men, bullying and destroying in order to bring about their New Jerusalem.

If we are unlucky, our descendants will read *Brave New World, 1984, The Space Merchants, We*, and will remark that the twentieth-century imagination registered as evil what they have come to see as progress.

8

Lukacs' Theory of Realism

The aim of this chapter is at the same time modest and bold. There is a tendency in contemporary Marxist thought to insist on seeing any individual work of Marxist theory as part of a developing system: Lukacs on realism can only be understood if it is seen as developing out of Lukacs on *History and Class Consciousness*, which in turn must be related to the tension between materialist and dialectical strains in Marxism, to understand which one must begin with Hegel.... I had better say at once that I am not a philosopher, am not competent to trace the relationship with Hegel, and do not know Lukacs' work well enough to study his literary theory as part of a developing philosophical position. In the eyes of many followers of Lukacs this confession will seem not merely modest but incapacitating; and to proceed to write a critique (and a hostile critique at that) of Lukacs on realism will be dismissed as presumptuous lunacy.

But the tendency I have described has one great, indeed enormous, defect. To relate a theory so elaborately to its genesis, to place it so thoroughly in a tradition, seems to prevent one from actually using it. I have been very struck, in almost all the discussions of Lukacs I have read, by how little they say about actual works of literature.[1] In spelling out the way one work of his led to another, or showing how much more fully we understand him if we understand Hegel, they say a good deal about his theory of the novel, but virtually nothing about novels. Now if literary criticism is treated in this way, it will be swallowed up by philosophy; and since Lukacs himself cannot be accused of ignoring actual works of literature, and since I do know and care for many of the novels he discusses, I shall make bold to treat his theory of the realistic novel as just that.

§

I must begin by expounding the theory as I understand it. For this I have relied mainly on the following books, all available in English: *Studies in European Realism, The Meaning of Contemporary Realism, Writer and Critic* and *The Historical Novel*. Lukacs is a prolific but also a repetitive writer, and from the recurrent assetions in these works a general picture of his theoretical position does emerge. This is what it says:

First, that realism involves social understanding, so that the individual is explained in terms of the social forces behind him. Central to the realistic novel, according to Lukacs, is the idea of the *type*, the outstanding individual who is at the same time the representative of significant social forces. 'The realism of Balzac rests on a uniformly complete rendering of the particular individual traits of each of his characters on the one hand, and the traits which are typical of them as representatives of a class on the other' (*SER*, ch. 1). Society must be depicted not simply as a backdrop to essentially individual conflicts, but as the necessary material for understanding these conflicts. 'The inner truth of the works of the great realists rests on the fact that they arise from life itself, that their artistic characteristics are reflections of the social structure of the life lived by the artist himself' (*SER*, ch. 6). 'Richness and depth in characterisation depend upon richness and depth in the grasp of the social process' (*W & C*, p. 173). If the social process is grasped in such richness and depth, then meticulous documentation is unnecessary: hence Lukacs' constant attack on the piling up of social detail by the naturalists, which he sees as a substitute for the 'intensive totality of essential social factors.'

We can pause here and ask: what is the opposite of realism? Is this a descriptive theory contrasting realistic with non-realistic modes, or a normative theory contrasting good literature with bad? It is a problem that theories of realism always encounter, because of the constant tendency to claim that there is a higher realism, a truer realism, that embraces the life of dream, of fantasy, of idealisation, which are just as real as (or even more real than) the surface of social behaviour. Dostoevsky saw himself as a realist; I have heard Kafka claimed as a realist. There is an insight here but it does take us to the point where we no longer need the term: for if *all* genuine literary expression is in some wider sense realistic, then there is only one true literary mode. A term like realism seems most useful to distinguish one way of writing from another (equally valid) one, such as fantasy or romance or symbolism.

It is not easy to be sure of Lukacs' position on this point. In *The Historical Novel* the contrast is with drama. Certain crises of human life issue naturally in dramatic form. In a play, these are shown as clashes of individuals: for Shakespeare and the classical dramatists, the world of human action is seen as the pure and direct relations of people to one another, and these people will therefore be those at the centre of the action. But the great historical figures who occupy the centre of the stage in a historical drama are only minor characters in the historical novel. The hero of a Scott novel is a middling, unheroic young man, whose personality develops as we watch, whereas the statesmen, generals and religious leaders enter the book, as it were, ready-made. It is not their development as individuals that concerns us, but the crisis in the lives of ordinary people that gives them their social significance. Lukacs quotes Balzac to the effect that Scott's plots march towards the appearance of great heroes in the same way that history itself did. In the historical novel, as in the epic which Lukacs sees as its origin, the personal crisis of the individual occupies a position in the total processes of life; in tragedy it occupies the centre.

That, then, is an instance of Lukacs using his idea of realism descriptively, as one of a number of equally legitimate modes. In his discussion of Theodor Fontane, however, (in *Deutsche Realisten des 19 Jahrhunderts*), Lukacs distinguishes two ways of depicting marriage in the *Eheroman*, the novel of marriage, and insists that when it is shown in purely individual terms as only personal, accidental, eccentric, even pathological, then we have dropped into mere *belles lettres*. This is certainly normative, and belongs with Lukacs' throughgoing attack on

naturalism and aestheticsm as the complementary substitutes
that appear when the great days of realism are over. If substitutes for realism are inferior, then the scope of the term
'realism' will be enlarged, and in *Writer and Critic* we do find
just that: 'It is not necessary that the phenomena delineated be
derived from daily life, or even from life at all. That is, free play
of the creative imagination and unrestrained fantasy are compatible with the Marxist concept of realism. Among the
literary achievements Marx especially valued are the fantastic
tales of Balzac and E. T. A. Hoffman.'

§

Realism then can be seen as one possible mode (when contrasted with drama) or as the one true mode (when contrasted
with naturalism, the *Eheroman*, or modernism). It is the
second of these that is central to Lukacs' theory, since he uses
the norms of realism for his celebrated attacks on modernism.
These attacks are the most famous element in Lukacs' criticism. The extreme contrasts between different streams that all
bear the modern label constitute for Lukacs a demonstration
of their weakness; naturalism and aestheticism (Hauptmann
and Huysmans), montage and fantasy (Dos Passos and Kafka),
stream of consciousness (Joyce) and the *Art poétique* of Ver-
laine — all these are partial, where Scott and Balzac are whole.
In the same way decadent bourgeois thought splits into mechanistic determinism on the one hand, idealism on the other,
whereas dialectical materialism is a unity. There is no doubt
about the strength of Lukacs' hostility to modernisation,
which sometimes sounds very like the hostility of the trad-
itionalist, indignant at the reductive cynicism that ignores the
nobility of man: 'If Joyce had set Napoleon on the toilet of the
petit bourgeois Bloom, he would merely have emphasised what
was common to both Napoleon and Bloom' (*W & C*, p. 180).

This of course is the point at which Marxist rejection of
Lukacs strikes. There is now a widespread view, almost an
orthodoxy, in the new generation of Marxist critics, that runs
like this: The marvellous insight which Lukacs brings into the
great realists of the last century has, alas, incapacitated him
from appreciating modernism. His dismissal of modernism as

static and unhistorical is just the kind of rigid Marxist dogma we have at last broken free of. The dismissal of Proust, Kafka and Joyce as decadent reactionaries is a narrowness for which Lukacs is partly responsible, and has impeded a truly flexible Marxist literary theory. And so instead of Lukacs the fathers of neo-Marxist criticism are Benjamin and Brecht: Benjamin because he is a natural materialist, constantly looking for explanations in terms of substructure, while at the same time subtly responsive to the shifts in sensibility that led to modernism; Brecht because he filled the techniques of expressionism with revolutionary social content, and because he offered modern Marxism another way of looking at tradition. He asked why the '*Restaurationschriftsteller*' (the post-1815 generation) should be preferred to the revolutionary aesthetic of the rising bourgeoisie. Why could not Voltaire, Diderot and Richardson, for instance, represent a better tradition than Scott and Balzac? The Brecht-Lukacs debate is now much discussed in both Germanies, and leads to a Marxist alternative to Lukacs' aesthetic.

I ought to say that that is not the position of this essay. Though to me Brecht is the greatest modern dramatist, and Benjamin a subtler critic than Lukacs, I have much sympathy with Lukacs' view of modernism. That Kafka, Eliot and Beckett, by seeing man as isolated, irrational and non-social, have reduced our conception of man, have invited us into rat's alley, is important and needs to be said. It has often been said crudely, and by those totally unable to respond to the genius of these modern writers. Worse still, the practice of saying it is intimately involved with censorship, repression and fulminations against capitalist decadence. Nonetheless, it needs saying and Lukacs' way of saying it can still teach us something.

But the area of Lukacs criticism I want to criticise here is just that area which is regarded as its strongest point: his theory of realism. It is on the nineteenth century that I want to test Lukacs. Before doing so, however, I must continue with the exposition.

§

The social process that lies behind the typical figure of realist fiction is to be understood in Marxist terms. What the novelist is depicting is a struggle between classes, and, in the nineteenth century, the rise of the bourgeoisie. In this process 1848 is a crucial moment: until then, the bourgeoisie is a progressive class and its literary mode — realism — is capable of producing masterpieces. But after 1848 the bourgeois revolution is over, and it is now a reactionary force: this means the end of great realistic fiction. 'In a Balzac novel a court of law is not simply an institution with certain social functions, as in the books written after 1848. It is a battlefield of various social struggles, and every interrogation of a suspect, every drawing up of a document, every court sentence is the result of intricate social tugs-of-war whose every phase we are invited to witness' *(SER,* ch. 6). That states very clearly what Lukacs has in mind when he insists on the social forces behind the individual; and the phrase 'as in books written after 1848' is no *obiter dictum,* for it is stated over and over again. In *HN* ch. 3 he lists examples of how the bourgeois ideology of progress, after 1848, becomes a class ideology, no longer appealing to the progressive element in *all* classes. The literary consequences of this were disastrous. 'The evolution of bourgeois society after 1848 destroyed the subjective conditions which made a great realism' *(SER,* ch 6). 'What was new after 1848 was not merely that writers used commonplace reality as thematic material but that writers limited themselves exclusively to the aspects and phenomena of everyday existence' *(W. & C.,* p. 164).

Lukacs is very careful not to turn his theory into a way of judging writers by their political position. He is concerned with novels, not with the opinions of those who wrote them. So Balzac's reactionary opinions do not prevent his novels from offering insight into the social forces depicted. The utopian schemes and economic panaceas that Balzac believed in have only the most shadowy and general appearance in his novels; whereas the noble, bourgeois and peasant who battle for power in his fiction are there in all their fullness of social reality. The fact that Balzac criticised capitalism from a feudal, Romantic, reactionary position did not prevent him from showing the brilliance and shrewdness of the capitalists, nor from depicting his beloved nobility as careerists, harlots and fools. This is the view of fiction we now know in Lawrence's aphorism, never trust the teller, trust the tale; and the critic who undertstands that is at any rate preserved from the extremes of political simplification.

Lukacs was not the first to see Balzac this way. His whole view of Balzac can be regarded as an elaboration of Engels' famous letter to Margaret Harkness, in which we find the claim that Balzac is 'a far greater master of realism than all the Zolas *passés présents et à venir*', and the same distinction, quite clearly drawn, between his reactionary political opinions ('his sympathies are all with the class doomed to extinction') and the penetrating honesty of the social vision conveyed in the novels, the fact that his satire is never keener than when depicting 'the very men and women with whom he sympathises most deeply', and that 'the only men of whom he always speaks with undisguised admiration are his bitterest political antagonists.' The letter in fact is a succinct and vivid summary of Lukacs' whole argument and makes one realise what a literary critic we might have had in Engels. And — a small ironic postcript — this view of Balzac had already been propounded (in an essay called *'Les romanciers naturalistes'*, 1881) by no less a person than Zola! Discussing Balzac's political opinions, he remarks on the striking contrast between his support of absolute power and the essentially democratic talent that produced the most revolutionary *oeuvre* we have; and goes on to speculate on the fascinating problem of how a man's genius can run counter to his convictions.

§

So much for exposition. In discussing the thesis, and proposing objections to it, I shall take the two parts separately. First, the more literary assertion, that realism must involve an understanding of social change. Can a novelist really understand his characters if he places them in a social situation that is static? Second, the more historical assertion, that since realism is a bourgeois form, its possibilities of greatness are exhausted after 1848. Is this a tenable view of nineteenth-century history? And is it a fair judgement on nineteenth-century literature? Since any literary theory must in the end be judged by what it can tell us about actual books, I shall then turn to particulars, and examine what Lukacs has to say about a few novels. And finally I shall return to the most general question of all, and ask what criteria Lukacs uses when judging literature.

Does the novelist need to show the forces of social change? Is the development of the hero in the *Bildungsroman* fully comprehensible only as a manifestation of conflicting social pressures? In the case of some novelists, the answer is clearly yes. Julien Sorel is the *petit paysan*, and the weakness of French society lies in the very fact that it needs the infusion of talent such upstarts provide, while at the same time being ready to despise them simply because they are upstarts. Balzac's concern with new money and old money, with the battle over property (*qui terre a guerre a*) and with rising and falling fortunes, is obviously central to his work. But Lukacs is not simply saying that realism *can* tell us about social change, he is saying that it *must*; so it is necessary to ask if any of the major novelists fail to do so. Like any theory, it must be tested on examples that don't seem to fit. Who are the novelists who offer us the growth and conflicts of the individual without locating that as part of the growth of society as the conflict of social forces? I can think of two: Jane Austen, whom Lukacs does not discuss, and Fontane, whom he does.

§

The central situation of a Jane Austen novel shows us the immature but delightful heroine learning to know herself, and so finding her place in society. The lessons she has to learn, and the place she has to fit into, are already there: it is she who has to change, not the situation. We can see this from the titles: what we are shown is the encounter of timeless passions like pride and prejudice, or the contrast between psychological types, like sense and sensibility; when the moral norm is socially embodied it is in the unchanging institution of the country house, like Mansfield Park. Jane Austen's whole literary method is traditional: fixed moral qualities and humour-figures lurk beneath the surface of her sparkling realism. Lately, this has become a less fashionable view of Jane Austen and critics have tended to tell us that she is well aware of the forces of change in her society. As an example of this newer fashion we can take David Daiches, writing in a book that takes its starting point from Lukacs (*Aspects of History and Class Consciousness*, edited by István Mészáros). He attributes to Jane Austen 'a modified aristocratic position moralised under bourgeois influence', and makes out a strong case: but such a description is the critic's explanation of attitudes that Jane Austen herself saw in terms of fixed personal morality. 'It is an aristocratic trait in Jane Austen that she should be frank about money', says Daiches. I am sure that Jane Austen did not see it as aristocratic but as comic: her motives were artistic, however ingeniously the socially-aware critic may relate them to social groupings. As an illustration of Jane Austen's awareness of 'the economic foundations of the society in which she lived', Daiches cites the marriage of Charlotte Lucas, desperate with spinsterhood, to the pompous and ridiculous Collins. But this is not the economic but the financial basis we are being shown — i.e. the importance of economic constraints on the individual, not their operation in society. What Jane Austen does not give us is an awareness that the institutional structures which have put so many Charlottes in that situation could conceivably be different. That would really be social awareness.

And Fontane? Fontane is a realist to the backbone. There is not the faintest trace in his work of the old Morality-figures that (perhaps) leave a clear imprint in Jane Austen. He is a marvellously perceptive observer of a particular social situation in nineteenth-century Prussia; but that need not mean that he explains it in terms of social *change*. *Irrungen-Wirrungen* is the story of a man's liaison, with a girl below him in social station, and his marriage, with a girl he is expected to marry, and why the one has to give place to the other. Nothing surprising happens — as so often in Fontane, there is very little plot — and the centre of the book is a long meditation by Botho, the hero, on why he ('an average member of the so-called upper class of society') will not do anything unexpected, much as he longs to. *'Das Herkommen bestimmt unser Tun'* is his conclusion: custom determines our actions. The corresponding moment in *Effi Briest* is Instettin's decision to fight a fuel with his wife's seducer. In a long and interesting debate, both with himself and with his friend Wüllersdorf, he asks himself why he has to do this. The affair happened six years ago and he feels no wish for revenge: common sense as much as compassion urges him to let the matter drop, but he cannot, because his life henceforward will be full of social situations in which he will not know where to look, in which he will glance at Wüllersdorf to see if he is smiling wryly. *Das Herkommen bestimmt sein Tun*: or, to use the corresponding sentence in this novel, '*man gehört einem Ganzen an*' — we are part of a whole.

Now in all this there is one point that is never made, nor even, so far as I can make out, hinted at: that what we have is an old morality against a new. It would have been easy to suggest that Instettin is following an ethos that is not only rigid but also obsolescent, that honour costs him his happiness in a way that (ironically) is ceasing to be necessary. Wüllersdorf, for instance, could have been made the spokesman for another and more utilitarian code; or some such clash of moralities could have entered into the very touching discussion between Effi's parents on whether to take her back. Not only does Fontane not do this, but the omission is ironically highlighted by a single word. Very prominent in Instettin's reasoning is the term *Verjahrung* — 'going out of date' or, in a legal sense, 'limitation.' Common sense insists that in affairs of honour there must be a *Verjahrung*, 'but where does it begin? Where is the boundary? Ten years require a duel — that's called honour — and after eleven years, or perhaps even after ten and a half it's called folly. The boundary, the boundary.' To the modern reader, the idea of going out of date must surely suggest a social as well as an individual meaning, i.e. that the code of honour to which Instettin is a reluctant slave might also go out of date; but no such meaning is intended.

§

Fontane has a strong and subtle awareness of social pressure: and family conflict is actually explained in terms of contrasting social milieux in two of his most delicate novels, *Frau Jenny Treibel* and *Unwiederbringlich*. But the society he presents, though complex, is static. There is hardly any possibility of individuals behaving differently from the way they behave, or feeling differently from the way the norms of their background prescribe. Effi's adultery is felt by her as sin, not as liberation: she has the makings of an Anna Karenina but it is not allowed to develop. Fontane's characteristic effect is a resigned and moving awareness of how great the price of acceptance is, by characters who could never have done anything but accept — less moving when they state their hopelessness than when it suffuses the reader's consciousness, which it so powerfully does in Lene's renunciation and Botho's marriage, or in the account of Effi living in desperate solitude in her flat.

Lukacs' essay on Fontane begins with an account of his political opinions, which appear to have moved steadily to the Left as he grew older, and in 1896 (when he was seventy-seven, and still writing fiction) he wrote that the truest interest now lay in the Fourth Estate, that 'what the working man thinks, says and writes has really overtaken the thinking, saying and writing of the old ruling classes.' The figures Fontane most admires in his novels are often from the lower classes, but their superiority, Lukacs admits, is not revolutionary; it consists in their not cherishing illusions and self-deceptions, in their accepting contemporary society as it is. Lukacs goes on to distinguish the successful from the bad novels according to whether the social situation is fully perceived: sometimes Fontane falls back into *belles lettres* because he doesn't follow through the tough consequences of his insights, but takes refuge in a happy ending or convenient death. The good novels are those that relate the quandary of their characters to the particular social situation in Prussia at the time, and which show how 'the victory of this social being over the consciousness, over the inclination and the striving of his figures, is anchored in the special conditions of that mode of existence.' Sometimes it was only a happy accident that led Fontane to give his story a setting that enabled him to do this. Lukacs' actual preferences are orthodox: *Irrungen-Wirrungen* and *Effie Briest* are the finest novels (also the novelette *Schach von Wutenow*, which I must confess to finding tedious), and these can be more fully explained in social terms than any of the others.

On all this I offer two comments. First, here is another example of never trust the teller, trust the tale, one that provides a neat contrast to that of Balzac. It is Fontane's explicitly held beliefs — his democratic and even radical sympathies — that will command the assent of Marxist readers;

but the novels themselves are pessimistic and resigned. Perhaps I would not expect Lukacs to make this point, but I can't help feeling disappointed when he doesn't: what was sauce for the reactionary goose is surely sauce for the progressive gander; and the happy endings that Lukacs finds so evasive surely correspond to the melodrama and rhetorical clichés that disfigure Balzac's novels even more, and against which the social insight has to fight. Furthermore, Lukacs writes as if there were no happy endings before 1848: his claim that Fontane's unease in the period after 1848 translates itself into a failure to follow through his social insights ignores the problem whether the plot devices he uses are indicative of the same failure when they are used at other periods. The elements of a novel are determined not only by the society in which it was written, but also (and Lukacs tends to ignore this) by the literary tradition from which it derives.

What is central to Lukacs' case is his attempt to assert that the best novels do show a social dynamic: he claims Effi as a figure of great vitality held down by being the slave of a decaying convention — like Anna Karenina. This is pure assertion. The crucial question about both Fontane and Tolstoy is whether they are depicting a conflict between natural passions and the institutional safeguards necessary in any society or a conflict between two social codes, one giving way before the other. Both of them thought they were doing the former; and I have explained why Fontane at any rate does often seem to me to have been doing the former in practice.

If by social change we really mean change, then I think Fontane upsets Lukacs' case, for his novels, realistic as they are, do not depict it. But there is a more flexible interpretation that could partly save the thesis. If the moral dilemma of the main characters is presented in terms of two moralities, and these in turn are seen as resting each on its own social basis — landed gentry *v.* commercial classes, or protestant piety *v.* aristocratic secularism, or professional *v.* leisured classes — then we have an understanding that can certainly be called social. Even if the novelist displays no interest in which is the rising class or the new morality, the critic can always maintain that such a situation is unstable and shows the seeds of change, and he may claim to know which *is* the rising class and which the declining. In this case there is some sense in saying that like a true realist the novelist explains the individual in social terms, and it is a kind of useful half-truth to say that the social context is dynamic. I am sceptical whether *Effi Briest* can be interpreted in this way, but I think *Irrungen-Wirrungen* and *Frau Jenny Treibel* possibly can, and *Unwiederbringlich* and *Der Stechlin* certainly can.

§

There is no doubt that Lukacs' assertion that the realist will see society dynamically is meant to be normative — i.e. it will be a measure of the excellence of the novel. But a view of society is not, in itself, an aesthetic quality. The argument would have to be that the creative energy itself of the great novelist issues in a certain vision of society — he sees beneath the surface of the individual, and this causes the static picture of society to be set in motion. But any social doctrine can be acquired theoretically: it does not have to be won by imaginative insight. Why should there not be superficial and mechanistic novels that see society as changing? Let us not be so theoretical — there *are* such novels, and by a particularly interesting figure, who held the view that society was changing as new classes arose, and wrote novels to show this, with a genius that was theatrical rather than narrative.

No one now reads Shaw's novels but they are lively and intelligent books, full of social perceptions, though the plots creak and the characters are too prone to make Shavian statements about their own lives and opinions. For this discussion the most interesting is *The Irrational Knot*, about a marriage which fails, almost recovers, then doesn't; with a subplot about the liaison of a wealthy man with an actress who shows more independence of spirit than expected (but not, in the end, enough). The plot involves us in several conventional situations, then develops them unconventionally. A father's assumptions on who is or is not a proper person to marry his daughter are not accepted by daughter or suitor not because they are conventionally romantic, but because they realise times have changed; the drunkenness of the kept actress is blamed not on moral but on social factors. Shaw has seen quite clearly that certain assumptions about society were made by traditional plots, and may no longer be valid; and in the preface which he wrote for the novel twenty-five years later, he congratulated himself as he realised, on re-reading, that it was 'a fiction of the first order.' He then goes on to distinguish between second-hand fictions, which accept 'ready-made morality' (Shakespeare, Scott, Dickens and Dumas), and those which replace it by original morality (Euripides, Ibsen — and himself). The former may be more readable, the latter may not be more constructive, but 'the first order remains the first order and the second the second for all that.'

Shaw is making the same point as Lukacs: fiction of the first order is that which shows an awareness of social change — and thus of the possibility of a morality becoming superseded. I am sure he is right, and his list of who belongs in which order is quite correct — but I do not see that the distinction is one of aesthetic merit. Shaw's novels are fascinating to the historian of ideas, they are (despite his disclaimer) very readable, but their neglect is not all that much of an injustice. Whereas Ibsen in *The Doll's House* showed true dramatic genius in translating a social insight into dramatic form, so that when Nora rejects her role as wife she destroys the anticipated shape of the action, Shaw merely inserts his insights, often undigested, into the dialogue. The attempt to blame society for Susanna's drunkenness, for instance, consists essentially of an analytic speech made by the hero two pages from the end: the true creative effort, that of telling the story differently so that it will lead up to this conclusion, has hardly been begun.

Perhaps Lukacs would accept this point, but it needs saying — and he does not say it. No political or social awareness by an author can be a guarantee of literary excellence. If awareness of social change is a necessary condition of great realistic fiction (I shall return to this), it is certainly not a sufficient condition: it can be used as mechanically as any other insight.

§

I turn now to the second, more historical part of Lukacs' thesis; and here it is impossible to ignore the fact the he writes as a Marxist. It is perfectly possible to believe that the concern of the novel is social change without basing this on Marxism: both Stendhal and Balzac, after all, believed it. This means that in his account of these novelists, Lukacs will be measuring their view of society against a theory they did not subscribe to (which is unimportant) and which they did not know about (which could be very important). Of course Marxist critics can illuminate non-Marxist novels, but only if they are careful about what they are doing; and I am not sure that Lukacs always is careful.

Lukacs' central point in his comparison between Balzac and Stendhal concerns their ambivalent attitudes to romanticism; and he defines romanticism, quite simply, as 'a deep and spontaneous revolt against rapidly developing capitalism' (*SER*, p. 67). And sure enough, when he looks at their view of society he looks at their view of capitalism. Balzac 'puts before us all the grotesque, tragic, comic and tragi-comic types engendered by this capitalist development'; Vautrin tempts the heroes 'onto the path of "reality", or, in other words, the path of capitalist corruption and unprincipled careerism.' The central weakness of Stendhal's view of society, for Lukacs, lies in his illusion that bourgeois society would by 1880 develop a cultural revival conceived in the spirit of the Enlightenment: he could not see the part the proletariat was to play in the creation of a new society. And so this great anti-romantic is himself the victim of romanticism: he does not understand the necessary social basis of a serious questioning of bourgeois society.

Now I believe that Stendhal offers, especially in *Le rouge et le noir*, a sophisticated social analysis of a complexity you would never suspect from reading Lukacs' account of it. For Stendhal the career of Julien Sorel illustrates three different social contrasts. There is the cultural contrast, between Paris and the Provinces, on which Stendhal himself is deeply ambivalent: the provinces are the home of provinciality, smugness and envy, but also of vitality and sincerity. This contrast is embodied in the two women of the novel, the sophisticated Mathilde and the provincial Mme de Renal, whom Julien finally prefers. Second, there is the social hierarchy, in which Julien is the '*petit paysan*' climbing the ladder, his sexual conquests a form of aggression towards his betters, culminating in his savagely triumphant (indeed Napoleonic) remark on Mathilde '*la voilà donc, cette orgueilleuse, à mes pieds!*'

Stendhal thrusts such explanations at us continually, but then he often undercuts them. The most prominent is put into Julien's own mouth, when he tells the jury at his trial that he has not the honour to belong to their class, and describes his own life as that of *'un paysan qui s'est révolté contre la bassesse de sa fortune.'* It is not at all certain that Stendhal himself endorses this account: Julien wants to be found guilty, and is goading the jury; and the shooting of Mme de Renal, for which he is being tried, was after all the most striking abandonment of his constant urge to rise socially. The supreme young role-player is here playing one of his finest roles. It is not possible in this essay even to indicate the complexity of Stendhal's own attitude to seeing the novel in terms of class opposition; and I am not convinced that class is the right concept, since he appears to see the social hierarchy as a continuum rather than as a set of contending groups.

Finally, there is *'le moment'*, the chronological contrast that for Stendhal often appears the most important of all. It is stated explicitly in his essay on the novel. There appear to be three Frances — that of the *ancien régime* (*'gaie, amusante, un peu libertine'*), that of Napoleon (when a common man could become a general), and the moral and morose France of the Jesuits and the Bourbons in which the novel is set.

The interaction of these three axes produces a view of society that is quite clearly not Marxist. This does not mean that it is not susceptible of a Marxist analysis — even an illuminating one — but only, surely, if the critic is prepared to turn Stendhal's concepts into his own, for instance by showing that the second contrast is in practice relied on more thoroughly than the others; or that the first and third are often seen in class terms; or by considering the difference between a continuum of social ordering and class opposition; or by asking if Stendhal's main symbols do correspond to his ideas. In the one essay on Stendhal by Lukacs which I am acquainted with (in *SER*) he does none of these, and the ignoring of the author's own social analysis is so blatant that I can only describe it as the imposition of a Marxist strait-jacket.

§

And 1848? It is a crucial moment for Lukacs, primarily for

political reasons, and consequently (in the best materialist tradition) for literary reasons too. It was the moment of the successful bourgeois revolution, after which the bourgeoisie is no longer a revolutionary force, and so no longer has an imaginative appeal to the realist. 'The really honest and gifted bourgeois writers who lived and wrote in the period following upon the upheavals of 1848 naturally could not experience and share the development of their class with the same true devotion and intensity of feeling as their predecessors' (*SER* p. 141).

Was 1848 the year of the bourgeois revolution? Have we succeeded in identifying that magical moment when the bourgeoisie ceased to rise? I shall not be rash enough even to begin discussing this. Part of the problem is the extreme difficulty of knowing what a revolution is. Even the Marxist definition — the transfer of political power from one class to another — would not necessarily involve all social activity; but Lukacs seems to be claiming that everything felt different after 1848. The honest writers could no longer feel the same about "the development of their class": to Lukacs that phrase will include family relationships, aesthetic activity and political debate. What evidence is there that writers felt differently about these in the 1850s and 1860s? What evidence could there be? In England the great debate between the political economists and the novelists on the 'Condition of England Question' preceded 1848; and if some of the debaters had grown more sour by 1860 (as Carlyle clearly had), this may be attributable to their having grown older. It would be easy to produce examples of sensitive men feeling they were 'unable to participate in the life of capitalism' from the 1840s — or the 1830s or the 1820s or any decade you care to name. I am prepared to listen to a case that there was a withdrawal from a feeling of social involvement, but only from an historian who has realised how difficult it would be to demonstrate, who looked at the subtlest kind of evidence — diaries, letters, glimpses of social attitudes — and was careful to compare the comparable. I find none of this in Lukacs, and conclude that his theory about the quality of thought after 1848 is simply imposed on the material.

Who are the great realists of the later nineteenth century? I suggest there are four: Dickens, George Eliot, Zola and Tolstoy — and, if we add drama, Ibsen. Does this represent a decline from the age of Scott, Balzac and Stendhal? Dickens is a special and difficult case. His work is so dominated by personal fantasy and by traditional literary devices that he probably should not be called a realist at all; and his later and greater work does reveal a deep alienation from society. All in all, I think it would be possible to make out a Lukacs-type case on Dickens. George Eliot as far as I know is never seriously discussed by Lukacs, who is not on the whole interested in English literature. Zola is discussed by him at length, in the spirit of Engel's hostile view: he is a naturalist, who shows the surface of social life without the essential deeper forces, so that his great genius was not able to rise to a true social vision. Whereas Balzac and Stendhal took part in the great social movements of their time, Zola represents the new positivist ideal of the writer as solitary observer and critical commentator (the Dreyfus affair does not count because it came so late in his career). Now I do agree that naturalism, with its biological analogies and its determinist view of man, reduces the possibilities of the novel; and the enormous local vitality of Zola's novels is not always matched by a total vision of man's potential as a social being. Yet the passions of which Zola's characters are such inescapable victims have much in common with the passions that dominate in the worlds of Shakespeare and Racine; so that this limitation may prevent a certain kind of positive social awareness in Zola without preventing him from being a great writer. As for the reduction of the writer to the observer, it is suggestive to relate this to positivism, but I do not believe Lukacs has the facts right. If we set up writers on a scale between detachment (Flaubert, Joyce, Keats) and practical involvement (Fielding, Disraeli, Shaw, Brecht), I do not believe that the latter will turn out to be either the greater artists or less numerous after 1848.

§

Finally, Tolstoy. The reason he was able to achieve the great realism of the earlier period, according to Lukacs, is that he represents the revolutionary peasantry, something that was then possible only for a Russian. The point goes back to Lenin (so many of Lukacs' best literary insights go back to someone else, Lenin or Engels, Balzac or Scott — though in fairness one must add that he never tries to hide this). 'Until this nobleman came along', Lenin said to Gorki, 'there was no real peasant in our literature.' This is no doubt true, but the fact that Tolstoy creates the peasant as he had never before been created in fiction does not mean that the standpoint of his novels is that of the peasants — still less that the peasant standpoint was revolutionary. The peasantry in *Anna Karenina* are presented as deeply conservative, not just politically but on the deepest level of their life-style. I find them interestingly similar to the farm-labourers of *Middlemarch* who attack the railway surveyors ('this is the big folks's world, this is'), except that Tolstoy goes on to suggest there is an inarticulate wisdom in their prejudices. Lukacs admits the reactionary outlook of Tolstoy, but claims that it is bound up with his awareness of the progressive popular movement of which the peasants are the weak point but also the revolutionary potential. I will leave to others the question whether the Russian peasantry were a revolutionary force, and say that the argument about Tolstoy seems based on a logical fiddle. 'What Tolstoy expressed was in Lenin's view the feeling of those millions of Russians who had already reached the point of hating their masters, but had not yet reached the stage of entering on a conscious, consistent and merciless struggle against them.' Suppose one rewrote this without the crucial assumptions revealed by such wording as 'already reached', 'not yet reached': then one could abandon the claim that hatred of the masters is a 'stage' towards revolutionary struggle, and is therefore progressive. For of course it is nothing of the sort: it is age-old, and Tolstoy sees it as age-old. Remove the contorted argument of the critic and you see Tolstoy for what he is, a great conservative novelist.

I do not believe that realism declined after 1848; and Lukacs' claim that it did seems to me to involve disposing of the great realists who upset his case by means of special pleading, misrepresentation and the suggestion that they are a special case. All great novelists, however, are special cases.

§

This next section may be felt as particularly unfair by admirers of Lukacs. I have already remarked that he does not seem very interested in English literature or English history; and since this is the literature — and the society — I know about, I have felt handicapped in discussing him. Now I am going to shift attention, without apology, from Lukacs' interests to mine: i.e. to pick out what he has to say, often rather briefly, about English writers, and ask how helpful it is. I have chosen two examples, Thackeray and Conrad.

Thackeray is discussed in *The Historical Novel* as an example of the tendency to 'make history private.' Thackeray's famous aim, to show history without her periwig on, is attributed by Lukacs to disillusion with the social and political life of his own time. What Thackeray gives us is, in consequence, the cynical underside of the great men, plus the honesty of simple, slightly above average men like Henry Esmond; what he omits is the people. As a result the historical figures who appear — Marlborough, Swift, Addison — are 'degraded', and history becomes a matter of 'the trivial and the private.'

Now it is certain that *Henry Esmond* is not the same kind of historical novel as Scott writes, just as it is clear that Thackeray's novels of contemporary life do not show the common people. *Esmond* is set at a time when 'the middle farmers, yeomanry and city plebeians were undergoing economic and moral ruin', and 'of this tragedy, which is the real basis of tragi-comedies and comedies occurring "on top" Thackeray sees nothing.' This is surely to give a very mechanical meaning to 'basis', assuming the crudest sort of Marxist model of superstructure as directly dependent on base. Does Thackeray misrepresent the life of the Castlewoods becaue he does not talk about the economic plight of the yeomanry? (This is the exact opposite of Charlotte Brontë's complaint, who thought he should have given us less history since his talent was 'to show us human nature at home, as he himself daily sees it.')

It is not that Thackeray did not realise what the gap between rich and poor was like. A powerful paragraph in *The Four Georges* contrasts the awful landscape — 'wretched wastes, beggardly and plundered; half-burned cottages and trembling peasants, gathering piteous harvests' — with 'the enormous,

hideous, gilded, monstrous marble palace where the Prince is
.... and the forest where the ragged peasants are beating the
game in (it is death to them to touch a feather).' If Lukacs is
accusing Thackeray of a lack of awareness, he is simply wrong.
It would, however, be right to say that Thackeray is not
concerned with the economic currents that may have been
making this gap wider or narrower; and that however important social awareness may be for him, his profoundest
effects spring from the interaction of these with the timeless.

One of the few glimpses of the common people in *Esmond* is
the death from smallpox of the blacksmith's daugher Nancy,
with whom Esmond had been flirting. The bereaved father
receives a visit from Lady Castlewood, 'but her visit brought
no consolation to the old father, and he showed no softness, or
desire to speak. "The Lord gave and took away", he said; and
he knew what His servant's duty was.' It is an impressive
glimpse of the piety and bitter pride of the lower orders, but of
course it is written on the assumption that in their consciousness, deprivation and death come from the Lord. In comparison with this, economic circumstances (perhaps there had
been two blacksmiths a generation earlier) would have seemed
superficial, both to Thackeray and to the character. The 'surly
bow' with which he bids Lady Castlewood good morning
expresses the contrast between social relationships and the
directness of death, and if Thackeray had made his blacksmith
mutter something about the ruin of village life, instead of 'The
Lord gave and took away', his historical understanding would
have been worse, not better.

§

Lukacs' brief paragraph on Conrad begins by claiming that
the opposition to socialism often causes distortion. 'Yet in his
best writings a strange phenomenon is observable: his faith in
capitalism is such that the narrative does not even touch on its
social implications. Conrad's heroes are confronted with exclusively personal, moral conflicts, in which their individual
strength or weakness is revealed. Put in more general terms
these conflicts might have attained a wider significance; but
such generalisation is excluded by the method of narration.
This gave Conrad's work its finished, self-sufficient quality,

but it also prevents him from portraying the totality of life; he is really a short-story writer rather than a novelist' (*MCR*, p. 71).

Conrad's faith in capitalism? *Nostromo* does show some confidence in the effect of foreign capitalism on an under-developed country, but *Heart of Darkness* emphatically doesn't: the foreign capitalists there are motivated only by greed, and their impact on the native society is disastrous. (Ironically, it is the long novel that fits Lukacs' account and the much-admired short story that doesn't: an illustration of how crass is his attempt to move from content to form in the last sentence.) As for the functioning of an advanced capitalist society, we can turn to *The Secret Agent*, that marvellously nihilistic study of how a set of contemptible revolutionaries are plotting to destroy a society that hardly seems worth saving.

The narrative does not touch on social implications? I find this assertion so astonishing I have to ask whether Lukacs has read *Nostromo*. The significance of Gould and the San Tomé mine is overwhelmingly social: it brings work, prosperity and peace. 'The security which it demands must be shared with an opporessed people.' This is the most profound study in all fiction of the connection between capitalism and the institutions of liberty; and its elaborate presentation of the separatist revolution of Sulaco traces the interaction of social force to produce a successful revolution (military-church-organised workers) in a way I have never seen in another novelist.

Of course Conrad does deal with personal and moral conflicts, and he does find in them an element of the timeless. Lukacs has given a correct description of, say, *Lord Jim* and *The Secret Sharer*, though I would not agree with his evaluation of them. But when it comes to *The Secret Agent*, *Heart of Darkness*, *Under Western Eyes* and *Nostromo*, he has not even described correctly.

§

The central concern of the Marxist critic must be the relation between ideology and form; and not only of the Marxist, but of any critic who sets out to interpret literature in relation to society. For on the one hand there are those for whom social content is the mere inert stuff out of which a formal structure is made: one piece of stuff is as good as another, and what makes art resides in the form alone. On the other hand there are the ideologists, from Plato to Zhdanov, who judge a work of literature by which side it is on. These are Scylla and Charybdis: between them are the attempts to see a particular formal effect arising out of the world view that infuses a work, new human and social content calling for new artistic techniques, which the truly innovatory author then supplies. Lukacs belongs — it is why he matters — among the Odysseus-figures who have tried to mark a course that avoids the extremes. We saw in the last sentence of his paragraph on Conrad an example (a very crass one, unfortunately) of his attempt to do this; a more impressive example would be his comparison of the horse races in *Nana* and in *Anna Karenina*, with its attempts to base narrative differences on the difference between direct involvement and the mere spectator.

For me this is the most exciting kind of criticism: though many of its finest practictioners — Auerbach, Empson, Trilling, Poggioli — are not, as it happens, Marxists. Lukacs has stated this critical programme admirably; and it is therefore particularly serious if we find that he has been gobbled up by Scylla after all. I will end with one glimpse of this happening, from his discussion of Balzac's *Les Paysans* (*SER*, p. 35). After describing the attempt of the landowner Montcornet to do away with the traditional rights of the poor, and so assist the move from feudalism to capitalism on the land (a description that certainly misrepresents the novel), Lukacs remarks that this 'presents in literary form the same essential development of the post-revolutionary small-holding that Marx described in *The Eighteenth Brumaire*.' Then comes a quotation, followed by the statement 'later Engels stated *more concretely* the tragic part played by the peasantry.' Then a quotation from Engels, and then: 'Naturally Balzac, the pro-aristocratic royalist, could not have had *a correct conception* of this process. But several of his characters ... reflect, *however indistinctly*, a similar evolution.' The italics are mine: do they show us what Lukacs, in the end, thinks of presentations in literary form? They seem to be measuring Balzac against Marx and Engels, and judging him by how well he attains to their insight. The one belief that is essential to the literary critic — the belief that however true the insights of Marx, there is a further kind of insight that is *only* available through the uneasiness and aware- ness of the characters in the novel, the insight into what the theory means, in human terms — seems completely missing from this passage. There are moments, we see, when Lukacs writes in a way acceptable to the bureaucrats of Marxism.

It is not easy to write a concluding paragraph to this chapter; for all the obvious ways of summing up — general remarks on his whole career, accounts of his development, indications of what tradition he belongs in — would be in- vitations to the other kind of discussion of Lukacs, the kind we have so much of, and with which I do not intend to compete. I have been concerned with how much use Lukacs is in inter- preting nineteenth-century literature, and how perceptive a literary critic he is. The answer, I suggest, is : not much and not very.

Note

1   For example: Werner Mittenzwei, the East German critic, describes the develop- ment of Lukacs' thought in an essay of 100 pages ('Gesichtspunkte: zur Entwicklung der literaturetheoretischen Position Georg Lukacs' in *Dialog & Kontroverse mit Georg Lukacs*, Reclam, 1975). It is an extremely informative general survey, which mentions in passing the 'extraordinarily valuable particular results' of his literary criti- cism, without feeling any need to specify, let alone defend, any of these. George Lichtheim went further still (*Lukacs*, in *Modern Masters*, Fontana, 1970). He con- sidered literary criticism an inferior activity to 'conceptual totalisation in the Hegelian-Marxist sense', and so distinguished Lukacs' 'genuinely theoretical studies' from those which discuss actual works of literature, and are, in comparison, trivial. The gap between that position and the position of this essay is unbridgeable. István Mészáros, Lukacs' most distinguished follower in the English-speaking world, shows the centrality in Lukacs' thought of the interacting concepts of totality and media- tion (*Lukacs' Concept of Dialectic*, Merlin Press, 1972), admitting that the theoretical nature of his conception of mediation can lead him to misdescribe historical situations — and, one might add, novels. 'Lukacs' achievements are outstanding', writes Mészáros, 'in those of his works in which the inquiry can legitimately remain at a more abstract level.' But can it ever, in literary criticism?

Other discussions of Lukacs available in English include: George Steiner, *Language and Silence*, Faber 1967; Fredric Jameson, *Marxism and Form*, Princeton 1971; Diana T. Laurenson and Alan Swingewood, *The Sociology of Literature*, MacGibbon & Kee 1972; Terry Eagleton, *Marxism and Literary Criticism*, Methuen 1976; and the following articles in *New Left Review*: Stanley Mitchell, 'Marxism and Art' in no. 23 (January-February 1964); 'Lukacs on his life and work' (an interview) in no. 68 (July- August 1971); Brecht, 'Against George Lukacs', with a good anonymous intro- duction, in no. 84 (March-April 1974); and Michel Löwy, 'Lukacs and Stalinism' in no. 91 (May-June 1975).

9

The Bourgeois Imagination

Literature and Class Prejudice in Mid-Nineteenth-Century England

With varying degrees of consciousness, the Victorian bourgeoisie had an ideology:

> "We have shown the example of a nation," said Palmerston, "in which
> every class in society accepts with cheerfulness the lot which
> Providence has assigned to it; while at the same time every individual
> of each class is constantly striving to raise himself in the social
> scale — not by injustice and wrong, not by violence and illegality, but
> by persevering good conduct, and by the steady and energetic ex-
> ecution of the moral and intellectual faculties with which his Creator
> endowed him."[1]

Palmerston may sometimes look like the rugged survivor of an
earlier age, but here he is speaking for the middle classes of
1850. Society is a struggle between individuals, a total but not
too unpleasant struggle, in which self-help, virtue, and initiative
lead to success. The fittest survive.

This picture of English society can be matched from a
thousand sources. Beatrice Webb's mother believed that 'it
was the bounden duty of every citizen to better his social
status; to ignore those beneath him, and to aim steadily at the
top rung of the ladder.'[2] A biographer wrote of Ebenezer
Elliott that 'free trade was his religion, and heaven was paved
with cheap bread and rich mozaics of golden untaxed grain.'[3]
Cobden delighted in telling his fellow-Britons 'that nobody
can help them until they are determined to help themselves.'[4]
Between self-help, moral improvement, *laissez-faire*, struggle
for survival, and progress there is sufficient resemblance for us

to see them as a single complex of ideas; because of the glow of approval that suffuses them we can call them an ideology; and there is no doubt which class they served the interests of. This ideology turns up in expected and unexpected places. Darwin's theory of natural selection has many resemblances to it; and in a famous passage in his autobiography he tells how he got the germ of his theory from reading Malthus' *Essay on the Principle of Population* in 1838 — an admission that Marx and Engels did not fail to pounce on: '... nothing discredits modern bourgeois development so much as the fact that it has not yet succeeded in getting beyond the economic forms of the animal world.'[5] In discussions of the history of ideas, too, we find a belief in the survival of the fittest — not, as it happens, in Mill, who believed that the best ideas could be defeated in the struggle, that truth unaided might lose to falsehood; but in, for instance, Robert Owen:

> Let truth unaccompanied with error be placed before them; give them time to examine it and to see that it is in unison with all previous ascertained truths, and conviction and acknowledgement of it will follow of course.[6]

To find a name for this ideology we can turn to George Eliot. 'If you are weary of English unrest,' she wrote from Weimar, 'of that society of "eels in a jar," where each is trying to get its head above the other, the somewhat stupid "bien-être" of the Weimarians will not be an unwelcome contrast.'[7] Eels in a jar: there, in a moment of irritation — or detachment — George Eliot has characterised the bourgeois ideal. The irked, acerb flavour of the phrase makes it all the more useful as a name: this is the acerbity that sees shrewdly, but without hostility. George Eliot is not wholly unsympathetic to bourgeois self-help, but she is not taken in by it. For more complete hostility, we can look to those critics whose very style rejects the comfortable assumptions around them, Carlyle and Ruskin. Carlyle respected — or was prepared to respect — the captains of industry, but only in so far as they renounced 'eels in a jar' for a traditional pre-bourgeois conception of service and responsibility: 'Enlightened Egoism, never so luminous, is not the rule by which man's life can be led ... "laissez-faire," "Supply-and-demand," "Cash-payment for the sole nexus," and so forth were not, are not, and will never be, a practicable Law of Union for a Society of Men.'[8]

The eccentric Germanising of Carlyle's language enacts the rejection that such a passage announces: it has individuality, but not the individuality his bourgeois readers expected. Carlyle's individuality is wholly a matter of style. He loves writing metaphysics about the absolute, but in this swamp where so many Victorians drowned formlessly he is continually giving vigorous linguistic kicks. He 'reaches forth into the void deep,' he is 'alone with the Universe,' but in the very act of telling us to look on man's soul instead of his appearance, he lays that appearance in front of us, dressed in pure Carlylese:

> Shall we tremble before clothwebs and cobwebs, whether woven in Arkwright looms, or by the silent Arachnes that weave unrestingly in our Imagination?[9]

The result is a strange mixture of perversity and insight, the one impossible without the other. Was it perversity or insight that eccentrically claimed in 1843 that advertising was a natural consequence of *laissez-faire* supply-and-demand, and that treated advertising as a cultural, and not merely as a commercial, phenomenon?

> Consider, for example, that great Hat seven-feet high, which now perambulates London streets; which my Friend Sauerteig regarded justly as one of our English notabilities, "the topmost point as yet," said he, "would it were your culminating and returning point, to which English Puffery has been observed to reach."[10]

Sauerteig, the comic, learned German who is wiser than the serious English, is of course an echo of Teufelsdröckh, professor of Allerlei-Wissenschaft at the Univesity of Weissnichtwo, the grotesque hero of *Sartor Resartus* (1835). Teufelsdröckh is a perfect persona for the comments that Carlyle offers in this book: he is created from the author's awareness that his own style is grotesque, comic, and indispensable. He is a true persona, for Carlyle is both detached from him and deeply identified with him: Teufelsdröckh is ridiculous but profound, the licensed fool who sees through the pretensions of English society. We can see the brilliance of this conception if we compare it with Matthew Arnold's pallid imitation in *Friendship's Garland* (1871), which presents a similar attack on 'eels in a jar' through the comments of the author's German friend Arminius. Is a self-administering community an ideal, Arminius asks himself. 'That depends entirely on what the self-administering community is like. If it has "Geist,", and faith in "Geist," yes; if it has not, no.'[11] Now if we replace 'Geist' by 'culture,' this this has the exact shape and tone of a sentence from *Culture and Anarchy*: Arnold has used a German word, but he has continued to talk in his own urbane, judicious, slightly self-satisfied voice, quite unlike the thin intense scream of Teufelsdröckh's brilliant grotesquerie. Arnold does not need the persona as Carlyle does, and therefore cannot use it so effectively.

The other great critic of bourgeois ideology is Ruskin. 'Your ideal of human life,' he told the bourgeoisie of Bradford, 'is that it should be passed in a pleasant undulating world with iron and coal everywhere underneath it.' He then went on to analyse what he called the Goddess of Getting-on. '"Nay," you say, "they have all their chance." Yes, so has every one in a lottery, but there must always be the same number of blanks.'[12] It is not easy to decide whether to call Carlyle and Ruskin reactionary or radical. Bourgeois ideology may be measured — and rejected — in comparison with the past or with the future. 'Insisting on the need for government and speaking with scorn of liberty' could sound like an old Tory or a new Socialist. The famous controversy on progress between Southey and Macaulay[13] is similarly ambivalent. Southey writes as a very old Tory indeed (the social comments of his *Colloquies* are delivered by the ghost of Sir Thomas More), yet his rejection of industrialism becaust it is ugly reads like a first crude sketch of the view of William Morris, and his trust in 'the intermeddling of Mr Southey's idol, the omniscient and omnipotent State,' would have been denounced as socialism two generations later. There is nothing misleading about this ambivalence: it is a reminder that the best way to analyse mid-nineteenth-century social attitudes is not — as Victorians such as Trollope assumed — by a two-fold division into conservative and liberal, but by a three-fold scheme such as Dicey's.[14] Analysing the relation between law and public opinion in England, Dicey divided the nineteenth century into three periods: a paternalist period in which the state was thought of as bearing social responsibilities; the (surprisingly brief) heyday of *laissez-faire*, in which the state was reduced to a night-watchman; and the beginnings of modern collectivism, in which the state once more extends its functions. It is easy to see how the first and last phases resemble each other in contrast to the individualism of the middle one; and it should not surprise us, therefore, to find Marx and Engels sympathetic to the 'reactionary' Carlyle, or to see the close resemblance between Ruskin's critique of Victorian England and that of Marx. 'The labourer is brought face to face with the intellectual potencies of the material process of production, as the property of another':[15] this is not very different from the analysis of the 'degradation of the operative into a machine,' the complaint that 'it is not, truly speaking, the labour that is divided; but the men.'[16] When Morris divides society into three classes — 'a class which does not even pretend to work, a class which pretends to work but which produces nothing, and a class which works, but is compelled by the other two classes to do work which is often unproductive'[17] — it is not easy to be sure if this is the disciple of Ruskin or of Marx that we are hearing. One conclusion that might flow from this will not be altogether palatable to the Marxist: that the brilliant analysis of 'the separation of the labourer from his means of production,' which comes in the first volume of *Capital*, is an analysis not of the effects of capitalism, but of industrialism itself.

Two brief examples will show the presence of 'eels in a jar' in the Victorian novel. Mark Rutherford's *Catherine Furze* contains some very shrewd analyses of social prejudices in a market town, and of the friction as one class rubs against the jagged edge of another. Old Mr Furze, the ironmonger, loses his shop in a fire, and is never the same man again; when his business re-opens, it is really held together by his young assistant Tom — clever, helpful, and the very model of the industrious prentice, nineteenth-century style, for he has mechanical ingenuity and the business sense of an *entrepreneur*. Tom's great enemy is Mrs Furze, who considers him pushing, and urges her husband to discharge him. There is no doubt that Mark Rutherford prefers Tom's enterprise to Mrs Furze's snobbery, but what is more interesting than his preference, and shows his sensitivity to social forces, is his awareness of Tom's power. Because he knows how to run a business unsentimentally, and Mr Furze no longer does, Tom is indispensable, and the haughty contempt of Mrs Furze ('send him about his business at once, before he ... gets hold of your connexion')[18] is the anger of a class whose status has outlived its function. Tom is not pushing, but his personal modesty cannot undo the effect of his expertise, and as customers notice that he is the one who understands the business, he will inevitably get hold of the connection — or would have, if the novelist had not taken over from the social historian and given the plot a twist.

Catherine Furze, set in the 1840s, was not published till 1893. But the early Victorian decades did not need to wait two generations for analysis: they were very well aware of themselves. Elizabeth Gaskell, for all her old-world charm, was a remarkably up to date writer; and her mixture of old and new appears very strikingly in one of her most vivid characters, Ebenezer Holman, the farmer and Congregationalist minister in *Cousin Phillis* (1865). This sad (and grossly neglected) little story is told by a young apprentice engineer who visits the Holman family, relatives of his mother, and watches a love affair ripen between their daughter Phillis and his attractive, ambitious boss, Holford. This love story is the main theme of *Cousin Phillis*, but quite as interesting is the undercurrent that shows us that four of the characters (Paul, the narrator; his father; Holford; and Ebenezer Holman, who is really the hero) share a bond: they are all at home with the Industrial Revolution. Holman, deeply conservative in his moral values, is very talented mechanically, and in one gay little scene he listens attentively while Paul's father demonstrates how a turnip-cutter could be improved, and scrawls his points in charcoal on poor Mrs Holman's immaculate dresser. When Paul's ignorance of humanistic learning is first exposed he feels an aggrieved wish to defend himself to Phillis ('"She shall see I know something worth knowing, though it mayn't be her dead-and-gone languages," thought I'); this is childish enough to be rather attractive, but later we realise that he has been inarticulately confessing his allegiance to another and newer culture, the culture of (say) John Thornton, the hero of *North and South* (1855), the practical manufacturer who understands the classics because he understands life, who explains to the

scholarly Mr Hale 'the magnificent power, yet delicate adjust-
ment of the might of the steam-hammer, which recalled to Mr
Hale some of the wonderful stories of subservient genii in the
Arabian Nights.'[19]

Such, in unavoidable brevity, is a possible sketch of the
bourgeois ideology, as seen by its defenders, its critics, and its
novelists. It was often the novelists who saw more clearly than
anyone that self-help and *laissez-faire* were the doctrines of an
industrial culture, and that the real cultural revolutionaries,
the men who were subverting traditional social assumptions,
were those who were inventive mechanically. They might be
conservative in many of their opinions, but their allegiance to
the new skills led to an acceptance of new forms of organisation, and made them, rather than those of advanced political
views, the true plotters for the future.

§

If this complex of ideas was truly an ideology, then it must
have shaped perception of social realities, and so have influenced the version of these that appears in Victorian literature. Let us therefore take a single social reality that could be
perceived in very different ways. When the Victorian bourgeoisie looked at their social worlds, the one thing they
constantly saw, and yet in a sense never saw, was the working
classes. Here is one crucial application of the ideology, which
will now form the subject of this essay. What did middle-class
Englishmen think of the 'operatives,' as they called them? And
what were the literary consequences of their attitude?

It was rare and difficult for a respectable middle-class Victorian fully to understand the working classes. Examples of
this difficulty litter the well-meaning exhortations of clergy,
governments, and newspapers. Throughout the early nineteenth century, a stream of pamphlets — conservative, Whig,
pro-capitalist, pro-government — gushed over the English
proletariat, and dropped away unheeded and unread. The
working classes found them unacceptable not only in doctrine,
but also in style: this is neatly illustrated in a letter of Francis
Place, writing about an article on trade unions in the *Com-
panion to the Newspaper*, a publication of the very middle-class
Society for the Diffusion of Useful Knowledge. Place is a good

man to consider here, because he was a believer in Political Economy, and a friend of working-men. He was thus sympathetic to the content of an article that urged labourers to save money and then withdraw from the market in order to raise the price of unskilled labour, and he is angry because he recognises in the article's style a cultural gulf that the author had not the imagination to bridge:

> Not a working-man will read it without condemning it, and looking upon the writer as his enemy; he will see that...he is treated as an irrational creature and he will be more than ever confirmed in his false notions.[20]

This complaint, that middle-class writers were incapable of treating the working classes as true equals, can be made of many in the nineteenth century: it has been made of Place himself. It can certainly be made of Lord Brougham, the great champion of education for the working man, the moving spirit behind the Mechanics' Institutes of the 1820s and 1830s. The bourgeoisie was divided about these institutes. The Tory view was usually that they were dangerous and would encourage working-men to forget their station and organise in discontent; the Liberal view was that education was a protection against revolution and would lead working men to an acceptance of the social order. The controversy has obvious parallels in the twentieth century, and it is very difficult, looking back, to decide who was right. What the institutes were aiming to do was to find a middle course between the open paternalism of traditional Toryism, which felt that an operative had no need of science or politics, and what seemed the revolutionary alternative of working-class organisation for working-class ideals. Tories felt that if working men were given opportunities they would use them in their own way, not in Lord Brougham's. In one way, both sides were wrong: the institutes had little impact on the working classes and (like the modern W.E.A.) they were more and more used by the bourgeoisie.[21]

As a contrast, let us look at a movement that genuinely belonged to the working class. There were three such movements in early Victorian times, all subversive, all interconnected: the Anti-Poor-Law Movement, the agitation for the Ten-Hours Act, and Chartism. There is an odd sense in which the opponents of the Mechanics' Institute treated working men as responsible adults: they believed that if they were offered opportunities, they would take them on their own terms. The opponents of the Ten-Hours Movement certainly believed this, and explicitly claimed it. Tooke, Chadwick, and Southwood Smith, the three Benthamites who formed the Royal Commission of 1833, opposed the Ten-Hours Movement because they objected to interfering with the freedom of contract between capital and labour. They saw very shrewdly that the adult operatives denounced the exploitation of children so that they could hide their own case behind this even stronger one; and they pointed out that the responsibility for child labour often lay with the working-class parents:

> Sometimes the sole consideration by which parents are influenced in making choice of a person under whom to place their children is the amount of wages, not the mode of treatment to be secured to them.[22]

It is easy for us to see nowadays that the commission's concern for freedom of contract was nonsense, and nonsense of a kind very useful to the masters: the working man who worked fourteen hours a day set no store by the freedom to make, if he wished, a contract that economic pressure had in any case forced on him. Nonetheless it is interesting that opponents of the movement use the rhetoric of responsibility, and use it both shrewdly and sincerely. Among the friends of the working class it does not survive so easily.

There is less patronage and condescension, however, among the friends of the Ten-Hours Movement than among those of the Mechanics' Institutes, and the reason is clear: the former was a movement of the proletariat, the latter a movement for them. Even the aristocratic Shaftesbury, with his eighteenth-century political views and his devout nineteenth-century religious views, was not a self-appointed leader like Brougham: he served what Marx and Engels enthusiastically hailed as a genuine proletarian movement, a step toward the workers' revolution in England. There is nothing in Brougham's career that corresponds to the 'astonishment, doubt, and terror' of Ashley (as Lord Shaftesbury was in 1832) when G. S. Bull, on behalf of the workers' delegates, asked him to represent their movement in Parliament.[23] Shaftesbury obviously belonged to another world from that of the operatives, but he was their servant and not their patronising adviser. Oastler, Bull, and Stephens, the grass-roots leaders, were not working men either, but they thought and wrote like the men they represented. Oastler, with true popular gusto, threatened the mill owners who broke the law in their factories that he would

> teach every factory child in the kingdom how to use a needle among the machinery. Oh yes, I'll do for them. I'm taking lessons how to teach little children how to do more harm than good.

The middle class answered, in the columns of the *Manchester Guardian*, that

> a man who can use language like this — who can talk of teaching children to destroy the property of their employers — may if he please call himself a Christian and a philanthropist, but he is either a madman or a most hardened and despicable villain.[24]

The typical 'friend' of the working class in the nineteenth century was not Oastler but Brougham, or Brougham's henchman Charles Knight, the secretary of the Society for the Diffusion of Useful Knowledge. Knight was a modest and pleasant man who believed that one should not condescend to the working class, but he did not have either the ferociousness or the common touch of Oastler.[25] And when working-men's clubs found their way into literature they were seen through the eyes of Knight and Brougham, not through radical or Chartist eyes. 'The Philosophers,' the group of working men with clay pipes and a look of concentrated intelligence who meet in Chapter 42 of *Daniel Deronda* (1876), are shown as a spontaneous band of seekers and friends, but they say nothing that the most timid politician or mill owner need be afraid of. They are seen from above, not from within.

Was the bourgeoisie applying or betraying its ideology when it held aloof from full imaginative understanding of the working class? The creed of self-help clearly held radical potentialities: whether they were realised depended on which way you leaned. Most Victorians did not lean too hard when the implications looked alarming. Self-help always remained a doggedly middle-class creed, because it was individual self-help. 'Much as I want to see workmen escape from their slavish position,' wrote William Morris, 'I don't at all want to see a few individuals more creep out of their class into the middle class; this will only make the poor poorer still.'[26] Whether Morris is right or wrong economically, he is certainly right ideologically. The great inarticulate alternative to 'eels in a jar' was class solidarity: inarticulate because the British working class did not know that Marx had stated it for them. Indeed, the 'working class,' in the sense I have been using the phrase, was still numerically small by the mid-century. Most working men were artisans whose modest employer may have worked beside them at the bench: but those whose factory experience had shown them the experience of alienation and led them to trade union organisation, though few, were the men of the future. And these few — the politically conscious — did not, for the most part, want to take middle-class advice and save:

> ...your happiness, your position in life, will depend neither on the franchise nor the charter, neither on what parliament does, nor on what your employer neglects to do; but simply and solely upon the use you make of the fifteen or thirty shillings which you earn each week, and upon the circumstances whether you marry at twenty or at twenty-eight, and whether you marry a sluggard and a slattern or a prudent and industrious woman.[27]

The 'objective' aim of exhortations like this is to urge self-help as an *alternative* to working-class organisation. John Barton the Chartist — the passage above comes from the *Edinburgh Review*'s attack on *Mary Barton* (1848) — has 'to thank himself for most of his sorrows and misfortunes.' Why? Because he spent his time and money on trade unions instead of prudently saving it. He behaved, in other words, like a man in whom class-consciousness had superseded Samuel Smiles. Articulate working men wanted to form trade unions and to demand the Charter — which *they* had drawn up — not to have the Corn Laws repealed, which the masters had told them was in their interests. And, meanwhile, with that unconscious cunning that the ideology of a class so often displays, self-help was pressed to the shape of greatest usefulness to the bourgeoisie. If the operatives helped themselves collectively by demanding political and economic rights, they were urged not to set class against class; if they helped themselves individually by 'duly husbanding' wages instead of squandering them on subscriptions, they were given cosy ideological pats of approval.

It is something like this point that Dickens makes in *Our Mutual Friend* (1865) through the character of Betty Higden; and, as so often, he offers us the opportunity to draw a more complex conclusion than he intended. Betty Higden represents self-help run mad: she is an eel who doesn't mind going to the bottom of the jar. Her one fixed aim in life is to refuse charity. At the suggestion that the sick child Johnny should be removed 'to where he can be taken better care of,' she picks him up 'with blazing eyes' and tries to run away: and when she herself is homeless and dying she will do anything — lie, starve, give away her money — rather than go on the parish. 'Patiently to earn a spare bare living and quietly to die, untouched by workhouse hands — this was her highest sublunary hope.' Now Dickens' point is that charity has been so callously used to degrade the recipient, that to a pauper the Good Samaritan now looks like a pursuing Fury, whom she flees 'with the wings of raging Despair': he does not say outright that Betty's refusal to be a burden on the rates is exactly that form of self-help most convenient to the rich, but he clearly suggests it. Ladies in carriages who buy from her persuade themselves that she is well-to-do in the world. 'As making a comfortable provision for its subject which costs nobody anything, this class of fable has long been popular.'

It is the same point as that made by Engels in *The Condition of the Working Class in England* in 1844: 'Can anyone wonder that the poor decline to accept public relief under these conditions? That they starve rather than enter these bastilles?' Dickens' brilliance lies in seeing the grotesque result both in its own weird individuality, and as the product of social forces. Now, for the full power of this effect to be felt, the grotesque element is essential. Betty Higden is obsessed, and her independence is irrational, even crazy: it is a story that needs Dickens' grisly humour. When he pauses to rebuke 'my lords and gentlemen and honourable boards' in solemnly moral language, he loses some of his power; when he ceases to regard the old woman as obsessed, the result is worse still:

"I understood too well. I know too much about it, sir. I've run from it too many a year. No! Never for me, nor for the child, while there's water enough in England to cover us."

When a Dickens character uses language like this, a red light shines in the reader's response. This is not the ruthless morality of Dickens the comic, it is the cant of Dickens the sentimentalist, the writer of melodrama. We sense now that unbearable note of moral approbation that other Victorian novelists could handle, but that Dickens seldom or never could. Moral approbation is a fatal attitude for the novelist to apply to Betty Higden, for in asking us to admire what she has become, it suggests that her reaction of sturdy independence is not only courageous but wise. When he suggests this, Dickens has become like the lords and gentlemen he claims to be mocking. The brilliance of his creation of Betty Higden lies in the way it shows us that her courage is crazy, that her independence will destroy her. Over this brilliance Dickens spreads an attitude of respectable approbation that seems to find her behaviour rational. The brilliance shows her rejecting real charity as well as false, so complete a victim of an inhuman doctrine that she loves the Big Brother of bourgeois ideology: the reassurances show her as martyr as well as victim, undo the suggestion that her independence destroys her, and smooth away the subversive edges.[28]

Why did the bourgeois ideology get twisted as it did? Why were sincere and intelligent Victorians able to mould it to the shape of class interest, while hardly noticing what they were doing? There may be no simple answer: partly, this is what always happens to ideologies. But one answer is obvious: the middle classes were afraid. Fear of mob violence and of insurrection was widespread and deep from 1789 until 1848. It ended almost suddenly: the Chartist hordes of the 1840s gave place, in the middle-class imagination, to the respectable working man, coming up to London by special train with his family to see the Great Exhibition in 1851. In so far as fear of the drunken and violent poor persisted after this, it was no longer primarily political, as in the eighteenth century it was not political. It is hard to decide how far the fear of insurrection in the earlier nineteenth century was justified: what is beyond doubt, however, is that it existed. Honest men believed (and spread) incredible scurrilities about Tom Paine; practical men offered impossible advice to the poor; intelligent men believed that poverty was the result of improvidence.

How could a middle-class Victorian find his way out of the prison of prejudice? How could he learn to listen, to stretch his imagination, to see the working classes as they were? I can see three possible ways. First, by personal contact: to live among working men and to serve them; to do, not what you wished to do for them, but what they wished you to do; to breathe their air and think their thoughts without a constant moral nag — in this way it was possible for a dedicated few to speak with an accent completely acceptable to the operatives (whom they would not, of course, call operatives). The two prime examples of this were William Cobbett and Richard Oastler; and both, significantly, began as Tories. Cobbett is the less significant here, because his aggressiveness was personal and eccentric, and because his contacts were with the rural rather than the urban poor: indeed, his picture of society is largely pre-industrial, and his greatest hatred is not for the capitalists but for the 'tax-eaters,' the recipients of government help. For Oastler, however, the great enemy was clearly the mill owners: he opposed the Reform Bill, because he could not bear the thought of the country being in the hands of the £10 householders. In the Huddersfield by-election in 1837, Oastler actually ran as a combined Radical and Tory candidate, and a shrewd document by the local Radical Committee explained why they supported a man 'who designated himself as an Ultra Tory.' As well as points of specific agreement (anti-Poor Law, Ten-Hours agitation, 'equal rights and equal laws'), they said, there was the fact that:

> He is our neighbour, and acquainted with the wants and wishes of the great majority of the inhabitants of the borough, and his previous conduct is to us a sufficient guarantee that he would do his duty.

No Whig or Philosophic Radical earned this kind of trust from the working men, or was called 'neighbour.'[29]

The second way is by complete integrity: not just ordinary honesty, but the ability to free one's mind from the pressures of class assumptions and conventional attitudes. The creed of self-help, we have seen, could be radical if you took it seriously: but such seriousness needed a rare integrity. If any man in the nineteenth century had a free mind, it was John Stuart Mill: he knew what responsibility meant, and he knew that:

The working classes have taken their interests into their own hands, and are perpetually showing that they think the interests of their employers are not identical with their own, but opposite to them... The poor have come out of leading strings, and cannot any longer be governed or treated like children. To their own qualities must be commended the care of their destiny.[30]

Mill's excursion into practical politics is often considered a failure; but his account in the *Autobiography* (1873) offers nothing that is at odds with this passage. He relates with special pride the occasion when he was asked at a meeting containing working men whether he had written a passage saying that the working classes were generally liars:

I at once answered "I did." Scarcely were these two words out of my mouth, when vehement applause resounded through the whole meeting. It was evident that the working people were so accustomed to expect equivocation and evasion from those who sought their suffrages, that when they found instead of that, a direct avowal of what was likely to be disagreeable to them, instead of being affronted, they concluded at once that this was a person whom they could trust.[31]

Why does this, in spite of the elaborate subordinate clauses in which Mill wraps all narrative, ring out with a note almost of its own? It is surely because we have here the voice of Chadwick and Southwood Smith, telling the working men that if they are adults they must be told home truths; and the voice, for once, is not being used to promote someone else's interests at their expense. A 'friend' of the working class has become a friend.

§

But of all ways to emerge from the limitations of one's ideology, it is the third that most concerns us: for that is the way of the imagination. The one body of men who, by their very function, are able to transcend class limitations, are the writers: for the act of literary creation *is* the entering into a human situation that is not altogether one's own. Of course the writer must find in his own emotional life the starting-point for understanding; but if he never goes beyond that life he will be a writer of so narrow a range that even the expression of his own life may fail for want of ballast.

Let us start with a very minor writer. Elizabeth Barrett

Browning has lost her once handsome reputation, and the high esteem in which the Victorians held her poetry now seems astonishing. In one of her lyrics she was moved to write about labour conditions, and for the most part it is a sloppy and indifferent lyric:

> "For oh," say the children, "we are weary,
> And we cannot run or leap..."

This compassion is too near the easy romantic sob for the health of the poem; yet in two stanzas toward the end it does stiffen into something more interesting. After describing God's love ('We know no other words except "Our Father"'),

> "But no!" say the children, weeping faster,
> "He is speechless as a stone,
> And they tell us, of His image is the master
> Who commands us to work on..."

Did the poet realise how subversive a point this was? The children look up to Heaven and see only 'dark wheel-like turning clouds': Heaven is the image of industrial society. And then, in a flash of subversion, or through the necessities of rhyme, she endorses the children:

> Do ye year the children weeping and *disproving*,
> Oh my brothers, what ye preach?
> For God's possible is taught by this World's loving,
> And the children doubt of each.

Mrs Browning may have meant only to shed a gracious, rhythmical tear in passing, but her poem turns, for a moment, into something really disquieting.[32]

For a more sustained and profound example, we can turn to Blake. Blake's response to his society is in one sense obscure, as all his poetry is obscure; in another sense it is vivid, compelling and direct. The simpler poems are often the most memorable.

London

> I wander tho' each charter'd street,
> Near where the charter'd Thames does flow,
> And mark in every face I meet
> Marks of weakness, marks of woe.

In every cry of every Man,
In every Infant's cry of fear,
In every voice in every ban,
The mind-forg'd manacles I hear.

How the Chimney-sweeper's cry
Every black'ning Church appalls;
And the hapless Soldier's sigh
Runs in blood down Palace walls.

But most thro' midnight streets I hear
How the youthful Harlot's curse
Blasts the new born Infant's tear,
And blights with plagues the Marriage hearse.[33]

Blake combines directness of passion with verbal subtlety in a way one would have thought hardly possible. Look, for instance, at 'charter'd.' It burns with indignation: yet what it means is strangely complex. There is, first of all, the ambiguity between a charter as a stuffy old document that grants privileges and restrictions, and a charter as offering freedom. This gives alternative readings (they can hardly be combined). The former is perhaps the more obvious, but as we get to know the poem it tends to be replaced by the latter. But that, in its turn, is rendered ironic by the repetition. Political freedom — what charters grant — is a mockery in a land such as England, and the rights on which the English pride themselves were granted with a casual stroke of the pen to the whole city — streets and river and all — and therefore to no one.

The third stanza is the subtlest, subtle almost beyond analysis. The cry 'appalls' the church, i.e. it both shocks it and casts a pall over it. 'The church' is both the institution and a building. 'Black'ning' can be active or passive: as an institution, the church blackens the moral scene; as a building, it grows blacker, from the soot shed by the chimney-sweeper. The two lines dodge with great skill between these two readings: the physical reading seems dominant in 'black'ning,' the institutional in 'appalls.' But neither of them interferes with the other. There is a rather different ambiguity in the next lines, depending on whether the soldier is a deserter being shot or (a subtler reading, surely) a reluctant trooper crushing a riot.

In Blake's vast, unwieldy, and ambitious prophetic books there are few (if any) passages as concentrated, or as successful, as this lyric, but there is a similar response to social injustice:

> They mock at the Labourer's limbs; they mock at his starv'd
> Children:
> They bury his Daughters that they may have power to sell his sons:
> They compell the Poor to live upon a crust of bread by soft mild arts:
> They reduce the Man to want, then give with pomp and ceremony.[34]

Most of the indictment of Marx and Engels, of the Chartists, of Arnold and Morris, is sketched out here: even the idea of alienation is present, for the labourer's limbs are mocked — he is estranged from his species-being. Blake's angry vision of the labourer, however, is more often about exploitation than about industrialism. Vala, compelled to labour among the brick-kilns, complains

> We are made to turn the wheel for water,
> To carry the heavy basket on our scorched shoulders.

This pre-industrial imagery renders some effects impossible, but permits others. The climax of Vala's complaint reads:

> Our beauty is covered over with clay and ashes, and our backs
> Furrow'd with ships, and our flesh bruised with the heavy baskets.[35]

Many of the complaints in *Vala* are merely repetitive, but this one ('our backs Furrow'd with ships') reaches a true climax, as the exploited workers are suddenly seen as the Earth itself.

These quotations, like all others in an essay of this sort, have been wrenched out of context; but in the case of Blake the context is such that we cannot be sure that the wrenching really matters. Even Blake scholars are not certain what story *The Four Zoas* is telling, what mythological or psychological reality is represented by Jerusalem, what points Blake is making by these analogies from work. These passages, and many others like them, illustrate a purpose that is obscure to us; and since they are so vivid and powerful in themselves, the reader seems justified in reversing the author's intention, and regarding the design of the poem as a means to achieving these brilliant local effects, and claiming that their true subject is not their actual subject — not Vala's night but the state of England. This is a sleight of interpretation that we do not need to carry out for the *Songs of Experience*.

My third example of the insight that creation brings is once again from a minor writer. A pooer and pious widow with a thirteen-year-old son is visited by missionaries, who leave behind a few tracts, in which the lad reads of 'pacific coral islands and volcanoes, coconut groves and bananas, graceful savages with paint and feathers'; and he lies in bed dreaming of how he will conver the Tahitians and the New Zealanders:

> And one day, I recollect it well, in the little dingy, foul, reeking, twelve foot square back-yard, where huge smokey party-walls shut out every breath of air and almost all the light of heaven, I had climbed up between the water-butt and the angle of the wall for the purpose of fishing out of the dirty fluid which lay there, crusted with soot and alive with insects, to be renewed only three times in the seven days, some of the great larvae and kicking monsters which made up a large item in my list of wonders: all of a sudden the horror of the place came over me; those grim prison-walls above, with their canopy of lurid smoke; the dreary, sloppy, broken pavements; the horrible stench of the stagnant cesspools; the utter want of form, colour, life, in the whole place, crushed me down, without my being able to analyse my feelings as I can now; and then came over me that dream of Pacific Islands, and the free, open sea; and I slid down from my perch, and bursting into tears threw myself upon my knees in the court, and prayed aloud to God to let me be a missionary.[36]

If the Rev. Charles Kingsley had been told that religion was the opium of the people, and that romantic poetry was the quickest way out of a London slum, he would have turned in distaste from these clever, cynical ideas; yet what else is he telling us here? The intensity of the boy's longing for romance is a reaction from the grim prison walls; his spurious religious zeal has a ring of dreadful authenticity. More than that: Kingsley has built toward the violent irony of the last line with a skill that is usually far beyond him. The dreary, sloppy, broken pavement has to be as real as possible, to engender that final cry; and so there is a ring of hard fact, a blunt quality of mere ineluctable *existence*, about the twelve-foot-square back-yard that frees it for an exhilarating instant from the shrouds of rhetoric and compassion. The imaginative excitement of the creative act has driven a moral man and ponderous writer out of his kind and into a new power.

§

Such are the possibilities of imagination; I turn now to its deflections. This discussion unfortunately has to be longer and more complicated: there is always more to say about the mixed cases, in which we are trying to perceive both the insights that imagination has brought and the failure that has come from not being able to sustain such insight.

For the first example, we can continue with *Alton Locke* (1850). Chapter 10 of this book is called 'How Folk turn Chartist', and was intended — as was a good deal else in the novel — to make respectable readers uncomfortable. Poverty and exploitation roused Kingsley to generous anger, and he wrote his novel — as he had written his Parson Lot articles — to arouse sympathy for the oppressed. Every now and then there is a gleam of the strange, intense sensibility that enabled him to write the passage about the water butt and the missionaries: Alton's speech to his mother against religion (nobody believes in it, he claims, except 'good kind people ... who must needs have some reason to account for their goodness'), or Crossthwaite's comment on the M.P. who shook his head and told the workmen about the iron laws of political economy ('he may have been a wise man. I only know that he was a rich one'). A reader half-way through *Alton Locke* might think it was a genuinely subversive novel: but as he read on to the end he would find that his fears (or his hopes) were unfounded. Almost everything that really disturbs complacency in this book is eventually retracted. The very plot is an account of how Alton acquired and then shed his Chartist views. His speech against religion is immediately followed by 'I had hardly spoken the words, when I would have given worlds to recall them — but it was to be — and it was.' The account of why folk turn Chartists is followed by the 'confession' that with him, 'and I am afraid with many, many more, the means become, by the frailty of poor human nature, an end, an idol in itself.' The chapter is, it turns out, ambiguously titled. It is not an account of the arguments for the Charter, offered for our inspection and possible acceptance, but an excuse, an explanation of how people are misled. 'Folk' means other folk. Writing under his pen name of Parson Lot, Kingsley had complained that the Charter did not go 'far enough'; as we read the end of *Alton Locke* we see just what he meant by saying that the Charter had become an end in itself or did not go far enough. He means that the Charter was political, and should not have been.

We can find an exact parallel to this in a far greater novel. George Eliot's Felix Holt is a radical who wants to get to deeper roots than his fellow-demagogues: 'I want to be a demagogue of a new sort.' Now the only important character in *Felix Holt* (1866) who seems to hold genuinely radical views is the Rev. Rufus Lyon, with whom Felix argues a good deal; and the only times when Felix advances opinions that are specifically political are when he makes a speech on nomination day — warning the workers (who have no vote, so hardly need the warning) that power can mean power to do mischief, that:

> all the schemes about voting, and districts, and annual Parliaments and the rest, are engines, and the water or steam — the force that is to work them — must come out of human nature — out of men's passions, feelings, desires;[37]

— or when he tells Mr Lyon ('being in a perverse mood') that 'universal suffrage would be equally agreeable to the devil.' 'Perverse' Felix no doubt was that day; but it is difficult to regard the author's parenthesis with much conviction when there is no trace of Felix's unperverseness — that is, his ordinary radicalism — anywhere in the novel. There is no sign that he has ever read Tom Paine or William Cobbett; nothing but the slightest of hints that he does not believe in God. His radicalism 'of a newer sort' is not radical at all, for when we look at its content we see that it consists of a mistrust of politics, a belief that the reform of institutions will achieve little without a change of heart. A generation earlier, Sidney Smith had seen that the change-of-heart doctrine could, in a political context, be a convenient way of blocking improvement. 'Instead of reforming the State, the constitution, and everything that is most excellent,' runs the conclusion of his Noodle's oration, 'let each man reform himself! Let him look at home, he will find there is enough to do, without looking abroad, and aiming at what is out of his power.'

A year or so after finishing *Felix Holt*, George Eliot wrote an article for *Blackwood's* magazine, on the occasion of the

181

Second Reform Act, that she called 'Address to the Working Men, by Felix Holt.'[38] It is a deeply conservative document, full of praise of 'the wonderful slow-growing system of things made up of our laws, our commerce and our stores of all sorts,' and warning against hurrying on political change. It should not surprise us that the article is so conservative and that its title should perhaps offend us. The great point about Felix in the novel is that he *is* a working man: the contrast with Harold Transom, the gentleman who holds more radical opinions more superficially, is clear and effective. But the article, removed from the context of fiction, contains the views of Marian Evans, who was not a working man, so that the use of Felix as a persona is actually misleading. There is so much profound political understanding in *Felix Holt* (the trade-union man whose speech Felix answers is a figure almost unique in nineteenth-century fiction), that this need the author felt to draw back, in the end, from politics, is a particularly significant deflection.[39]

§

For a more extended example, I turn to Dickens. What is the social point of *Hard Times* (1854)? 'It's a' a muddle,' says Stephen Blackpool to Bounderby; and if ever a system cried out for mending, it is the one that put Bounderby in charge and sent Stephen tumbling down a mineshaft; that built the tall chimneys, out of which 'interminable serpents of smoke trailed themselves for ever and ever, and never got uncoiled.' Now there are two characters in the book who are trying very hard to improve the system, and they correspond to the two main attempts historically, one from the centre, one from below. These two are Gradgrind and Slackbridge, and their efforts get small sympathy from Dickens. What is Gradgrind doing, among his army of blue-books, or travelling up to London to sit in Parliament, the national dust-heap? 'Proving that the Good Samaritan was a Bad Economist,' Dickens tells us, and of course he is right, for the utilitarians designed the New Poor Law, justly loathed by its 'beneficiaries'. Yet he does not realise how radical a thing this is for Gradgrind to prove. Charity supports, it does not overthrow, the social structure: the manufacturers had nothing to fear from the

Good Samaritan. If Gradgrind was a typical utilitarian, he spent his time in the national dust-heap trying to get dangerous machinery fenced in, or to improve the sanitation of Coketown, not simply serving the interests of the masters. It was not really fair of Dickens to make him a friend of Bounderby.

Slackbridge's answer to the muddle is that the workers should organise and so make their power felt. It is a doctrine that could be held in all sobriety by a thoughtful working man, but Slackbridge the demagogue is neither thoughtful nor a real working man. Dickens has disdained no tricks to make him vulgar:

> An ill-made, high-shouldered man, with lowering brows, and his features crushed into an habitually sour expression, he contrasted most unfavourably, even in his mongrel dress, with the great body of his hearers in their plain working clothes.[40]

In the mouth of such a man, what can the trade union be but part of the organiser's rhetoric, what effect can it have but to oppress the well-meaning working man who stands out? Whatever solution to the muddle lay here, Dickens has simply dismissed it.

There are two comments to be made on Slackbridge, one external, one internal. As a portrait of the typical trade-union organiser of the time, he is a calumny, and Dickens knew that he was a calumny: for Dickens had been to Preston to gather material when he was planning *Hard Times*, and had attended a trade-union meeting. There he had heard a demagogue, whom he names Gruffshaw, and had seen how, when Gruffshaw tried to push oratory and politics in the way of practical business, he was firmly put down. 'My friends,' the chairman said, 'these are hard words of my friend Gruffshaw, and this is not the business.'[41] This scrupulousness of the reporter was laid aside when the novelist took over.

The internal comment concerns the implausibility of the whole trade-union episode. The satire on Slackbridge is Dickens at his crudest: he knits his brows, he sets his teeth, he pounds with his arms. When he speaks, his rhetoric is too broad to be worth seeing through. Yet though he makes so easy a target, Dickens will not let well alone; and the chapter is crammed with anxious authorial commentary, telling us over and over again that he was below the level of his audience. The novelist did not even take over here, the reporter changed sides. Even more implausible is Stephen's involvement. Slackbridge, to show his blackness, must victimise the hero, and therefore the hero must refuse to join the union. We are never told why: certainly it is not through loyalty to Bounderby. Stephen uses some utterly vague phrase ('I mun go the way as lays afore me') and refers to a promise he made to Rachel, which turns out to be even vaguer (if, as seems possible, it was a promise to keep out of trouble, he can hardly be said to have acted on it). Finally, against all probability, Stephen is dismissed: for no particular reason, and in a sense for not joining the union. In this episode Dickens betrayed the truth and made a mess of his novel. It is tempting to see the two — the external and the internal flaw — as connected.[42]

Everyone agrees that *Hard Times* is unusual among Dickens' novels: it lacks some of his faults and many of his merits, and its opinions are, for Dickens, freakish. Certainly it suggests a violently anti-bourgeois writer, who could look like a radical if he had not taken such pains not to do so. Is this the real Dickens we are glimpsing? Was he at the deepest level naturally hostile to the bourgeois ideology? The sensibility shown in his novels is more complicated and shifting than the technique, and it is not easy to know what his deepest attitudes on social questions were. I have already cited that paragon of irrational self-help, Betty Higden; but he was also able to see self-help as an assertion of working-class independence. One of the sketches in *The Uncommercial Traveller* (1861) describes the 'self-supporting COOKING DEPOT for the Working Classes.' 'Whatever is done for the comfort and advancement of the working-man,' Dickens asserts, 'must be so far done by himself as that it is maintained by himself. And there must be in it no touch of condescension, no shadow of patronage.' He is in favour of the Cooking Depot because the staff are adequately paid, the food is good, and the books are properly kept; his only objection is that no beer is served because this shows a distrust of the working man. It is an institution almost exactly similar to the canteen opened by the men of John Thornton's factory, which he is so careful not to interfere with, and where he is invited, as an equal, to sit down and take a snack on hot-pot days:

> If they had not asked me, I would no more have intruded on them than I'd have gone to the mess at the barracks without invitation.[43]

Self-help here is not, or not obviously, a doctrine convenient to the middle class, and it is not altogether surprising to find Dickens saying 'there are in Birmingham at this moment many working-men infinitely better versed in Shakespeare and Milton than the average of fine gentlemen in the days of bought-and-sold dedications and dear books.'[44] Here middle class and working class are one: they both, in their sturdy independence, contrast with the 'fine gentlemen.' And often Dickens' sympathy for the working class ran deeper than this: he liked them for what set them apart from the bourgeoisie as well, and dismissed patronage in favour not of sturdy self-help but of entertainment — that is, what the working men actually wanted. In his essay 'Two Views of a Cheap Theatre,'[45] for instance, he shows the sympathy we should expect for the project of Sunday-night prayer-meetings in the Britannia Theatre, Hoxton, yet he is not altogether satisfied with the preacher who condescended, who kept calling his audience fellow-sinners, and above all who set himself 'in antagonism to the natural inborn desire of the mass of mankind to recreate themselves and be entertained.'

Dickens (as this last sentence should suggest) is the greatest philistine in English literature. His ideal of the good life was cosy: Christmas at Dingley Dell; Traddles playing Puss-in-the-Corner in his chambers with his innumerable jolly sisters-in-law and his Sophy, who had 'a loving cheerful fireside quality in her bright looks';[46] Esther the domestic paragon, settled in a Bleak House that turns out not to be bleak at all, but 'quite a rustic cottage of dolls' rooms' set in 'a pretty little orchard, where the cherries were nestling among the green leaves.'[47] It is not quite the ideal of any one class. Sometimes it seems to emphasise the nuclear family: Wemmick at Walworth, with the Aged Parent making buttered toast and Miss Skiffins brewing tea behind the security of the raised drawbridge, in a home arranged around the traditional metaphor that an Englishman's home is his castle.[48] Sometimes it emphasises the wider unit of popular culture: the party at Todgers' Boarding House, which included a gentleman of a sporting turn, a gentleman of a theatrical turn, a gentleman of a debating turn, and a table groaning beneath the weight of 'boiled beef, roast veal, bacon, pies, and abundance of such heavy vegetables as are favourably known to housekeepers for their satisfying qualities.'[49] The arts, the intellect, and the religious life are almost totally absent from Dickens' conception of happiness.

Victorian fiction has two great satiric portraits of philistines, by its two great novelists: Mr Bult in *Daniel Deronda* and Mr Podsnap in *Our Mutual Friend*, both minor characters, yet both, somehow, complete. The contrast between them is the contrast between George Eliot and Dickens. Mr Bult is completely credible: he had 'the general solidity and suffusive pinkness of a healthy Briton on the central tableland of life'; he 'was amiably confident, and had no idea that his insensibility to counterpoint could ever be reckoned against him.'[50] Mr Podsnap is gloriously incredible. When introduced to a foreign gentleman (Podsnap believes 'the whole European continent to be in mortal alliance against the young person') he asks '"How do you like London?" as if he were administering something in the nature of a powder or potion to the deaf child; "London, Londres, London?"'

> "The Constitution Britannique," Mr Podsnap explained, as if he were teaching at an infant school; "We say British. But you say Britannique, you know" (forgivingly, as if that were not his fault). "The Constitution, Sir."[51]

And now comes a paradox. We might expect that the caricature would come from the author who was looking from the outside, the realistic portrait from the author who felt close to what he was showing and so subtly attacking. Yet the opposite is true. George Eliot, the European traveller, the polyglot, the ex-editor of the *Westminster Review*, is genuinely free of all temptation to be Bult; Dickens, the laureate of fireside slippers and home-made punch, the *entrepreneur* who made £30,000 a year from his readings, the novelist who could portray an artistic poseur such as Henry Gowan but never, in all his books, a true artist — Dickens had a smack of Podsnap, all right. From which we must conclude that his brilliant caricature is drawn from a wholly external vantage-point to which Dickens had to retreat for safety; whereas the calmly brilliant sober portrait is the work of the writer who knew she could come very close without catching anything.

Dickens' ideal of personal relations, then, is balanced between the culture of two classes, inclining now to one, now to the other, and always to the solid centre of each. What of his picture of society as a whole? To answer this we must distinguish, even more clearly than criticism usually needs to, between the man and the writer. Dickens the man was a busy and practical reformer, eager to help in a thousand schemes, never much doubting that they were worthwhile: in spite of all the coyness with which he handles sex, and the melodrama with which he shows vice, he must have known exactly what prostitutes were like, especially after the help he gave with Miss Coutts' home for fallen women. Dickens the novelist often set out to work for Dickens the man, and to expose abuses in society so that they could be reformed: the law's delay, imprisonment for debt, transportation, civil-service muddle. We know now that he was cautious about this, and that the abuses he noticed were those that most people had already noticed; but this strengthens rather than weakens the case that his purpose in writing was a reforming one.[52]

But what we have seen in *Hard Times* is not an isolated case. Dickens attacks abuses, but he does not really believe that they can be cured. The evil in *Bleak House* and *Little Dorrit* is inescapable. The fog that opens the former is a social abuse turned into a natural phenomenon, and so made permanent; the powerful descriptions of Tom-All-Alone's, the tenement that may even be the property in Jarndyce and Jarndyce, are sadly contemptuous of attempts to put it right ('There is not a drop of Tom's corrupted blood but propagates infection and contagion somewhere'); even the death of Jo, nicely balanced between the restrained and the over-eloquent, owes its artistic success to its refusal to be explicitly reformist, to suggest remedies. The view of society in *Little Dorrit* is just as black. Because all society is a prison, the only possibility of happiness is in a pastoral retreat: Mr Meagles' residence at Twickenham, or Bleeding Heart Yard. And because these are not quite safe

— Bleeding Heart Yard belongs to the extortionate Casby, Twickenham lets Henry Gowan in and he captures Pet — the best retreat is behind the walls of the Marshalsea. There the Circumlocution Office can do no damage, nor can Merdle break through and steal. And the world outside? Dickens originally intended to call the novel *Nobody's Fault*. It is a good reformer's title, if it is ironic; but is it? Merdle, who ruined thousands, is seen as the most pathetic victim of all; young Barnacle, when we finally get inside the Circumlocution Office, turns out to be rather likeable, and as helpless as anyone else. On the deepest level Dickens seems to have believed that it really was nobody's fault.

Dickens has the opinions of a reformer, but the imagination of despair. The opinions found their way into his books, and were prominent in his life, and they urged that something must be done; the creative imagination shut its ears, knowing that nothing could be done, that society was a fog, a prison, a muddle; that those who wanted change were helpless before the Establishment.

We can now explain the anomaly of *Hard Times* and its attack upon industrialism. When Dickens died, Ruskin wrote that he had been 'a pure modernist — a leader of the steam-whistle party *par excellence*.... His hero is essentially an ironmaster.'[53] This is true of *Bleak House*; in *Dombey and Son* the railway is on the whole benevolent; and like any good modernist, Dickens loved to make fun of the Wisdom of our Ancestors ('Dirt, Ignorance, Superstition and Disease'). Why did he change sides in *Hard Times*? Clearly because *Hard Times* is set entirely in Coketown, a town that belongs to the ironmasters. Dickens feared and hated authority; he saw the community as groaning under the inevitable yoke of whatever powers may be. When industrialism is an independent force, a ray of light in the fog, an inventor defying the Circumlocution Office, he is all for it; but when industrialism has become the Establishment, fear and hatred are the only possible reaction.

§

Elizabeth Gaskell is a less complex writer than Dickens, and the deflections of the creative imagination in her work can be discussed more briefly. It will be simplest to take the earlier and less powerful of her two industrial novels, *Mary Barton* (1847), which was written to take the side of the working man. That, at any rate, is what she *thought* she had done, and she even felt uneasy at the charge that she had given a one-sided picture, at the thought that 'people at a distance should be misled and prejudiced against the masters, and that class be estranged from class.'[54] 'Some say the masters are very sore,' she says in another letter, 'but I'm sure I *believe* I wrote truth.'[55] This apologetic tone is revealing. Is it present in the book itself? Is *Mary Barton* less whole-heartedly on the side of the workers than the author thought? The answer is surely Yes. There is a great deal of compassion in the novel, and some very honest and realistic description of poverty in Manchester; but it is deeply committed to, and at the end explicitly states, the doctrine of harmony of interests between classes, which (as we have seen) was a middle-class doctrine. The book's change of title is revealing. Originally it was to be called *John Barton*, for 'he was my hero, *the* person with whom all my sympathies went, with whom I tried to identify myself at the time.'[56] But John Barton is not, in the end, a very prominent character, for the book grew, it turned into something more conventional: daughter displaced father, and love displaced politics. One crucial detail in the plot betrays this deflection: Jem Wilson's trial, the climax of the book, is for murder, and the concluding action is all concerned with this 'violation of the eternal laws of God.' But by turning her Chartist into a murderer, Mrs Gaskell shifted from the laws of men to those of God (a less dangerous subject), replaced a political by a criminal trial, and shirked the true challenge of working-class radicalism. And she spoilt her novel: for John Barton, external and cursory as his final treatment is, remains the most impressive character in the book.[57]

In her industrial novels Mrs Gaskell handled material she could not altogether control. Her imagination led her to an understanding of working-class attitudes, but she could not sustain this when its implications were too disturbing. Something like the opposite is true of Disraeli. He has appeared to some to be the great adventurer of Victorian politics, but it is as a novelist, rather than as a statesman, that he showed a really bracing irresponsibility. Disraeli's handling of human relationships is almost always stagey and unconvincing; but *Sybil* (1845) has an interest rare among his novels because of its taste for the lurid. *Sybil* comes to life best when Disraeli is describing scenes he knew nothing about: riot at the tommy-shot; the career of Devilsdust, the clever and impudent foundling; the naked brutality of life in Wodgate:

> There are no landlords, head lessees, main-masters, or butties in Wodgate. No church there has yet raised its spire.... The streets are never cleaned; every man lights his own house; nor does any one know anything except his business. The most usual stimulus to increase exertion, is to pull an apprentice's ears till they run with blood.[58]

It does not matter — though the fact is interesting — that Disraeli got the material for these scenes from blue-books. It is clear that these documentary accounts of the 'other nation' took his fancy. The representation of the unfamiliar exploited a sense he had of the dangerous forces in society, and when writing out of bravado he showed a social intelligence far greater than his powers as a novelist. Again, George Eliot provides a contrast. The riot in *Felix Holt* is described scrupulously and at length; that in *Sybil* is wilder, more colourful, more entertaining. Disraeli's was the imagination that was titillated by danger.

The fear from which Mrs Gaskell's imagination fled was faced calmly by George Eliot, and set the adventurous fancy of Disraeli racing. Let us turn now to a novel written primarily out of fear, where riot is not incidental, nor a thrilling climax, but is the central theme of the book. Whatever else *Barnaby Rudge* (1841) is about, it is certainly about riot — a riot that turns into pure irrational violence, as irresistible as fire or flood. Dickens' intention was undoubtedly to rebuke the rioters, and to express his sense of shock at their savagery. Yet once again achievement did not square with intention: for as Dickens takes us through the streets of burning London, showing by the vivid light of the flames the crazy crowd looting, burning, drinking, dying, he is led to identify himself deeply with what he set out to deplore:

> There were men there, who danced and trampled on the beds of flowers as though they trod down human enemies, and wrenched them from the stalks, like savages who twisted human necks. There were men who cast their lighted torches in the air, and suffered them

to fall upon their heads and faces, blistering the skin with deep unseemly burns. There were men who rushed up to the fire, and paddled in it with their hands as if in water; and others who were restrained by force from plunging in, to gratify their deadly longing. On the skull of one drunken lad — not twenty by his looks — who lay upon the ground with a bottle to his mouth, the lead from the roof came streaming down in a shower of liquid fire, white hot; melting his head like wax. When the scattered parties were collected, men — living yet, but singed as with hot irons — were plucked out of the cellars, and carried off upon the shoulders of others, who strove to wake them as they went along, with ribald jokes, and left them, dead in the passages of hospitals. But of all the howling throng not one learnt mercy from, or sickened at, these sights, nor was the fierce, besotted, senseless rage of one man glutted.[59]

Any reader must feel the heavy thump of that last moralising sentence; and must realise by contrast how vivid the rest of the paragraph was, how all detachment is swept away, all disapproval overwhelmed, by the sheer intensity of fascination. The men paddling as if in water, the ribald jokes to wake the dead: these are details that testify to the writer's eye being on the object and not on his own moralising. And when the rioters reach Newgate and burn it, something in Dickens seems to have stood up and cheered at the power and ingenuity of pure violence, destroying the hated institutions of authority.

§

Mary Barton, North and South, Our Mutual Friend, Alton Locke and *Felix Holt*: all draw back from their own subversive implications and the insights they provide are weakened by the endings. This weakening is a classic example of overdetermination: it can be attributed either to political factors (an inability to stay with insights that undermined the author's own position) or to the constraints imposed by convention (abandonment of the political theme for the love-interest and the happy ending). The two are connected, for the effect of the love-interest is to turn the political into the personal, and to 'solve' an impasse that results from class hostility through the successful achievement of an individual relationship.

Belief in harmony of interest between classes was, in 1848, a belief held by the bourgeoisie and its apologists, but that does not make it wrong: it has proved truer, in the end, than the belief that class conflict must lead to revolution and the dictatorship of the proletariat. Of course the argument between a conflict view and a harmony view is partly a matter of degree: how much conflict has to be admitted, how many concessions have to be made by the possessing class, before the fundamental harmony will be accepted? The withdrawal from radicalism at the end can be seen as a too hasty falling back on the belief in harmony of interest, and so can be criticised from a non-revolutionary position.

But as well as the ideological question itself, this discussion has brought us up against the problem of how literary and political values are related. Have I not assumed that the artistic success of all these novels is identical with their subversive insights? Is this not to subordinate artistic criteria to political? Are radical novels good and conservative novels bad?

Of course there are bad radical novels. Ernest Jones the Chartist, for instance, wrote a number; and in *Woman's Wrongs* (1855) we can see how lack of talent can impose the wrong moral on a book. John Haspen, the bullying husband, is shown as a mere brute when at home; he squanders his money on drink, beats his wife, and is condemned with all the clichés of sobriety, kindness, and thrift. At the factory, however, he offers heroic resistance to the bad employer who lovers wages and offers his workers the 'freedom' to starve instead of working for him: here Haspen is praised with the clichés of radicalism. So easily has Jones fallen into each set of clichés that he does not notice that they are inconsistent with each other: Margaret Haspen rebukes her husband in the language of the *Edinburgh Review*, but Jones keeps that in one pigeon-hole, and the factory scenes in another; or rather he ought to, but they eventually mingle in some confusion.

No, it is not because radicalism is a virtue in any novelist that Condition of England novelists renege on their own strengths in the end: it is because they set out to describe politically conscious working men to a bourgeois audience. Such an audience was very ready to assimilate these men, even when it admired them (perhaps most when it admired them) to what it wished them to be like, and so underestimate their rejection of the *status quo*. Insofar as these novels aim to present the unfamiliar truthfully, they will undermine the pieties which author and reader believe in, and will be successful according as they are subversive: retreat into the familiar ideology will mean imaginative withdrawal from its critics. To counter the subversive insights with other and incompatible insights would show an awareness of the complexities of politics, but to sweep them away and impose easy conversions on their adherents can only damage the novel.

§

Is it possible to relate the ideological questions so far canvassed to the artistic success or failure of the novels? Clearly no ideology has the convenient consequence of ensuring good novels, just as no opinion precludes the possibility of powerfully imagining its consequences. But even though there will be no clear-cut answer, it is worth asking whether the emotional conflicts we have looked at in the novelists were artistically damaging or artistically fruitful.

The fear which the novelists felt had two consequences, as fear always does: to distort and to make vivid. Because Kingsley was frightened, he drew back from the consequences of his own novel, and set out to undo his achievement; because Mrs Gaskell was frightened of political crime, she shunted John Barton's murder on to the merely personal level, or turned the troubles at Thornton's mill into an episode in a love affair. Fear has done artistic damage there. But the reason why the mob of *Barnaby Rudge* is so much more powerful than the mob of *The Old Curiosity Shop* is that Dickens is now more involved and, if not more afraid, is certainly more uncomfortable, more disturbed — disturbed, perhaps, at his own involvement. In *Hard Times*, too, the industrial landscape is an uncomfortable one. 'The piston of the steam-engine worked monotonously up and down, like the head of an elephant in a state of melancholy madness.' That is comic, but it brings a giggle, not a laugh: it is frightening too. Fear has been artistically fruitful here.

How can the same feeling have such opposite consequences? The reason of course is that two different criteria of excellence can be applied. Here we can call them power and truth, and they correspond to the one fundamental division that runs through all evaluation of literature. The Condition of England novelists were all realists: they all believed that the purpose of the novel was the faithful representation of social reality. Hence the parallel (a favourite with George Eliot) between the novelist and the Dutch painter — a parallel also drawn by the early photographers. For Ruskin truth (it is, admittedly, a rather elastic term in his hands) is essential to art: 'Nothing can atone for the want of truth, not the most brilliant imagination, the most playful fancy, the most pure feeling (supposing that feeling *could* be pure and false at the same time).'[60] Realism in the mid-nineteenth century was not a conservative creed but was embraced with the exhilaration of those who felt they were freeing themselves from stereotypes: some of George Eliot's finest effects involve the explicit rejection of previous conventions. This exhilaration accounts for — even justifies — the extreme positions that attribute an artistic power to facts, and that fail to distinguish between literature and social investigation. When Huxley wrote to Kingsley in 1860 'Sit down before fact as a little child, be prepared to give up every preconceived notion, follow humbly wherever to whatever abysses nature leads, or you shall learn nothing'[61], the context was a discussion of science not of literature, but he is offering a creed that the realists accepted for art as well. This helps to explain why our response to the Condition of England novels spills over the edge of literature: why the voices of the witnesses reporting to Parliamentary Committee on Child Labour in 1832, or to the Children's Employment Commission of 1842, can move us as much as the voices in the novels — more, sometimes, if we feel the novelist has betrayed reality, has not sat down before fact as a little child. 'I think you must observe what is *out* of you, instead of examining what is *in* you' was Elizabeth Gaskell's advice to the novelist[62]. It is good advice for writing *Mary Barton*, but if we look at literature as a whole it is patently inadequate. 'Look in thy heart and write': the commonplace is far older than the Romantics, though it is their doctrines of expression and spontaneity, as it is their great poems of fantasy, that most obviously insist that literature comes from the depths of the creative self. Mrs Gaskell's advice would be merely absurd if

applied, say, to Coleridge's *Dejection*, that poem on the uselessness of observing what is out of you.

Realism urges the imagination to take the shape of observed
reality, to check the content of one's fiction against the ability
to watch, to listen and to deduce. Those literary forms that
embody fantasy shape reality to the wishes, dissatisfactions,
ideals and fears of the writer and (since literature is communication) of the readers. The two can merge: in many of the
greatest writers they are held in fruitful tension. But in other
writers (and those too, sometimes, of the greatest) it is possible to say that one aim is dominant. Mrs Gaskell and George
Eliot were clearly realists. Their genius was for observation
and understanding, and although they drew on their own
emotional life, they disciplined it with care; whenever they
abandoned realism they fell into the commonplace. This is
especially clear with Mrs Gaskell, because she had a fondness
for romance: all her stories of bandits, murders, and conceal-
ment are mere cliché. She is sometimes praised for the honesty
she showed in introducing Esther, the heroine's prostitute
aunt, into *Mary Barton*. But although she was honest enough
to admit Esther's existence, honesty collapsed when it came to
her portrayal. Embarrassment, perhaps even ignorance, hin-
dered truth-telling, and Mrs Gaskell had to fall back on her
fantasies, which turn out to be utterly commonplace.

The case is less clear with George Eliot, because what she fell
into was less obviously cliché. But the dreamlike journey of
Romola in the little boat to the plague-stricken village, for
instance, cannot compare with the marvellous realism of
Hetty's journey to Windsor and back; nor the obvious symbolism of Eppie's golden curls with the brilliant psychological
realism of Gwendolen deciding when to wear which of her
no doubt symbolic jewels. Both these women — like most women writers — had an imagination that was essentially realistic.

And Dickens? He too made realistic claims. *Sketches by
Boz* is subtitled, 'Illustrative of Every-day Life and Every-day
People', and the Preface to *Bleak House* insists on the fact of
spontaneous combustion, as if the value of its brilliant chapter
32 depended on the accuracy of the chemistry. Over and over,
Dickens defends his work by telling us that the world is like
that, that he has avoided the distortions of fantasy; but he has

done nothing of the sort. It was no realist who imagined meeting 'a Megalosaurus, forty feet long or so, waddling like an elephantine lizard up Holborn Hill'. What weird truths we learn from the grotesqueries of Quilp, from the vision of a London mob led by a half-wit, a bastard, and a hangman, from the mutterings of that unending law-suit, and even from the spontaneous combustion of Krook! But they are not the truths of George Eliot, for they feed on the distortions of fear and longing.

§

In conclusion, I return to the social attitudes from which we began. Must we take our picture of Victorian society entirely from the bourgeoisie, or is there an alternative vision? Must we, in spite of our adjustments of the middle-class imagination, accept it as the only imaginative vision of that world available to us, or did working-class culture produce its own literature, with its own (different) version of human relationships — 'eels in a jar' seen from below?

The answer, on the whole, is No. The literature of the Victorian bourgeoisie is one of the world's supreme artistic achievements; it is unreasonable to expect a less articulate, far less educated section of the community to have produced anything to compare with it. Yet lack of education, although it obviously incapacitates a class from producing a complex literature, has certain small advantages; and though there is no real proletarian literature in the nineteenth century, there may at least be a proletarian voice, whose sound can help us to correct the limitations of the bourgeois imagination.

Where can we look? First, and most obviously, to the memoirs of working men, such as William Lovett, Thomas Cooper, and Samuel Bamford.[63] These three were remarkable men and their books are fascinating, but if we look in them for a true subculture, we may be disappointed. Samuel Bamford, the weaver-poet and radical leader (whom I suspect to have been the original of Felix Holt), belonged to two worlds. On the one hand, he is continually slipping into genteel language. Describing the Blanketeers setting off to London in 1817, he writes of 'a youth...waving his hand to a damsel pale and tremulous with alarm',[64] meeting a couple on a walk, he falls into conversation, and talks of 'the noble and exalted pleasures of true affection, and . . . the sickening pangs of love betrayed, and the unhappiness which must eventually haunt the betrayer, whether man or woman.'[65] If this is the style to which the self-educated aspired, the advantages of illiteracy were greater than one realised.

But Bamford also belongs to a world of Lancashire superstition and plant-lore, of fights and dialect and quack-doctors. He was in a splendid position to describe, for example, the incident when his friend Healey pulled two teeth instead of one and knocked over a jug of cream — and then had to haggle with the patient's mother over who owed money to whom. As we read Bamford's account of this episode,[66] we can see that he both does and does not belong to the world he is describing. He was Healey's friend, and like him was on the run from the law; yet he seems to see the whole adventure with a touch of the outsider's amusement. We have here something of the mixture of irony and love that Hardy brought to his Wessex peasants.

Like Hardy, Bamford is showing us a world that may belong in the nineteenth century if we count heads, but not if we measure the direction of change: it is an old, a static, a pre-industrial, even a pre-Reformation world. For this reason, Bamford cannot show us the industrial bourgeoisie from below.

Bamford, who was present at Peterloo, was too old to be a Chartist. Although he lived till 1872, he felt that working-class politics had passed him by, and he urged the Chartists to 'turn from the precipice whither you have been led blindfold.' Yet he was the same kind of man as they were: his great belief was in do-it-yourself. This was a doctrine, as we have seen, that the propertied and voting classes found it hard to accept. Carlyle was no friend of the bourgeoisie, yet he was quite as unable as they were to understand Chartism. What is the meaning of the Charter, he asked:

> What are all popular commotions and maddest bellowings, from Peterloo to the Place-de-Grève itself? Bellowings, inarticulate cries as of a dumb creature in rage and pain; to the ear of wisdom they are inarticulate prayers: "Guide me, govern me! I am mad and miserable, and cannot guide myself!"[67]

Now if there is any one thing that the Chartists did not want, it was this 'What is our present relation to you as a section of the middle class?' the Sunderland Chartists said to the Anti-Corn-Law League in 1840. 'It is one of violent opposition. You are the holders of power, participation in which you refuse us.'[68] That the sympathetic Carlyle could so misinterpret Chartist aims is a clear sign of a vast cultural gulf. Chartism was not a plea for guidance, it was an emphatic repudiation of guidance, an assertion by the working class that they would run their own affairs — and, if possible, the country too. The assertion can sometimes have an attractive breeziness. 'Well done, Thornton,' said Fergus O'Connor after one William Thornton had opened a Chartist meeting with a prayer. 'When we get the Charter I will see that you are made the Archbishop of York.'[69]

It was not only politics that the Chartist leaders felt the working class should do for themselves. Thomas Cooper urged working men to 'join hands and heads to create a library of your own. Your own prose and your own poetry: you ought to be resolved to create these.'[70] This programme did not succeed, for the lure of bourgeois culture, like the lure of bourgeois ideology, was too strong. The English working class may never have felt enthusiastic about 'eels in a jar,' but they have never really rejected it, never told the Edinburgh Reviewers that they would have none of them, never really followed the call of Marx and Morris and Ernest Jones. Scholarships have tamed a thousand Coopers.

So there is no working-class culture as a presence in Victorian literature, there is only a working-class voice. It is a blunt voice that hates cant and is cynical about high-minded professions. It is the voice of not wanting to be helped. 'Heaven preserve us from kind masters,' it says. 'Duty to your employer? Your duty is to have no employer at all,' it says.[71] It must have heckled a thousand anti-Corn-Law speakers, a thousand Gladstonian Liberals, but it has usually (thank God? alas?) be content to heckle.

And to hear it, we do best to open the bourgeois authors. 'I want an end of these liberties took with my place,' said the workman to Mrs Pardiggle:

An't my place dirty? Yes, it is dirty — it's nat'rally dirty, and it's nat'rally onwholesome; and we had five dirty and onwholesome children, as is all dead infants, and so much the better for them, and for us besides. Have I read the little book wot you left? No, I an't read the little book wot you left. There an't nobody here as knows how to read it; and if there wos, it wouldn't be suitable to me. It's a book fit for a babby, and I'm not a babby. If you was to leave me a doll, I shouldn't nuss it.[72]

A workman said it, but it took Dickens to hear it. Mrs Gaskell, Kingsley, George Eliot, Dickens, all heard and captured this voice; then, somewhere or other, in the same book, they anxiously retracted what they had made it say. One function of the literary critic, reading their work today, is to guard these moments of insight against the inevitable withdrawal symptoms: moralisings, authorial reassurances, contrived happy endings. It is not necessary to argue that this working-class voice is truer or wiser than the more complex voice of the bourgeoisie: the total impact of *Bleak House* is more profound than the impact of Mrs Pardiggle's workman. All we need to argue is that the voice is worth hearing. All voices are worth hearing: to the lover of literature this must be an article of faith. And at times there are voices that are especially worth hearing. The voice of working-class resentment is especially valuable when authority is being sanctimonious. This is neither rare nor confined to the nineteenth century. 'Methinks I could not die anywhere so contented as in the king's company,' said Henry V before Agincourt, comfortable in the knowledge of his little joke, and the fact that he had archbishops to keep his conscience clear, 'his cause being just and his quarrel honourable.' 'That's more than we know,' growled this same sullen voice in reply.[73]

Notes

1 Lord Palmerston in the Don Pacifico debate in the Commons (1850). Quoted in Asa Briggs, 'The Language of "Class" in Early Nineteenth Century England,' in Asa Briggs and J. Saville (ed.), *Essays in Labour History* (London 1960).
2 Beatrice Webb, *My Apprenticeship* (London 1926), Ch. 1.
3 'January Searle,' *The Life of Ebenezer Elliott* (1850).

4 To Mr Hargreaves, 5 April 1863; quoted in John Morley, *Life of Cobden* (London 1881), Ch. 34.

5 Frederick Engels to Albert Lange, 29 March 1865. Cf. Gertrude Himmelfarb, *Darwin and the Darwinian Revolution* (London 1959).

6 Robert Owen, *A New View of Society* (1813).

7 George Eliot, 'Three Months in Weimar,' *Fraser's Magazine*, LI, (June 1855).

8 Thomas Carlyle, *Past and Present* (1843), Book 1, Ch. 6.

9 Thomas Carlyle, *Sartor Resartus* (1831), Book 1, Ch. 10.

10 Carlyle, *Past and Present*, Book III, Ch. I.

11 Matthew Arnold, *Friendship's Garland* (1871), Letter 2.

12 John Ruskin, *The Crown of Wild Olive* (1866), Lecture II: Traffic.

13 Robert Southey, *Sir Thomas More, or Colloquies on the Progress and Prospects of Society* (1829); Lord Macaulay, 'Southey's Colloquies,' *Edinburgh Review* (January 1830).

14 A. V. Dicey, *Lectures on the Relation between Law and Public Opinion in England during the 19th Century* (London 1905).

15 Karl Marx, *Capital* (1867), Vol. I, Part IV, Ch. 14.

16 John Ruskin, 'The Nature of Gothic,' Section 16, in *The Stones of Venice*, Vol. II (1851).

17 William Morris, *Useful Work Versus Useless Toil* (1885).

18 Mark Rutherford, *Catherine Furze* (1893), Ch. 11.

19 Elizabeth Gaskell, *North and South* (1855), Ch. 10.

20 Francis Place to Joseph Parkes, 7 December 1833; quoted in R. K. Webb, *The British Working Class Reader, 1790-1848* (London 1955), Ch. 7.

21 Cf. Richard D. Altick, *The English Common Reader* (Chicago 1957), esp. Ch. 9.

22 *Report of Commissioners on the Employment of Children in Factories* (1833); quoted in G. M. Young and W. D. Handcock (ed.), *English Historical Documents* (London 1956), No. 250 f.

23 Edwin Hodder, *The Life and Work of the 7th Earl of Shaftsbury, K.G.* (London 1886), Vol. I, p. 148.

24 Richard Oastler, *The Law and the Needle* (1836); the *Manchester Guardian*, 24 September 1836.

25 Cf. Charles Knight, *Passages of a Working Life* (1864-5).

26 William Morris to Mrs Burne-Jones, 1 June 1884; quoted in Asa Briggs (ed.), *William Morris: Selected Writings and Designs* (Harmondsworth 1962), p. 149.

27 Review of *Mary Barton* by W. R. Greg in the *Edinburgh Review* LXXXIX (April 1849).

28 *Our Mutual Friend* (1865), Book I, Ch. 16; Book II, Ch. 9 and 14; Book III, Ch. 8.

29 Cecil Driver, *Tory Radical: the Life of Richard Oastler* (New York 1946), Ch. 25, Section 3.

30 J. S. Mill, *Principles of Political Economy* (1848); quoted in Webb, *op cit*.

31 J. S. Mill, *Autobiography* (1873), Ch. 7.

32 E. B. Browning, 'The Cry of the Children' (1844).
33 William Blake, 'London,' in *Songs of Experience* (1794).
34 William Blake, *Jerusalem* (1804-20), Section 30.
35 William Blake, *Vala, or The Four Zoas* (1797), Night the Seventh (a).
36 Charles Kingsley, *Alton Locke* (1850), Ch. 1.
37 George Eliot, *Felix Holt* (1866), Ch. 30.
38 'Address to the Working Men, by Felix Holt,' *Blackwood's* C III (January 1868).
39 Cf. David Craig, 'Fiction and the Rising Industrial Classes,' *Essays in Criticism* XVII (January 1967); Arnold Kettle, 'Felix Holt the Radical,' *Critical Essays on George Eliot*, ed. Barbara Hardy (London 1970).
40 *Hard Times* (1854), Book II, Ch. 4.
41 'On Strike,' *Household Words* VIII (11 February 1854)
42 Cf. Geoffrey Carnall, 'Dickens, Mrs Gaskell, and the Preston Strike,' *Victorian Studies* VIII (September 1964); also George Orwell, 'Charles Dickens' (1939), in *Critical Essays* (London 1946).
43 Gaskell, *op cit.*, Ch. 42.
44 Speech in Birmingham, 6 January 1853; Collected Papers II, 400-6.
45 *The Uncommercial Traveller* (1861), Section 4.
46 *David Copperfield* (1850), Ch. 59.
47 *Bleak House* (1853), Ch. 64.
48 *Great Expectations* (1861), Chs. 25, 37, and 55.
49 *Martin Chuzzlewit* (1844), Ch. 9.
50 George Eliot, *Daniel Deronda* (1876), Ch. 22.
51 *Our Mutual Friend* (1865), Book I, Ch. 11.
52 Cf. Humphrey House, *The Dickens World* (London 1941); Edgar Johnson, *Charles Dickens: His Tragedy and Triumph* (New York 1952); Philip Collins, *Dickens and Crime* (London 1962) and *Dickens and Education* (London 1963).
53 John Ruskin to Charles Eliot Norton, 19 June 1870.
54 J. A. V. Chapple and A. Pollard (ed.), *The Letters of Mrs Gaskell* (Manchester 1966), No. 42: Elizabeth Gaskell to Mrs Gregg, 1849.
55 *ibid.*, No. 35: Elizabeth Gaskell to Catherine Winkworth, 23 December 1848.
56 *ibid.*, No. 42.
57 Cf. John Lucas, 'Mrs Gaskell and Brotherhood,' in D. Howard, J. Lucas, and J. Goode (ed.), *Tradition and Tolerance in 19th-Century Fiction* (London 1966), Ch. 4.
58 Benjamin Disraeli, *Sybil* (1845), Book III, Ch. 4.
59 *Barnaby Rudge* (1841), Ch. 55.
60 Ruskin, Modern Painters (1843), Part II, I, Ch. 1.
61 Huxley to Kingsley, 23 September 1860, in *Life and Letters of T. H. Huxley*, ed. Leonard Huxley (1900) I, 219. See Sheila M. Smith, *The Other Nation: the Poor in English Novels of the 1840s and 1850s* (1980) especially Chs. 1-3.
62 Elizabeth Gaskell to Marianne Gaskell, 15 March 1859, in *The Letters of Mrs Gaskell* ed. J. A. V. Chapple and A. Pollard (1966), No. 420.

The Literary Imagination

63 Samuel Bamford, *Passages in the Life of a Radical* (1844); *Early Days* (1849); Thomas Cooper, *The Life of Thomas Cooper* (1872); William Lovett, *Life and Struggles in Pursuit of Bread, Knowledge, and Freedom* (1876).

64 Bamford, *op cit.* (1844), Ch. 6.

65 *ibid.*, Ch. 71.

66 *ibid.*, Ch. 9.

67 Thomas Carlyle, *Chartism* (1839), Ch. 6.

68 Quoted in Mark Hovell, *The Chartist Movement* (Manchester 1904), Ch. 13. Cf. Lucy Brown, 'The Chartists and the Anti-Corn-Law League,' in Asa Briggs (ed.), *Chartist Studies* (London 1959).

69 Benjamin Wilson, *The Struggles of an Old Chartist* (1887); quoted in J. F. C. Harrison (ed.), *Society and Politics in England, 1780-1960* (New York 1965).

70 Quoted in Altick, *op cit.*, Ch. 9, Section IV.

71 Ernest Jones, *The People's Paper* (13 November 1852); quoted in G. D. H. Cole and A. W. Filson (ed.), *British Working Class Movements: Selected Documents, 1789-1875* (London 1951), Ch. 15, No. 16.

72 *Bleak House* (1853), Ch. 8.

73 William Shakespeare, *Henry V*, Act IV, Scene 1.

Index